HKAC

APPOMATTOX

APPOMATTOX

THE LAST DAYS OF ROBERT E. LEE'S ARMY OF NORTHERN VIRGINIA

MICHAEL E. HASKEW

ZENITH
PRESS

To my family, Elena, Amanda, Adam, and Allie, who have traveled with me to many distant battlefields.

First published in 2015 by Zenith Press, an imprint of Quarto Publishing Group USA Inc., 400 First Avenue North, Suite 400, Minneapolis, MN 55401 USA

The information in this book is true and complete to the best of our knowledge. All recommendations are made without any guarantee on the part of the author or Publisher, who also disclaims any liability incurred in connection with the use of this data or specific details.

We recognize, further, that some words, model names, and designations mentioned herein are the property of the trademark holder. We use them for identification purposes only. This is not an official publication.

Zenith Press titles are also available at discounts in bulk quantity for industrial or sales-promotional use. For details write to Special Sales Manager at Quarto Publishing Group USA Inc., 400 First Avenue North, Suite 400, Minneapolis, MN 55401 USA.

To find out more about our books, visit us online at www.zenithpress.com.

Library of Congress Cataloging-in-Publication Data

Haskew, Michael E.
  Appomattox : the last days of Robert E. Lee's Army of Northern Virginia / Michael E. Haskew.
    pages cm
  Includes bibliographical references and index.
  ISBN 978-0-7603-4817-8 (hc)
  1. Appomattox Campaign, 1865. I. Title.
  E477.67.H37 2015
  973.7'38--dc23
                            2014042901

Acquisitions Editor: Elizabeth Demers
Project Manager: Madeleine Vasaly
Art Director: James Kegley
Cover Designer: Juicebox Designs
Layout Designer: Kim Winscher

On the front cover:
Confederate flag: General J. E. B. Stuart's personal flag
Background image: *Battle of Five Forks*, Kurz & Allison. *Library of Congress*

Printed in the United States of America
10 9 8 7 6 5 4 3 2 1

CONTENTS

INTRODUCTION

The message was clear. "Tell General Lee that my command has been fought to a frazzle and unless Longstreet can unite in the movement, or prevent these forces from coming upon my rear, I can not long go forward," said Gen. John B. Gordon, whose understrength corps of the Army of Northern Virginia had advanced against Union forces blocking the route of march toward Lynchburg on the morning of April 9, 1865.

General Robert E. Lee, the venerated commander of the army since the spring of great promise in 1862, knew well the ominous meaning of Gordon's dispatch. The beleaguered Army of Northern Virginia was doomed. For ten months, Lee's tattered and famished soldiers had fought, languished, and died in the trenches stretching around the Confederate capital of Richmond and the vital supply center at Petersburg on the Appomattox River, twenty-three miles south of the capital city.

Lee had long realized that his command could not survive the war of attrition in the trenches of Petersburg. General Ulysses S. Grant, commander of all Union forces in the field, had changed tactics. Although destroying the Army of Northern Virginia in a decisive battle had been his early objective, Grant had overwhelming superiority in men and materiel. He knew that the siege was slowly strangling the Army of Northern Virginia and that if Lee lost Petersburg he could not hold Richmond.

The last and best hope for Lee's command was to move west toward Lynchburg or Danville, where his troops might find rations and the rail line could supply them on a trek southward to join the Army of Tennessee, under Gen. Joseph E. Johnston, in North Carolina. Johnston faced a vastly superior foe as well: the Union Army of the Tennessee under Gen. William T. Sherman. Lee entertained the notion that the consolidated Confederate armies might deal successfully with Sherman and then turn to confront Grant.

In late March, Union troops moved to cut the South Side Railroad and the Boydton Plank Road, Lee's tenuous supply line and his only avenue of escape from Petersburg. Defeat at the Battle of Five Forks on April 1 compelled him to abandon Petersburg and advise Confederate President Jefferson Davis to evacuate Richmond. The ten-month siege was over, and the Army of Northern Virginia began marching for its life, dogged by three Union armies—its longtime adversary, the Army of the Potomac, as well as two smaller forces, the Army of the James and the Army of the Shenandoah.

Lee's haggard command reached Amelia Station a day ahead of the pursuing Federals only to find that railcars that were expected to contain rations for starving soldiers held ammunition, artillery caissons, and horse bridles. An appeal to the local farmers, already depleted of foodstuffs, went for naught, and the delay allowed hard-riding Union cavalry to close the gap. The long retreat had continually sapped the strength of Lee's army. Exhausted soldiers wandered into the woods and did not return. Men and horses collapsed with fatigue.

Grant's relentless pursuers thwarted Lee at every turn. On April 6, a quarter of the Army of Northern Virginia was forced to surrender at the Battle of Sailor's Creek, and nine Confederate generals were captured. Lee watched the debacle unfold and uttered, "My God, has the army dissolved?"

Union cavalry destroyed wagon trains and harassed the Confederates as they continued west. Lee received word that the Confederate commissary had sent supplies to Farmville, but the constant threat of being cut off obliged his tired, hungry men and horses to keep moving and pass by those provisions. Another train had reached Lynchburg and moved on to Appomattox Station, twenty-five miles from Farmville.

The situation was desperate. Grant sensed that victory was near and sent a message to Lee on the evening of April 7: "The results of the last week must convince you of the hopelessness of further resistance on the part of the Army of Northern Virginia. I feel that it is so, and regard it as my duty to shift from myself the responsibility of any further effusion of blood, by asking of you the surrender of that portion of the Confederate States army known as the Army of Northern Virginia." Lee received the message at 9:30 that night. He read with no emotion and, without a word, passed it to one of his trusted corps commanders, Lt. Gen. James Longstreet. A moment later, Longstreet advised, "Not yet."

Lee played for time and replied to Grant, "Though not entertaining the opinion you express of the hopelessness of further resistance on the part of the Army of Northern Virginia, I reciprocate your desire to avoid useless effusion of blood, and therefore, before considering your proposition, ask what terms you will offer on condition of its surrender."

Playing his last card, Lee pressed on to Appomattox Court House, a little town two miles northeast of the rail station.

Grant was aware of his adversary's predicament, and Gen. Phil Sheridan's Cavalry Corps was moving across the route of march of the Army of Northern Virginia. On the afternoon of April 8, Gen. George Armstrong Custer's cavalry division rode into Appomattox Station and seized the supplies meant for Lee's staggering soldiers.

That evening, Lee called his senior commanders together. There were no tents, no chairs. The headquarters baggage had been lost to the raiding Union horsemen. One glimmer of hope remained: Gordon, with the cavalry of Gen. Fitzhugh Lee (Robert E. Lee's nephew) in support, might break through Sheridan's cavalry cordon and cover the road to Lynchburg. As long as the enemy to its front consisted only of cavalry, there was a chance. The approach of Federal infantry, however, would mean the end.

Early the following morning, Gordon's proud II Corps stepped off with Fitzhugh Lee's cavalry moving to protect its flanks. The attack made good progress as the lightly armed Union troopers fell back, opening a gap in their thin line. Gordon's men gave the "Yip! Yip!" of the Rebel yell and surged ahead. Then, as they reached the crest of a ridge, a veritable sea of blue deployed before them: three divisions of the Army of the James under Maj. Gen. Edward O. C. Ord.

Gordon dashed off his message to Robert E. Lee, who read it with dismay. He turned and slowly intoned, "Then there is nothing left for me to do but to go and see General Grant, and I would rather die a thousand deaths."

PART I
SUMMIT AT CITY POINT

CHAPTER 1

THE TIGHTENING NOOSE

The end of the Army of Northern Virginia began with the stroke of a pen. The lobby of the Willard Hotel in Washington, DC, was bustling on the afternoon of March 8, 1864, and the appearance of a disheveled army officer, his fourteen-year-old son in tow and his uniform stained and dusty from just-concluded travels and partly covered by a nondescript linen duster, was nothing of particular importance.

The disinterested clerk turned the register toward the guest and mumbled that a room was available on the top floor. Baggage would have to be manhandled up several flights of stairs. The officer replied that the accommodations would do and dutifully signed, "U. S. Grant and son, Galena, Ill."

As he read the signature, the clerk responded as though stunned by electric shock. Immediately, a suite on the second floor became available, and he took the guests' bags under his arms and proceeded hastily to its door. For all the officer's unimpressive looks, this man was extraordinary. Lieutenant General Ulysses S. Grant had been summoned to the nation's capital by President Abraham Lincoln to take command of all Union armies in the field, well over half a million men.

The president personified the mood of a war-weary Washington, and by the spring of 1864, the infernal Civil War had dragged into its thirty-fifth month. Grant had won significant victories in the Western Theater of the war, at Forts Henry and Donelson in early 1862, Shiloh that April, Vicksburg in the summer of 1863, and Chattanooga that autumn. In the East, the Union Army of the Potomac, under Maj. Gen. George G. Meade, had turned back the Confederate Army of Northern Virginia and its dauntless commander, Gen. Robert E. Lee, at Gettysburg. However, in the eyes of many civilian and military observers alike, including Lincoln, Meade had failed to pursue Lee and destroy his army after Gettysburg. The fullness of victory had been denied.

Meade retained command of the Army of the Potomac through the end of the war, but as long as Lee and the Army of Northern Virginia survived in the field, the heart of the Confederacy continued to beat. Before Gettysburg, Lee had vexed and confounded a trio of Union generals, George B. McClellan, Ambrose Burnside, and Joseph Hooker, each rash, timid, or inept in his own way. General Irvin McDowell, who led the Union Army of Northeastern Virginia—the nucleus of the force that soon became the Army of the Potomac—in the war's first major battle, the debacle at Bull Run in 1861, also preceded Meade.

The task then fell to Grant to provide the leadership, the relentless drive, that would bring Lee's Rebel army to battle and end the bloodletting that had torn the nation apart. Few life stories in the history of the United States, however, would begin so inauspiciously and seem so unlikely to portend such tremendous command responsibility. Though Lincoln had been intrigued by Grant's conduct of the Vicksburg Campaign, he dispatched advisors to gauge the man responsible, determined to avoid the unpleasantness and discord engendered by earlier generals who were often blinded by ambition or proved more blather than substance.

A few days after the surrender of Vicksburg, Lincoln wrote to Grant, "I do not remember that you and I ever met personally. I write this now as a grateful acknowledgement for the almost inestimable service you have done the country."[1]

Born Hiram Ulysses Grant on April 27, 1822, in Point Pleasant, Ohio, the future general was the son of a tannery operator, Jesse Root Grant, and when the boy reached the age of seventeen, his father secured an appointment to the United States Military Academy at West Point through Ohio congressman Thomas L. Hamer. Although his son had shown no inclination to embark on a military career, the father believed the West Point experience and the army would guarantee him the ability to earn a living.[2]

Accounts vary as to just how it happened, but either Congressman Hamer completed the nomination form incorrectly with "Ulysses S. Grant of Ohio" or a clerk at the Academy posted the plebe's name to the roll as Ulysses Simpson Grant, and Hiram's original name faded from view. Grant later asserted that the "S" did not stand for anything specific. He graduated twenty-first of thirty-nine in the class of 1843, admitting that he took no particular interest in academics and had spent much of his time reading novels.

"A military life had no charms for me, and I had not the faintest idea of staying in the army even if I should be graduated, which I did not expect," Grant wrote in his 1885 memoirs. "I never succeeded in getting squarely at either end of my class, in any one study, during the four years. I was anxious to enter the cavalry, or dragoons as they were then called . . . I recorded therefore my first choice, dragoons; second, 4th infantry; and got the latter."[3]

The infantry posting was not the last disappointment of Ulysses S. Grant's adult life. While he opposed the Mexican War, he served nevertheless, experiencing his first enemy fire while bringing ammunition forward to troops during an engagement. In 1848, he married Julia Dent, the daughter of Col. Frederick Dent, a slaveholder and merchant who owned White Haven Plantation, west of Saint Louis, Missouri. Grant was then posted to Detroit, "where two years were spent with but few important incidents," and then to the Pacific coast, where his wife and children could not follow. He developed a fondness for whiskey.

"My family, all this while, was at the East," Grant remembered. "It consisted now of a wife and two children [eventually Grant became the father of four children, three sons and a daughter]. I saw no chance of supporting them on the Pacific coast out of my pay as an army officer. I concluded, therefore, to resign."[4]

By the autumn of 1854, Grant had separated from the army and moved to a farm that belonged to his father-in-law near Saint Louis. He built a crude house and worked to make a go of it, referring to the plot of land as "Hardscrabble Farm." He sold firewood on the streets of Saint Louis to make ends meet. More than a year of sickness limited his ability to labor in the fields, and by 1858 he had sold his equipment and tools at auction and given up farming. A real estate partnership foundered, and by the spring of 1860, he was in Galena, Illinois, working as a clerk in his father's leather goods store.

With the outbreak of war in April 1861, Grant failed to regain a commission in the regular army. He did, however, receive an appointment as a colonel of Illinois volunteers. By November 1861, he was promoted to brigadier general and commanded twenty thousand troops. That month, he led a small Union force against the Confederates at Belmont near the boot heel of Missouri—and overran a Confederate encampment before the arrival of fresh enemy troops forced a hasty retreat. In mid-February 1862, Grant moved against Forts Henry and Donelson on the Tennessee and Cumberland Rivers in upper Middle Tennessee.

Fort Henry fell to Union naval forces before the army arrived, but at Fort Donelson, Grant demanded, "No terms except an unconditional and immediate surrender can be accepted."[5] When Confederate Gen. Simon Bolivar Buckner relented, more than twelve thousand Rebels were taken prisoner. Northern newspapers seized upon the opportunity to turn a catchy phrase, and General U. S. Grant became "Unconditional Surrender" Grant.

Grant was promoted to major general and given command of the Army of the Tennessee. Two months after Fort Donelson, his army was surprised at Shiloh and narrowly avoided disaster before rallying on the second day of the battle to retake ground that had been previously lost and drive the Confederates back. After the first day's fighting had ended, Grant's friend Brig. Gen. William T. Sherman came upon the commander sheltering under a tree from a driving rain and puffing on a cigar.

"Well Grant, we've had the devil's own day, haven't we?" Sherman offered. Grant puffed and replied, "Yes. Yes. Lick 'em tomorrow though."[6]

On July 4, 1863, just a day after Meade's victory at Gettysburg, Grant accepted the surrender of Vicksburg, a fortress city on the bluffs above the Mississippi River, after a campaign and siege of forty-seven days. With the capture of Vicksburg, the lower Mississippi was under Union control and the states of the western Confederacy—Louisiana, Arkansas, and Texas—were effectively cut off from those to the east.

In October, Grant arrived at Chattanooga, where the Union Army of the Cumberland was besieged by the Confederate Army of Tennessee, following the former's defeat at the Battle of Chickamauga. Marshaling elements of three Union armies, Grant opened a supply line to the hungry soldiers in Chattanooga and then lifted the siege with consecutive victories against the Rebels at Orchard Knob, Lookout Mountain, and Missionary Ridge from November 23 to 25.

The high butcher's bill at Shiloh and accusations that Grant had been in a drunken stupor on the first day of the battle had raised an outcry from Northern newspapers and politicians, who clamored for Grant's removal, but Lincoln had already begun to believe in the tough soldier who did not shrink from the enemy. Senator Alexander McClure of Pennsylvania wrote:

> I appealed to Lincoln for his own sake to remove Grant at once, and, in giving my reasons for it, I simply voiced the admittedly overwhelming protest from the loyal people of the land against Grant's continuance in command. I could form no judgment during the conversation as to what effect my arguments had upon him beyond the fact that he was greatly distressed at this new complication. When I had said everything that could be said from my standpoint, we lapsed into silence. Lincoln remained silent for what seemed a very long time. He then gathered himself up in his chair and said in a tone of earnestness that I shall never forget: "I can't spare this man; he fights."[7]

After a brief rest in their suite at the Willard Hotel, Grant and his son Fred, recently recovered from a bout of typhoid and pneumonia, went to the dining room. A whisper was followed by a groundswell of excitement, and then cheers of "Grant! Grant! Grant!" Fred watched as his father stood, waved his napkin, and bowed several times before sitting back down to eat, and remembered the spectacle to his dying day.[8]

After dinner, Grant walked unnoticed, just as he had been when he arrived at the train station earlier in the day, two short blocks to the White House. President and Mrs. Lincoln were hosting a reception, and Grant was expected to make an appearance. When he arrived, Lincoln smiled warmly and extended his hand.

"Why, here is General Grant!" Lincoln exclaimed as he enthusiastically grasped the general's right hand. "Well, this is a great pleasure, I assure you!" At five feet eight inches tall, Grant was momentarily dwarfed by the lanky, six-foot-four-inch Lincoln.

Secretary of State William Seward then shuffled Grant to the East Room to meet Mrs. Lincoln and pause amid the throng of guests that included not only politicians, but also military men— with some of whom Grant had recently experienced professional difficulties. The crowd roared its approval and pressed close to him. So many wanted to shake his hand that Grant had to retreat to a sofa and stand on it.

Noah Brooks, a reporter for the Sacramento *Daily Union* newspaper and friend of the president, remembered that the crowd was "the only real mob I ever saw in the White House. . . . For once at least the President of the United States was not the chief figure in the picture. The little, scared-looking man who stood on a crimson-covered sofa was the idol of the hour."[9]

The next day, Grant went to the White House again, this time to accept command of the Union armies with the rank of lieutenant general, recently reinstated by Congress. Lincoln had been reluctant to make Grant the first lieutenant general in the US Army since George Washington, particularly since rumors had surfaced that some senators might support Grant as the Republican nominee for president rather than Lincoln himself in the election of 1864. Grant, however, had no such political ambition and publicly said so.

Lincoln spoke briefly during the ceremony, and Grant responded, "Mr. President, I accept the commission with gratitude for the high honor conferred. With the aid of the noble armies that have fought on so many fields for our common country, it will be my earnest endeavor not to disappoint your expectations. I feel the full weight of the responsibilities now devolving on me and know that if they are met it will be due to those armies, and above all to the favor of that Providence which leads both nations and men."[10]

Lincoln staked his presidency and the fate of the nation on Grant. He was not alone in his assessment of Grant's willingness to see the war through to the end.

Confederate general James Longstreet, the trusted subordinate of Robert E. Lee and commander of the I Corps, Army of Northern Virginia, soon learned of Grant's appointment to command the Union armies and judged, "I was with him for three years at West Point, I was present at his wedding, I served in the same army with him in Mexico, I have observed his methods of warfare in the West, and I believe I know him through and through. And I tell you we cannot afford to underrate him and the army he now commands. We must make up our minds to get into line of battle and stay there, for that man will fight us every day and every hour till the end of this war. In order to whip him we must outmaneuver him, and husband our strength as best we can."[11]

Rarely in warfare has there been a contrast in the lives of opposing military commanders more perceptible than that between Ulysses S. Grant and his adversary, Robert E. Lee. Although both were West Point graduates, Grant was a middling performer. Among forty-six graduates of the Class of 1829, Lee stood second, and during four years at the Academy he did not receive a single demerit. In the spring of 1864, Lee was fifty-seven years old, more than a decade senior to the forty-two-year-old Grant.

The greatest contrast lay in Grant's average upbringing and Lee's aristocratic pedigree. Robert E. Lee was born January 19, 1807, at Stratford Hall, overlooking the Potomac River in Westmoreland County, Virginia. His father, Henry Lee III, was better known as Light-Horse Harry, one of Gen. George Washington's cavalry commanders during the Revolutionary War. His mother, Ann Hill Carter Lee, was of the distinguished and influential Carters and allied families of Virginia.

An extravagant spender who squandered the fortunes of two wealthy wives, Light-Horse Harry Lee was sentenced to debtor's prison in 1809. After his release a year later, he moved the family, which included five children (a sixth had died in infancy), to Alexandria. By 1813, he had been seriously injured in a riot in Baltimore between Federalists and Democratic-Republicans over the prosecution of the War of 1812 and left the United States for Barbados. Robert, the fifth child, was six years old and never saw his father again.

In March 1818, Light-Horse Harry Lee died, and the widowed Ann Lee struggled to support her family. A relative, William H. Fitzhugh, who owned the house where the family lived in Alexandria, also welcomed the Lees to Ravensworth, his plantation in Fairfax County. When Robert reached the age of seventeen and began giving serious consideration to his future, Fitzhugh encouraged him to seek an appointment to West Point. The competition was keen, and Fitzhugh wrote a letter of recommendation directly to Secretary of War John C. Calhoun.

Rather than mailing the letter, young Robert delivered it to Calhoun in person. On March 11, 1824, the coveted appointment was secured; however, his admission was delayed more than a year, until July 1, 1825, due to the large number of plebes already accepted. His outstanding performance at the Academy was merely postponed. Those who excelled in their studies were placed on the list of distinguished cadets, whose names were then certified by

General Lee posed for this portrait by photographer Julian Vannerson in March 1864. Within days, Lee was in the field with the Army of Northern Virginia countering the offensive thrust of General Ulysses S. Grant's Federal armies during the Overland Campaign, which culminated with the Siege of Petersburg. The siege lasted nearly ten months and significantly eroded the fighting capability of Lee's army. *Library of Congress*

the secretary of war and included in the army register. In his first year, Robert made the list with "special proficiency" in French and mathematics. He was also promoted to the rank of staff sergeant, the highest rank any rising second-year cadet could achieve.

At the beginning of his second year at West Point, Lee and three other cadets were appointed acting assistant professors of mathematics. He engaged in extensive outside reading but gave that up when his academic performance slipped slightly. During his third year, his performance in and out of the classroom was exceptional. He remained near the top in every subject and managed to resume his outside reading, borrowing fifty-two books from the library during a four-month period.

As a first classman, Lee was named adjutant of the corps of cadets. Graduating second in the class behind Charles Mason of New York, he was allowed to choose his arm of service and selected the US Army Corps of Engineers. He cut a dashing figure in uniform, was well liked by his classmates, and was referred to as the "Marble Model." Another cadet remembered, "His personal appearance surpassed in manly beauty that of any cadet in the corps. Though firm in his position and perfectly erect, he had none of the stiffness so often assumed by men who affect to be very strict in their ideas of what is military."[12]

Second Lieutenant Lee's first army posting was to Cockspur Island, Georgia, where he worked on the drainage system at the future site of Fort Pulaski. He later served at Fort Monroe near Hampton, Virginia, and in Washington, DC. He helped to survey the state line between Ohio and Michigan and mapped the Des Moines Rapids on the Mississippi River.

On June 30, 1831, Lee married Mary Anna Randolph Custis, his fourth cousin. Mary's father, George Washington Parke Custis, was the step-grandson and adopted son of George Washington and the grandson of Martha Washington. The Lees had seven children; three of them were sons, and all three would serve in the Confederate Army during the Civil War. George Washington Custis Lee achieved the rank of major general and served as an aide to Confederate President Jefferson Davis. William Henry Fitzhugh Lee, called "Rooney," was a major general and cavalry commander. Robert E. Lee Jr. was a captain in the Rockbridge Artillery. After giving birth to their second child, daughter Mary Custis Lee, in 1835, Mary was stricken with rheumatoid arthritis, which grew progressively worse and eventually relegated her to a wheelchair.

During the Mexican War, Lee distinguished himself on the battlefield, and Gen. Winfield Scott commended him as "the very best soldier that I ever saw in the field." At Veracruz, an artillery battery under Lee's command pounded the fortress and compelled its surrender. At the Battle of Cerro Gordo, he participated in a movement behind enemy lines that forced the Mexicans to withdraw. In the vicinity of Mexico City, he commanded troops that outflanked Mexican positions by marching through a jumbled, rocky lava field that was considered impassable. Lee was brevetted for bravery three times, and though his permanent rank was that of a captain in the engineers, he achieved the temporary rank of colonel.[13]

Following the Mexican War, Lee was posted to Fort Carroll in Baltimore Harbor and was detailed to survey and map parts of Florida. In 1852, he was named superintendent of West Point and occupied the post when his son Custis Lee graduated in 1854. The following year, he transferred to the cavalry and served with the 2nd Cavalry Regiment in Texas. In October 1859, he led a force of ninety-three US Marines against the radical abolitionist John Brown at Harpers Ferry, quelling Brown's attempt to incite a slave rebellion.

On February 6, 1860, Lee was appointed to command the army's Department of Texas. At the age of fifty-three, he had spent thirty-one years in the army, and promotion from captain to lieutenant colonel had required twenty-two. Lee's chosen career had long been at odds with his desire to be close to his family and his home at Arlington, and his anxiety at separation was heightened by the gathering storm of secession and the probability of civil war.

Lee's stand on the institution of slavery remains open to debate to this day. Although he never personally owned a slave, Arlington had been his wife's family estate, built by Mary's father, and among her property were 250 slaves. When George Washington Parke Custis died in 1857, Lee became the executor of his will and dealt with the slaves, emancipating those who remained in the winter of 1862, five years after Custis's death, in accordance with his instructions.

With the election of Lincoln, the parade of secession commenced, with South Carolina first in December 1860 and then Mississippi, Florida, Alabama, and Georgia in January 1861. Lee wrote to his son Custis, "The Southern states seem to be in a convulsion. . . . My little personal troubles sink into insignificance when I contemplate the condition of the country, and I feel as if I could easily lay down my life for its safety. But I also feel that would bring but little good."[14]

Lee was a proponent neither of secession nor of slavery. He was loyal to Virginia and considered himself duty bound to defend his home state. On January 22, 1861, he wrote to a friend, "I wish to live under no other government, and there is no sacrifice I am not ready to make for the preservation of the Union save that of honour. If a disruption takes place, I shall go back in sorrow to my people and share the misery of my native state, and save in her defence there will be one soldier less in the war than now. I wish no other flag than the 'Star spangled banner' and no other air than 'Hail Columbia.' I still hope that the wisdom and patriotism of the nation will yet save it."[15]

Louisiana seceded on January 26, and Texas followed four days later. On March 15, Lee was offered a brigadier general's commission in the Confederate Army, an overture to which he most likely did not respond since Virginia still remained in the Union. He was promoted to colonel at the end of the month while en route to Washington, where he was ordered to report by April 1.

War broke out on April 12, with the Confederate bombardment of Fort Sumter in the harbor of Charleston, South Carolina. Lee was offered command of the Federal Army that was to be raised to put down the rebellion. The offer was tendered through Francis Blair, the former editor of the *Congressional Globe*, the official record of the proceedings in Congress.

Lee later recalled his response to Blair: "I declined the offer he made me to take command of the army that was to be brought into the field, stating as candidly and as courteously as I could, that though opposed to secession and deprecating war, I could take no part in an invasion of the Southern States."[16] He stopped by to see his old commander in Mexico, Gen. Winfield Scott, who had been instrumental in the offer of command being extended to Lee. Scott advised Lee that if he were unable to command the Union army he should resign his commission.

The following day, April 19, Lee learned of Virginia's secession. Just after midnight on the twentieth, he wrote a short note to Secretary of War Simon Cameron, resigning his commission as colonel of the 1st Cavalry Regiment. On the twenty-second, he accepted the post of "commander of the military and naval forces of Virginia." Subsequently, he was commissioned in the Confederate States Army.

Lee's debut was inauspicious, and his reputation suffered. He lost the Battle of Cheat Mountain in September 1861, unable to coordinate an effective attack against Union entrenchments. In November, he was transferred to command coastal defenses in Georgia, South Carolina, and Florida, and later he returned to Richmond as an adviser to President Jefferson Davis. He was derided as the "King of Spades" due to his penchant for digging trenches around the Confederate capital.

Despite these setbacks, when his West Point classmate Gen. Joseph E. Johnston was wounded at the Battle of Seven Pines on June 1, 1862, Lee was placed in command of the Army of Northern Virginia, which he would hold through the end of the war. The Richmond press blamed Lee for the loss of western Virginia to Unionists and howled against the appointment. Fearing he would lack aggressiveness, opponents dubbed him "Granny Lee."

Nevertheless, Lee shouldered the responsibility for the defense of Richmond and drove the Army of the Potomac, then under McClellan, from the peninsula and routed Maj. Gen. John Pope at Second Manassas. He fought McClellan to a standstill at Antietam and withdrew in good order from Northern territory. In December 1862, he inflicted grievous losses on the Union army under Burnside's command at Fredericksburg.

As he had done during the Antietam campaign, Lee defied military convention and divided his forces at Chancellorsville in the face of the Army of the Potomac, then under Maj. Gen. Joseph

Hooker. The ensuing battle, fought during the first week of May 1863, was a resounding Confederate victory, considered by many to be Lee's greatest. Two months later, Lee's second invasion of the North was turned away at Gettysburg. His decision to fight at that time and place has been questioned by historians and military analysts, but the Army of Northern Virginia quite nearly succeeded in winning a decisive victory on Northern soil.

During the course of a year, Lee's reputation as a battlefield commander soared. He was proclaimed the great defender of the Confederacy and gained the undying loyalty of his subordinate commanders, his often barefoot and hungry soldiers in the ranks, and of President Davis. Now, as Grant took command of the Army of the Potomac in Washington, Lee's weary Army of Northern Virginia was in winter quarters in Orange County, Virginia, just south of the Rapidan River.

Meade's army wintered at Brandy Station, Virginia, just twenty-six miles from Lee and on the other side of the Rapidan. The camp of more than one hundred thousand soldiers blanketed an area greater than ten square miles. Still smarting from the harsh criticism due to his failure to follow up the victory at Gettysburg, Meade speculated as to whether he would be relieved of command. On March 10, Grant came calling at Brandy Station. Meade welcomed him and dutifully offered to resign. Grant refused.

On March 16, 1864, Meade wrote to his wife, "I was much pleased with Grant. . . . You may rest assured he is not an ordinary man." Two days later, he added, "I see General Grant's assuming command and announcing that his headquarters will be with the Army of the Potomac, is in the public journals, and by to-morrow will be known in Richmond. Of course this will notify the rebels where to look for active operations, and they will prepare accordingly. You need not think I apprehend any trouble about my being relieved. I don't think I have at any time been in any danger. It would be almost a farce to relieve the man who fought the battle of Gettysburg, nine months after the battle."[17]

Grant made no secret that his place was in the field, away from the politics and pomposity of Washington, and Meade took no issue with the fact that his boss was always at his elbow. For Meade, the absence of independent command may even have been something of a relief. Grant developed strategy, and Meade became responsible for its execution.

The strategy that Grant envisioned with the spring campaigns of 1864 was indeed grand. The Army of the Potomac would cross the Rapidan in early May and threaten Richmond from the north. Meanwhile, Gen. Benjamin Butler and the Army of the James were to approach Richmond from the south. Lee would be drawn into a decisive battle and hopefully destroyed. If the Rebels were not defeated on the field and retired to the defenses of Richmond, the Union armies would lay siege to the city and slowly but surely choke the Army of Northern Virginia to death. At the same time, more than twenty-five thousand Union troops under Gen. Franz Sigel would march south through the Shenandoah Valley, cutting rail lines and depriving the enemy of food and materiel. In the West, Sherman was instructed to drive into Georgia, defeat Johnston's Confederate Army of Tennessee, and capture Atlanta.

Grant would utilize the telegraph to remain in contact with Union forces in the East and West. He grasped the war-winning capacity of Northern industry and the overwhelming superiority in manpower and supplies that would eventually mean victory. His grand strategy would stretch the already hard-pressed Confederates to the breaking point.

At the end of March, Grant reorganized the Army of the Potomac, disbanding the I and III Corps, both of which had been ravaged at Gettysburg, and reassigning their depleted regiments. Although the move was not popular within the ranks, it improved command and control during the coming campaign. The 110,000-man army then included three corps: the II under Maj. Gen. Winfield Scott Hancock, the V commanded by Maj. Gen. Gouverneur Kemble Warren, and the VI under Maj. Gen. John Sedgwick. The independent IX Corps, under Burnside, was also at Grant's disposal. During the conduct of the Chattanooga campaign seven months earlier, Grant was impressed with Gen. Phil Sheridan, who stood only five feet six inches tall and weighed a scant 115 pounds. He brought Sheridan to Virginia to command the Cavalry Corps.

At last, on the morning of May 4, 1864, the great Army of the Potomac and the Overland Campaign were set in motion, toward Germanna and Ely's Fords on the banks of the Rapidan. As the army prepared to move, a chaplain watched in awe. "We, with the entire Grand Army of the Potomac, were in motion toward the Rapidan. The dawn was clear, warm and beautiful. As the almost countless encampments were broken up bands in all directions playing lively airs, banners waving, regiments, brigades, and divisions falling into line . . . the scene even to eyes long familiar with military displays, was one of unusual grandeur."[18]

For the next forty days, Grant attempted to move around the right flank of the Army of Northern Virginia. Each time, Lee parried the thrust and thwarted Grant's maneuver. He realized that the last, best hope for the Confederate States of America was to make the war as costly as possible for the North, fighting on favorable ground, matching maneuver for maneuver. The population of the North might then grow tired and discontent as the long casualty lists seemed endless. With Lincoln standing for reelection in November, perhaps Confederate aims could be achieved at the ballot box when they could not on the battlefield.

The Army of Northern Virginia numbered about sixty-five thousand veteran soldiers, half the strength of the Union host that splashed across the Rapidan. Lee's army was organized in three corps, with Lt. Gen. Richard Ewell's II Corps, Stonewall Jackson's old command, near Mine Run and closest to the Federals. Lt. Gen. Ambrose Powell Hill commanded III Corps south of Ewell along the Rapidan, and Longstreet's I Corps, just returned after a long and difficult autumn campaign in Tennessee, was about ten miles farther south at Gordonsville. Lee's eight thousand cavalrymen, commanded by the dashing Maj. Gen. Jeb Stuart, were foraging to the east of the infantry formations.

Beyond the Rapidan in the Virginia countryside lay a broad expanse of second-growth timber, brambles, and thickets known as the Wilderness, where Hooker had come to grief at Chancellorsville the previous year. Grant hoped to move his large army through the difficult country before Lee could react in force and then confront the Confederates in the open. However, as the sun was still rising on May 4, Lee received the news that the enemy was on the move. He had correctly surmised that Grant's offensive would begin on his right flank.

The Army of the Potomac camped in the Wilderness on the night of May 4, and Lee moved more quickly than Grant expected. About noon the following day, the opposing forces collided in the Wilderness, where the rough terrain negated the Federals' numerical superiority. Confusion reigned. Fires broke out in the underbrush, consuming wounded men who could not move, and friend fired on friend. Longstreet was one of the casualties, caught in the crossfire as Virginia troops delivered a volley into their own men.

Not far from where Lee's forces now fought, Stonewall Jackson had been mortally wounded under eerily similar circumstances during the Chancellorsville fighting a year earlier. Longstreet survived, but his recovery took months.

Born on January 8, 1821, in Edgefield District, South Carolina, James Longstreet was forty-three years old in 1865, and he had earned the undying respect and affection of Robert E. Lee, who referred to the senior lieutenant general in the Army of Northern Virginia as his "Old War Horse." Longstreet's other familiar nickname, "Old Pete," was said to have been given to him by his father, who appreciated his rocklike and stoic demeanor.

As a boy, Longstreet lived for an extended period on his uncle's plantation in Augusta, Georgia. Congressman Reuben Chapman of Alabama, a relative, secured an appointment for James to the United States Military Academy in 1838, and four years later his poor performance placed him third from the bottom, fifty-fourth of fifty-six graduates, in the class of 1842. A veteran of the Mexican War, he was promoted for heroism at Churubusco and Molino del Rey, and badly wounded at Chapultepec. He resigned his commission in the Federal Army in June 1861 and accepted a Confederate commission as a lieutenant colonel. After a subsequent meeting with President Jefferson Davis, Longstreet was promoted to brigadier general.

After fighting at Bull Run and leading a division under General Johnston in the spring of 1862, and despite being accused of slowness at the Battle of Fair Oaks, Longstreet was considered a solid field commander. He opposed Lee's invasion of the North in 1862, but he fought well at Antietam, and with the reorganization of the Army of Northern Virginia in October of that year he was promoted to lieutenant general and given command of the I Corps.

Longstreet vehemently opposed Lee's decision to attack Meade's entrenched Federal army at Gettysburg in July 1863. He was thought by some observers to have moved slowly on July 2, thwarting an otherwise promising attack, and was reluctant to order Gen. George Pickett's division forward in its fateful charge the following day. In later years, Longstreet's conduct at Gettysburg became fodder for his detractors.

During the course of the war, though, Lee never lost confidence in Longstreet. This conclusion is evidenced by his longevity as Lee's chief subordinate. Indeed, Longstreet is considered by many historians and military analysts to have been the finest corps commander in the Confederate armies.

After two days of inconclusive fighting in the Wilderness, the Army of the Potomac had sustained eighteen thousand dead and wounded, the Army of Northern Virginia eleven thousand. Unlike his predecessors, who might have considered the cost too high, Grant did not withdraw. He continued southeastward, still trying to turn Lee's flank and get between the Rebel army and Richmond. As Stuart's cavalry harassed Grant's vanguard, the two armies raced for the village of Spotsylvania Court House. Lee got there first.

The tired Confederate soldiers set immediately to digging and erected strong earthworks above the town. An assault against the fixed positions would be costly. At about 6:00 a.m. on May 8, the Battle of Spotsylvania Court House began near a crucial road junction that Lee had to hold to maintain his supply line. Grant pounded Lee's left flank at Laurel Hill, and on the morning of May 9, a Confederate sharpshooter took aim at General Sedgwick, the VI Corps commander. Trying to encourage his men while bullets whizzed by, Sedgwick exclaimed, "They couldn't hit an elephant at this distance!" Seconds later, he was struck below the left eye. Grant mourned, "Is he really dead?"[19]

On May 10, frontal assaults against Lee's left flank and a prominent earthwork known as the Mule Shoe produced only more casualties. On May 11, Grant telegraphed an anxious Lincoln in Washington, "We have now ended the sixth day of very heavy fighting . . . the result up to this time is much in our favor. I intend to fight it out on this line if it takes all summer."[20]

The following day, a heavy attack by twenty thousand men of Hancock's II Corps was thrown back after bitter hand-to-hand fighting. At one point, Lee rode forward, personally rallying his troops. Intense fighting along another point of the Confederate line left the area nicknamed the "Bloody Angle." The armies were at each other's throats for twenty-two hours.

After six more days of fighting, Grant recognized the futility of trying to overcome Lee's fortified positions. More than 18,000 Union soldiers were lost at Spotsylvania Court House, over 2,700 of them killed. The Army of Northern Virginia lost 1,500 dead and more than 11,000 wounded or taken prisoner. Again, Grant sidled southeast, this time crossing the North Anna River only to find that Lee had deployed the Army of Northern Virginia in an upturned V formation with its tip resting on the North Anna at Ox Ford.

Grant crossed the river on May 23 and discovered that Lee's position was virtually unassailable. The apex of the V was against the river, and in the crossing the Army of the Potomac was split. Lee could use the advantage of interior lines to shift troops from one side to the other if either were assaulted. Lee wanted to attack, but he was suffering from a debilitating case of diarrhea. Unable to lead an attack himself, he did not believe A. P. Hill possessed the fortitude to lead such an enterprise, while Ewell was physically exhausted and Gen. Richard H. Anderson, who had replaced the wounded Longstreet, was new to corps command. Whatever opportunity there was to assume the offensive slipped away.

Grant crossed the Pamunkey River on May 26 and continued toward Richmond. Lee entrenched at Totopotomoy Creek, and the armies fought for two days along the creek and in the vicinity of Bethesda Church.

By June 1, Grant had reached Cold Harbor in Hanover County, just ten miles northeast of Richmond. The armies concentrated there, and Lee's troops built a strong line of earthworks some seven miles long and studded with artillery. On the dismal night of June 2, the Union soldiers knew to a man that the coming day would be one of great carnage. Lieutenant Colonel Horace Porter, a member of Grant's staff, came upon a group of soldiers during the night and was taken aback at what he saw.

"As I came near one of the regiments which was making preparations for the next morning's assault, I noticed that many of the soldiers had taken off their coats, and seemed to be engaged in sewing up rents in them," Porter wrote years later. "This exhibition of tailoring seemed rather peculiar at such a moment, but on closer examination it was found that the men were calmly writing their names and home addresses on slips of paper, and pinning them on the backs of their coats, so that their dead bodies might be recognized upon the field, and their fate made known to their families at home."[21]

Before dawn on June 3, elements of three Union corps, fifty thousand men in all, stepped off toward Lee's well-entrenched veterans. A slaughter ensued. One Union brigade suffered a thousand casualties in less than twenty minutes. A Confederate sergeant recalled that enemy soldiers fell "like rows of blocks or bricks pushed over by striking against one another." General Evander Law, commander of a Confederate brigade, summed it up. "It was not war; it was murder."[22]

General Ulysses S. Grant took command of all Union armies in the field in March 1864. He chose to make his headquarters on the march with the forces that eventually compelled Gen. Robert E. Lee and the Confederate Army of Northern Virginia to surrender. Grant's tactics differed from his predecessors in that he chose to maintain the offensive against Lee even while absorbing staggering casualties. This photo was taken after the Civil War ended, probably during Grant's second term as President of the United States. *Library of Congress*

Estimates of the Union dead and wounded that day ranged from 5,600 to 7,000 men. For the twelve days the armies faced one another at Cold Harbor, Grant had paid in blood with a total of 13,000 casualties. Writing his memoirs in 1885, Grant admitted, "I have always regretted that the last assault at Cold Harbor was ever made. . . . At Cold Harbor no advantage whatever was gained to compensate for the heavy loss we sustained."[23]

The Overland Campaign cost the Union sixty thousand killed, wounded, or captured—a toll nearly equivalent to the entire strength of the Army of Northern Virginia at the beginning of the campaign that covered approximately one hundred miles. The Army of Northern Virginia suffered thirty-five thousand casualties, and many of these could not be replaced. The fearful toll opened Grant to serious criticism, and in some quarters he was referred to as "Butcher."

Yet, Grant was relentless. On the night of June 12, he moved the Army of the Potomac by the left flank to the James River and crossed his army by ferry and pontoon bridge. Although Lee had thus far successfully avoided a climactic battle, he was now confronted by his greatest fear. Grant did not move directly on Richmond but against Petersburg, Virginia, twenty-three miles south, a vital supply base for both the Confederate capital and the Army of Northern Virginia.

Attempts to seize Petersburg in mid-June failed, and Grant changed his strategy. Lee had been run to ground, obliged to defend both Richmond and Petersburg. Grant was determined to conquer and initiated a siege that would last nine months—until April 1865.

Delivering his second inaugural address from the Capitol on March 4, 1865, President Abraham Lincoln stands before a large crowd and urges "malice toward none . . . charity for all." Later that month, Lincoln traveled to the Union supply base at City Point, Virginia, to confer with Generals Grant and Sherman and remained there for two weeks. During that time, he visited war-torn Petersburg and the Confederate capital at Richmond after the city fell on April 3, 1865. *Library of Congress*

CHAPTER 2

GRAND STRATEGY AND THE LAST CAMPAIGN

On Saturday, March 4, 1865, a year after Ulysses S. Grant assumed command of all the Union armies, Abraham Lincoln rose on the East Portico of the US Capitol to take the oath of office and deliver his second inaugural address as president of the United States.

The previous twelve months had been momentous. Although Grant had failed to defeat Lee and the Confederate Army of Northern Virginia in a decisive battle, the Rebels had been tethered to Richmond and Petersburg, the vital supply base a few miles to the south, under siege since the previous June. General William T. Sherman's Army of the Tennessee had taken Atlanta, completed its March to the Sea, and turned northward into the Carolinas in hot pursuit of Gen. Joseph E. Johnston's Confederate Army of Tennessee.

Concerns as to Lincoln's ability to gain reelection had persisted well into 1864, given the high cost of the protracted war in lives and treasure. The former commanding general of the Army of the Potomac, George B. McClellan, stood as the Democratic Party's nominee against the Republican incumbent, and if McClellan won the White House, it was fully expected that he would negotiate peace with secessionist states and the war would end with the nation divided.

By November, however, Sherman's triumph in the West at Atlanta and Grant's investment of Petersburg provided the glimmer of hope that total Union victory was still attainable. Lincoln prevailed with 55 percent of the popular vote, boosted by a large majority of the ballots cast by soldiers in the field. He trounced McClellan in the Electoral College, 212 votes to 21.

Now, Lincoln spoke of atonement for the institution of slavery and the reconciliation that must come with the end of the terrible war. "Fondly do we hope, fervently do we pray, that this mighty scourge of war may speedily pass away," he pleaded. "Yet, if God wills that it continue until all the wealth piled by the bondsman's two hundred and fifty years of unrequited toil shall be sunk, and until every drop of blood drawn with the lash shall be paid by another drawn with the sword, as was said three thousand years ago, so still it must be said 'the judgments of the Lord are true and righteous altogether.'"

Then, the tall, gaunt Lincoln, the strain of four years of war visibly etched upon his face, provided a glimpse of his vision for the reunited country. "With malice toward none, with charity for all, with firmness in the right as God gives us to see the right, let us strive on to finish the work we are in, to bind up the nation's wounds, to care for him who shall have borne the battle and for his widow and his orphan, to do all which may achieve and cherish a just and lasting peace among ourselves and with all nations."

Lincoln did not intend to mete out harsh justice to the defeated Confederates when the war was won. However, nearing the end of such a long national nightmare, he still harbored the fear that the war might drag on interminably. He could not allow himself to fully accept that the Confederacy was nearly finished. Although some observers indeed saw it as fact, there were issues still to be decided on the battlefield.

Urged to do so by his wife, on March 20, General Grant invited Lincoln to come to his headquarters at the bustling supply depot of City Point, Virginia, at the confluence of the Appomattox and James Rivers seven miles from the siege lines at Petersburg. The invitation was extended "for a day or two," and the general added, "I would like very much to see you and I think the rest would do you good."[24]

Lincoln welcomed the opportunity, and his stay was considerably longer than a day or two; he did not depart City Point until late on the night of April 8. Shortly after his arrival, he was asked by Gen. Henry Collis how long he planned to stay. Lincoln replied, "Well, I am like the western pioneer who built a log cabin. When he commenced he didn't know how much timber he would need, and when he had finished, he didn't care how much he had used up. So you see I came down among you without definite plans, and when I go home I sha'n't regret a moment I have spent with you."[25]

City Point was a diversion from the highly charged political scene of Washington, which Lincoln viewed as a nest of self-serving officials, pompous businessmen vying for government contracts, and a ceaseless flow of office seekers. There was also a sense of significance that spurred the president to leave his capital. Sherman was coming up from the Carolinas, and Rear Adm. David Dixon Porter, adopted brother of contemporary naval hero Adm. David Farragut, would be there as well. Porter commanded the navy's North Atlantic Blockading Squadron, which strangled Confederate trade, preventing the export of cotton and other commodities and the import of foreign weapons and supplies that were vital to the Rebel war effort. He was also responsible for maintaining control of inland waterways, such as the James, and defeating any challenge mounted by the Confederate Navy, such as it was.

This was not Lincoln's first visit to City Point. In June 1864, he spent two days there, warmly received by the troops, particularly the black soldiers of Gen. William F. "Baldy" Smith's XVIII Corps. These soldiers had taken part in the first Union attempts to seize Petersburg a week earlier and had actually captured some of the outermost Confederate entrenchments.

Lincoln's initial reception on June 21, however, was anything but cordial as he looked for Grant. Sylvanus Cadwallader of the *New York Herald* wrote in a dispatch:

> Yesterday about one o'clock a long, gaunt, bony man with queer admixture of the comical and doleful in his countenance . . . undertook to reach the General's tent by scrambling through a hedgerow and coming in the back way alone. He was stopped by one of the hostlers, and told to "keep out of here." The individual replied that he thought Genl. Grant would allow him

inside, and strode ahead. On reaching the guard, he was stopped with "No sanitary folks allowed inside." After some parleying, the intruder was compelled to give his name, and announced himself to be Abraham Lincoln, President of the United States, desiring an interview with Genl. Grant. The guard saluted and allowed him to pass. Genl. Grant recognized him as he stepped under the large "fly" in front of his tent, rose and shook hands with him cordially . . . it was ascertained that the President had just arrived . . . and was accompanied by his son "Tad" . . . [At dinner] the President was duly seated, ate much as other mortals, managed to ring in three favorite jokes during the meal, under the plea of illustrating the topics discussed.[26]

In the spring of 1865, Lincoln traveled to City Point with an agenda that was intended to be transformative. He not only sought assurance that the end was near—that Lee would not be allowed to slip the noose at Petersburg and head south to unite with Johnston and that Sherman would vanquish his foe in the Carolinas once and for all. There was also the matter of managing the anticipated peace. Lincoln intended to forego harsh treatment for former Rebels, bringing them back into the Union as citizens as rapidly as possible.

At 1:00 p.m. on March 23, the president and his entourage—which included his wife, Mary Todd Lincoln; their twelve-year-old son, Tad; Capt. Charles Penrose, assigned as a bodyguard by Secretary of War Edwin M. Stanton; White House guard William H. Crook; and Mrs. Lincoln's maid—boarded the steamer *River Queen* at the Arsenal Dock, 6th Street Wharf, for the voyage of several hours down the Potomac and then up the James. Before the war, City Point had been a typical riverside town, slow and sleepy. That all changed as the conflict progressed. By the autumn of 1864, City Point was the focus of Union command and logistics in the Eastern Theater of the Civil War. The waterfront stretched more than a mile along the banks of the James and the adjacent Appomattox rivers. Wharves had been hammered together for the offloading of merchant ships, both steam and sail, that averaged 140 comings and goings each day. At any given time, more than one hundred supply-laden barges were tied up along the docks.

City Point was teeming with Union soldiers, and feeding and supplying them required the construction of vast warehouses, barracks, blacksmith shops, and bakeries that produced thousands of loaves of bread daily. The quartermaster general asserted that his operation was capable of supporting an army of half a million men, and those who observed did not doubt his claim. A pair of steam engines pumped water to supply the bustling city, while hammers rang and saws buzzed, wagons were repaired, soldiers drilled, and horses seemed to be everywhere. Several wagons were fitted with ingenious sprinkler systems and plodded along the dirt streets to keep the dust down.

To facilitate the movement of supplies to the front lines at Petersburg, an existing short-line railroad was extended to twenty-one miles with all the necessary support, including repair facilities, coal stockpiles, and equipment for loading freight. The City Point Railroad eased the daunting task of supplying hundreds of thousands of soldiers, even in disagreeable weather.[27]

Located on a bluff overlooking City Point, the Depot Field Hospital was capable of caring for ten thousand patients. One visitor related, "Lice may have been the only problem the staff of the Depot Field Hospital could not handle. The largest of seven hospitals built at City Point during the Siege of Petersburg, the facility put to use all the Union army had learned since the beginning of the Civil War. While severely wounded soldiers were sent to the North, those who remained in the field received the best medical care available. Running water, pumped from the Appomattox River, helped keep this 200-acre complex as neat as a pin."[28]

City Point provided persuasive evidence that the vast might of the Union army, supported by the massive industrial and manpower base of the North, would inevitably defeat the Confederates, and probably any other military force on the Earth. Considering the spectacle here, one overriding conclusion was inescapable. The Confederacy and the proud Army of Northern Virginia could not win.

If the visit to City Point was intended to provide rest for the Lincoln family, it did not. During the trip, only Tad seemed to enjoy himself. William Crook, who worked at the White House for more than fifty years and served a dozen presidents, remembered that the boy "studied every screw of the [*River Queen*'s] engine and knew and counted among his friends every man of the crew." The president was uncomfortable much of the time, suffering a stomach ailment probably brought on by tainted drinking water. A brief stop was made at Fortress Monroe in Hampton Roads to take on a fresh supply. Mrs. Lincoln, meanwhile, was beside herself with worry after the president casually mentioned that he dreamed the White

House had caught fire. Mary insisted twice that telegrams be sent to reassure her that the presidential residence was still intact.[29]

The *River Queen* arrived at City Point and anchored off the riverfront at 9:00 p.m. on March 24, and General and Mrs. Grant greeted the presidential party. There were introductions and a few moments taken to discuss the current military situation.

The following morning, the president was up early. He ate very little, and those around him remembered that he still did not look well. His son Robert, an officer on Grant's staff, boarded the *River Queen* and advised that fighting had erupted on the Petersburg front during the predawn hours. Throughout the Siege of Petersburg, Grant had extended his lines, reaching for the railroads that supplied the Confederates, who doggedly held out. Each time Grant moved to the west, Lee was required to do the same, stretching his already thin line to the breaking point.

The action of March 25 has been recorded as the Battle of Fort Stedman, Lee's last failed attempt to break the siege. Accounts vary as to who made the initial suggestion, the president himself or Grant, but someone broached the idea of going forward to visit the scene of the action. A train was made ready, and a large group rode to Meade's headquarters at the front. When the visitors arrived, the president mounted a horse and rode across portions of the battlefield. Dead men lay where they fell, and wounded soldiers had yet to be evacuated.

Lieutenant Colonel Horace Porter, a staff officer, remembered:

General Grant proposed to the President that forenoon that he should accompany him to the Petersburg front. The invitation was promptly accepted, and several hours were spent in visiting the troops, who cheered the President enthusiastically. He was greatly interested in looking at the prisoners who had been captured that morning; and while at Meade's headquarters, about two o'clock, sent a dispatch to [Secretary of War Edwin M.] Stanton, saying: "I have nothing to add to what General Meade reports, except that I have seen the prisoners myself, and they look like there might be the number he states—1600." The President carried a map with him which he took out of his pocket and examined several times. He had the exact location of the troops marked on it, and he exhibited a singularly accurate knowledge of the various positions.[30]

After breakfast the next morning, Lincoln took a small boat to shore and ambled into the telegraph operator's tent at Grant's headquarters. He noticed three small kittens that had wandered into the tent. Their mother had died, and Horace Porter remembered them "expressing their grief by mewing piteously." The president picked them up and placed them in his lap. He whispered, "Poor little creatures, don't cry; you'll be taken good care of." Porter further remembered that Lincoln turned to a nearby officer and said, "Colonel, I hope you will see that these poor little motherless waifs are given plenty of milk and treated kindly." The officer replied, "I will see, Mr. President, that they are taken in charge by the cook of our mess, and are well cared for."

Several times during his stay, Porter later wrote, the president was seen "fondling these kittens. He would wipe their eyes tenderly with his handkerchief, stroke their smooth coats, and listen to them purring their gratitude to him."[31]

Later that morning, the presidential party set out to review formations of Maj. Gen. Edward O. C. Ord's Army of the James camped on the old battlefield of the Seven Days at Malvern Hill. Stops to observe formations of Sheridan's cavalry splash across the James and to review a naval flotilla were also scheduled. The barge left City Point about 11:00 a.m., and horses were brought along for the land portion of the tour. Grant offered his own mount, Cincinnati, to the president.

When the barge reached the north side of the James, those riding horses started off to the reviewing ground about two miles

Mary Todd Lincoln, wife of President Abraham Lincoln, posed for this portrait sometime between 1855 and 1865. Mrs. Lincoln hailed from Kentucky, and her family included men who fought for the Confederacy. She endured great personal tragedy during her lifetime with the deaths of her husband and three sons. Mrs. Lincoln suffered from depression and mental illness. Her eldest son, Robert, committed her to an asylum for a time. She died in 1882. *Library of Congress*

away. Colonel Porter had been entrusted with caring for Mrs. Lincoln and Mrs. Grant and helped them into an ambulance for the ride along a road that was so muddy that its wheels sank to the hub at times. When Mrs. Lincoln insisted that the pace was too slow, she decided to walk. However, the depth of the mud and the urgings of Porter and Mrs. Grant coaxed her back into the ambulance. She then asked the driver to pick up the pace.

"We were still on a corduroyed portion of the road, and when the horses trotted the mud flew in all directions, and a sudden jolt lifted the party clear off the seats, jammed the ladies' hats against the top of the wagon, and bumped their heads as well," recalled Porter. "Finally we reached our destination, but it was some minutes after the review had begun. Mrs. Ord and the wives of several of the officers, who had come up from Fort Monroe for the purpose, appeared on horseback as a mounted escort to Mrs. Lincoln and Mrs. Grant. This added a special charm to the scene, and the review passed off with peculiar brilliancy. Mrs. Grant enjoyed the day with great zest, but Mrs. Lincoln had suffered so much from the fatigue and annoyances of her overland trip that she was not in a mood to derive much pleasure from the occasion."[32]

In his recollection of the day, Porter was, no doubt, trying to be discreet, and remain within the boundaries of good taste. For those present, it was impossible to ignore Mrs. Lincoln's conduct. The first lady observed Mrs. Ord and other women escorting the president during the review and became incensed that the lovely young woman, a number of years her junior, had been so close to her husband. When Mrs. Ord rode up to greet Mrs. Lincoln after the review, she received a tongue lashing.

Mrs. Lincoln had been involved in a carriage accident in 1863, and the rough ride may have conjured up reminders of it. The bump on the head during the ambulance ride may also have induced a headache. Her anger went unabated throughout the evening, and during dinner aboard the *River Queen*, she continually berated the president for "flirting" with Mrs. Ord and even insisted that General Ord be removed from command. The president was deeply embarrassed, and Mrs. Lincoln remained in her cabin aboard the steamer for the rest of her visit, which mercifully for all ended when she returned to Washington on April 1. Tad remained at City Point.[33]

During his extended visit to City Point, the president slept fitfully as the matters of state and other distractions weighed heavily on his mind. For years, Lincoln was known to suffer bouts of depression and insomnia. His dreams were often disturbing and—he seemed to believe—prophetic. He once cabled Mary, on a shopping trip with Tad in Philadelphia, to take the boy's cap pistol away after a nightmare. He told army officers that a recurring dream always meant the coming of momentous news.

About the time of Mary's departure from City Point, Lincoln's most disturbing and predictive dream was said to have occurred. He waited, however, until three days before he was shot by John Wilkes Booth at Ford's Theater in Washington, to tell the terrible tale. Ward Hill Lamon, an old Illinois friend, law partner, and self-appointed bodyguard of the president, wrote years later of the eerie evening. While visiting with a small group of acquaintances in the Red Room of the White House, Lincoln seemed to emerge from long moments of melancholy and began to talk about the significance of dreams.

"It seems strange how much there is in the Bible about dreams. There are, I think, some sixteen chapters in the Old Testament and four or five in the New in which dreams are mentioned," Hill remembered the president saying. "If we believe the Bible, we must accept the fact that in the old days God and His angels came to men in their sleep and made themselves known in dreams. Nowadays, dreams are regarded as very foolish, and are seldom told, except by old women and by young men and maidens in love."[34]

Mrs. Lincoln pressed her husband for details. She said, "Why, you look dreadfully solemn; do you believe in dreams?"

"I can't say that I do," returned Mr. Lincoln, "but I had one the other night which has haunted me ever since."[35]

Mrs. Lincoln then saw her husband's demeanor change and urged, "You frighten me! What is the matter?" The president responded, "I am afraid that I have done wrong to mention the subject at all; but somehow the thing has got possession of me."[36]

Then the president slowly began:

About ten days ago, I retired very late. I had been up waiting for important dispatches from the front. I could not have been long in bed when I fell into a slumber, for I was weary. I soon began to dream. There seemed to be a death-like stillness about me. Then I heard subdued sobs, as if a number of people were weeping. I thought I left my bed and wandered downstairs.

There the silence was broken by the same pitiful sobbing, but the mourners were invisible. I went from room to room; no living person was in sight, but the same mournful sounds of distress met me as I passed along. I saw light in all the rooms; every object was familiar to me; but where were all the people who were grieving as if their hearts would break? I was puzzled and alarmed. What could be the meaning of all this? Determined to find the cause of a state of things so mysterious and so shocking, I kept on until I arrived at the East Room, which I entered. There I met with a sickening surprise. Before me was a catafalque, on which rested a corpse wrapped in funeral vestments. Around it were stationed soldiers who were acting as guards; and there was a throng of people, gazing mournfully upon the corpse, whose face was covered, others weeping pitifully. "Who is dead in the White House?" I demanded of one of the soldiers, "The President," was his answer; "he was killed by an assassin." Then came a loud burst of grief from the crowd, which woke me from my dream. I slept no more that night; and although it was only a dream, I have been strangely annoyed by it ever since.

"This dream was so horrible, so real, and so in keeping with other dreams and threatening presentiments of his that Mr. Lincoln was profoundly disturbed by it," wrote Lamon.[37]

Even without the complications of dreams, Lincoln's life had been filled with sadness and anxiety for some time. He and Mary had lost two sons, Edward, who died in 1850 at the age of four, and Willie, who died at age eleven in the White House in 1862. In the latter years of the war, Mary was distraught following Willie's recent death and concerned about their oldest son, Robert, joining the army. The pressures of domestic life were heavy enough for the president, but the larger concern always was the welfare of the nation in the midst of the dreadful war. For Lincoln there was precious little time to rest, as Grant had suggested, while visiting City Point.

President Lincoln, General Grant, General Sherman, and Admiral Porter gathered in the same place for the only time during the Civil War as they anticipated the final days of the conflict while at City Point. At the same time Lee had launched the Confederate strike against Fort Stedman, Grant was planning the final push against the defenses of Petersburg. Sherman had driven Johnston's Confederate army into North Carolina and tenaciously refused to

This photograph of Gen. William T. Sherman was taken at the Brady National Photographic Art Gallery in Washington, DC. Sherman prosecuted a relentless war of attrition against Confederate forces in Georgia and the Carolinas, recognizing the cruel nature of total war. However, with the surrender of the Confederate forces under Gen. Joseph Johnston in North Carolina on April 26, 1865, Sherman offered generous terms. *Library of Congress*

give him respite. The Confederate Navy was at bay in the James near Richmond. Lincoln wanted assurances that the Rebels would not escape any Union commander's grasp and that an end without retribution was close at hand. He also wanted to impress upon his generals that the government was responsible for conducting any overarching peace negotiations beyond the surrender of the enemy armies.

Sherman was confident that the situation was well in hand on his front. Born in Lancaster, Ohio, on February 8, 1820, the red-haired general was one of eleven children of Charles Sherman, an attorney and Ohio Supreme Court Justice. Charles Sherman died when his son was nine years old, and William was raised by Senator Thomas Ewing, a family friend who secured the young man an appointment to the US Military Academy at West Point in 1836. Sherman graduated sixth in the class of 1840. He fought in the Seminole Wars and spent the Mexican War posted in California. By 1853, he believed his military career was going nowhere and resigned his commission. The Panic of 1857 extinguished his banking career in the Golden State, and a law practice in Kansas foundered.

In 1859, Sherman accepted the position as the first superintendent of the Louisiana State Seminary of Learning and Military Academy, which later became Louisiana State University. He performed well in the role, but when Louisiana seceded from the

Union, he moved to Saint Louis and asked his younger brother, Senator John Sherman of Ohio, to arrange a commission in the army. His early performance in command was lackluster, and he was eventually considered unfit for duty. There was speculation that he was mentally unstable and may have suffered a nervous breakdown.

After returning to service at the end of 1861, Sherman was relegated to backwater commands in Missouri. Then, his support of Grant at Forts Henry and Donelson gave his career new life and reassignment to work under Grant. The two forged a lasting friendship on the field at Shiloh. In the spring of 1865, Sherman commanded the Military Division of the Mississippi, including all Union armies in the Western Theater of the Civil War.

Years later, Sherman remembered fondly, "Grant stood by me when I was crazy, and I stood by him when he was drunk. Now we stand by each other."[38]

On March 25, Sherman left Gen. John Schofield in command at Goldsboro, North Carolina, and traveled by train to Morehead City. There, he boarded the captured steamer *Russia* and, following a brief stop at Fort Monroe to telegraph his brother, the senator, with an invitation to join him on the return trip to Goldsboro, arrived at City Point on the afternoon of March 27. Horace Porter was with Grant when Sherman arrived and remembered:

> General Grant and the two or three of us who were with him at the time started down to the wharf to greet the Western commander. Before we reached the foot of the steps, Sherman had jumped ashore and was hurrying forward with long strides to meet his chief. As they approached, Grant cried out, "How d'you do, Sherman!" "How are you, Grant!" exclaimed Sherman; and in a moment they stood upon the steps, with their hands locked in a cordial grasp, uttering earnest words of familiar greeting. Their encounter was more like that of two school-boys coming together after a vacation than the meeting of chief actors in a great war tragedy.[39]

After the two commanders had talked for about an hour, Grant mentioned that it might be appropriate to call on the president aboard the *River Queen* before dinner. Grant is strangely quiet regarding Lincoln's visit to City Point and any discussions that went on there. Sherman and Admiral Porter, however, provided vivid recollections. Sherman had met Lincoln only once, four years earlier, and had not been favorably impressed. This meeting began well.

"We walked down to the wharf, went on board, and found Mr. Lincoln alone, in the after-cabin," recalled Sherman in his postwar memoirs. "He remembered me perfectly, and at once engaged in a most interesting conversation." Lincoln asked numerous questions about Sherman's March to the Sea and the subsequent campaigning. He also inquired about Sherman's "'bummers,' and their devices to collect food and forage when the outside world supposed us to be starving." The pleasant discussion ended, and Sherman later wrote, "Having made a good, long, social visit, we took our leave and returned to General Grant's quarters, where Mrs. Grant had provided tea."[40]

The following morning a number of senior officers at City Point visited Sherman, and soon he, Grant, and Admiral Porter boarded a small tug to carry them to the *River Queen*, now anchored in the river. "No one accompanied them," remembered Horace Porter. "There now occurred in the upper saloon of that vessel the celebrated conference between these four magnates . . . It was in no sense a council of war, but only an informal interchange of views between the four men who, more than any others, held the destiny of the nation in their hands."[41]

Grant explained the movements of Sheridan's cavalry, intent on cutting Lee's supply lines along the South Side and Danville railroads. Attempting to allay any fears that Lincoln harbored of a Confederate escape from the Carolinas or from the vicinity of Richmond and Petersburg—particularly one that might result in the two enemy armies combining—Sherman assured the troubled chief executive that his army at Goldsboro was strong enough to fight either Rebel army or both of them provided that Grant came up in support within a day or so.

The two generals then agreed that one more bloody battle would be necessary to subdue the Confederate armies once and for all. Lincoln then probed the officers for an alternative to further loss of life. Horace Porter wrote later that Grant relayed the discussion to him and to Mrs. Grant on the evening of March 28. "Mr. Lincoln asked if it would not be possible to end the matter without a pitched battle, with the attendant losses and suffering;

but was informed that that was a matter not within the control of our commanders, and must rest necessarily with the enemy."[42]

Inevitably, the subject turned to the future, to the situation after the war. Sherman, as aggressive in the presence of Lincoln as he was on the battlefield, spoke first. He later wrote:

> During this interview, I inquired of the President if he was all ready for the end of the war. What was to be done with the rebel armies when defeated? And what should be done with the political leaders, such as Jeff. Davis, etc.? Should we allow them to escape, etc.? He said he was all ready; all he wanted of us was to defeat the opposing armies, and to get the men composing the Confederate armies back to their homes, at work on their farms and in their shops. As to Jeff. Davis, he was hardly at liberty to speak his mind fully, but intimated that he ought to clear out, "escape the country," only it would not do for him to say so openly. . . I made no notes of this conversation at the time, but Admiral Porter, who was present, did, and in 1866 he furnished me an account thereof.[43]

There appears to have been some confusion between General Sherman and Admiral Porter as to the date of the meeting when the admiral took extensive notes. Whether it occurred on March 27 or 28, Porter wrote the following year in response to officials, chiefly Secretary of War Edwin M. Stanton, who had severely criticized Sherman for his liberal terms to Johnston at the end in North Carolina.

"My opinion is that Mr. Lincoln came down to City Point with the most liberal views toward the rebels," Admiral Porter wrote. "He felt confident that we would be successful and was willing that the enemy should capitulate on the most favorable terms. . . . The conversation between the President and General Sherman about the terms of surrender to be allowed Jos. Johnston continued. Sherman energetically insisted that he could command his own terms and that Johnston would have to yield to his demands; but the President was very decided about the matter and insisted that the surrender of Johnston's army most [sic] be obtained on any terms."[44]

Regardless of the timeline, when Sherman departed City Point on the fast steamer *Bat*, which Admiral Porter had offered to speed his journey to Goldsboro, there was no ambiguity as to Lincoln's stance on the restoration of peace and the beginning of reconciliation. Sherman also left the meeting with an abiding appreciation of Lincoln. The general wrote, "We parted at the gangway of the River Queen, about noon of March 28th, and I never saw him again. Of all the men I ever met, he seemed to possess more of the elements of greatness, combined with goodness, than any other."[45]

In retrospect, it is plausible that Sherman sought the shelter of Lincoln's revered stature in the controversy over the surrender terms that swirled in the wake of the president's death. However, Grant, Sherman, and Porter each heard Lincoln proclaim his perspective on the future of the nation that day at City Point, just as he had done during his inaugural address.

"Let them once surrender and reach their homes," Lincoln told the military men. "They won't take up arms again. Let them all go, officers and all, let them have their horses to plow with, and, if you like, their guns to shoot crows with. I want submission and no more bloodshed. . . . I want no one punished; treat them liberally all round. We want those people to return to their allegiance to the Union and submit to the laws."[46]

Lincoln remained at City Point another eleven days, and to his dismay more serious fighting did occur. Before peace returned, the loss of life continued, and the president himself was among the last of the casualties.

PART II

THE FORLORN HOPE

IN THE TRENCHES
OF PETERSBURG

The landscape at Petersburg was desolate and treeless in some areas, scarred by shell holes and the upturned earth that marked miles of trenches. The scene was a harbinger of the western front during World War I half a century later.

During the Overland Campaign, Gen. Ulysses S. Grant had made four direct thrusts at the Confederate capital of Richmond, fighting in the Wilderness, at Spotsylvania, along the North Anna River, and at Cold Harbor. Lee had deflected each one in a series of violent and costly battles punctuated by rapid maneuver. Rather than Gen. George Meade and the Army of the Potomac hastening to harry Lee as Grant had intoned at the beginning of the campaign, it was Lee who anticipated the Federal movements time and again and put his haggard but spirited Army of Northern Virginia across the path of the Union advance.

Years later, Confederate general John B. Gordon wrote wryly of his commanding officer:

> Verily, it would seem that Grant's martial shibboleth, "Where Lee goes, there you will go also," had been reversed; for, in literal truth, Meade was not going where Lee went, but Lee was

going where Meade went. It was General Grant's intention that General Lee should learn from every Union cannon's brazen throat, from every hot muzzle of every Union rifle, that nothing could prevent the Army of the Potomac from following him until the Confederate hosts were swept from the overland highways to Richmond. The impartial verdict of history, however, and the testimony of every bloody field on which these great American armies met in this overland campaign, from the Wilderness to the water route and to the south side of the James, must necessarily be that the going where the other goes was more literally the work of Lee than of Grant.[47]

Gordon went on to point out that in twenty-eight days of fighting the soldiers of the Army of Northern Virginia had killed, wounded, captured, or otherwise rendered ineffective as many Union troops as General Lee actually commanded. "Or, to state the fact in different form," he asserted, "had General Grant inflicted equal damage upon Lee's troops, the last Confederate of that army would have been killed, wounded, or captured, still leaving General Grant with an army very much larger than any force that had been under Lee's command at any period of the campaign."[48]

Lee fought a superb defensive campaign during the spring of 1864 but could not muster the strength to bring on a decisive battle—a victory that could change the course of the war. His peak strength at the beginning of the Overland Campaign approached seventy thousand, but by early June he had lost nearly half his command to combat deaths, wounds, or a growing rate of desertion.

Over the course of the campaign, Grant had also revisited a hard lesson he absorbed at Vicksburg. Direct assault against fortified and entrenched enemy positions is a costly and often futile endeavor. Spotsylvania and Cold Harbor had driven the lesson home once again. General Meade's Army of the Potomac had already suffered a staggering fifty thousand casualties. Among them was Maj. Gen. John Sedgwick, felled by a sniper's bullet at Spotsylvania Court House.

Connecticut-born Horatio G. Wright replaced Sedgwick in command of VI Corps on May 9, 1864, and was promoted to major general. The US Senate confirmed this second recommendation for Wright's promotion. The first, in recognition of his achievements against the Confederates along the Florida coast, was not confirmed in the Senate and later rescinded. Although his rank reverted to brigadier general, Wright performed well in Kentucky during the repulse of Gen. Braxton Bragg's offensive in 1862. He commanded a reserve division at Gettysburg and led his troops through the Overland Campaign.

Wright commanded the three army corps defending Washington, DC, during Lt. Gen. Jubal Early's raid in the summer of 1864 and marched with Sheridan during the Valley Campaign in the autumn. He was instrumental in Sheridan's victory at Cedar Creek in October 1864.

Three days after the bloodletting before the entrenched Confederates at Cold Harbor, Meade concealed his frustration in a letter to his wife. "Do not be deceived about the situation of affairs by the foolish despatches in the papers," he wrote. "Be not over-elated by reported successes, nor over-depressed by exaggerated rumors of failures. Up to this time our success has consisted only in compelling the enemy to draw in towards Richmond; our failure has been that we have not been able to overcome, destroy or bag his army. His success has been in preventing us from doing the above, and in heading us off every time we have tried to get around him. . . . The great struggle has yet to come off in the vicinity of Richmond. . . . We shall have to move slowly and cautiously, but I am in hopes, with reasonable luck, we will be able to succeed."[49]

While the devastating drama at Cold Harbor played out, Grant decided that he had no further options for a direct assault on Richmond. Therefore, he intended to move the army to the left, south of the James River, against the rail and road center at Petersburg, where the South Side Railroad ran from Lynchburg to the west, the Norfolk & Petersburg line came up from the southeast, and the Weldon Railroad entered from North Carolina, while supplies reached Petersburg and eventually Richmond on several plank roads as well.

The city in Union hands meant that either the Army of Northern Virginia would eventually be starved into capitulation while the Confederate capital fell, or that Lee would be required to come out of his long trench lines, abandoning both Petersburg and Richmond, in a desperate fight for survival. For the Confederacy, the situation grew more perilous by the hour.

For Grant, the Petersburg effort meant more than a simple advance around Lee's right flank. It would involve his large army and its supporting element crossing first the Chickahominy River and then the James, twelve miles to the south. The James crossing would be particularly hazardous. The river's strong currents complicated the movement, and its width of nearly 2,100 feet and depth of 100 feet at Wilcox Landing, the chosen point for the bulk of the Army of the Potomac to execute the maneuver, were problematic for engineers, who constructed a massive pontoon bridge across the James in less than eight hours.

In describing the tactical deployment of the contending armies at Petersburg, the word "siege" is something of a misnomer. The Union armies did not completely surround the city, and there was movement as Grant lengthened his lines and forced Lee to do so as well. When Grant set his vast Army of the Potomac in motion late on the afternoon of June 12, the II, VI, and IX Corps slipped from their entrenchments at Cold Harbor, while the V Corps made demonstrations against Lee's right flank to convince the enemy that another direct advance against Richmond was underway. Meanwhile, if all went according to plan, Grant would concentrate his forces in the Confederate rear, forty miles beyond Lee's Cold Harbor lines.

As a prelude to his movement to invest Petersburg, Grant sent Phil Sheridan with two divisions of cavalry fifty miles northeast, to Trevilian Station, where his troopers could tear up the tracks of the Virginia Central Railroad for miles, disrupting the supply line from Staunton in the Shenandoah Valley to Richmond. Union forces under Maj. Gen. David Hunter had occupied Staunton, and the two commands might join forces and press Lee from the west as well.

Lee got wind of the Union cavalry movement and ordered two divisions of his own horsemen, under Maj. Gen. Wade Hampton and Maj. Gen. Fitzhugh Lee, to intercept the marauding Federals. The cavalry command was split between Hampton, a capable forty-six-year-old South Carolinian, and Fitzhugh Lee, the twenty-nine-year-old nephew of the commanding general, since the flamboyant Jeb Stuart, the grandest cavalier of the Confederacy, had been killed at the Battle of Yellow Tavern a month earlier.

With a shorter distance to travel, the Confederate cavalry reached Trevilian Station first. Fighting erupted on the morning of June 11, and one of Sheridan's brigades, Michigan troopers commanded by Brig. Gen. George Armstrong Custer, slipped between the two Confederate divisions and fell upon Hampton's unprotected supply train, capturing some wagons and scattering others full of ammunition and provisions. Hampton heard the ruckus in his rear and sent the 7th Georgia Cavalry to meet the threat just as Fitzhugh Lee came up from Louisa Court House to the east.

Custer was surrounded and fought desperately to escape the encirclement. His command was nearly overrun, and the general tore his regimental colors from their staff and stuffed them into his coat. Sheridan sent timely reinforcements and rescued Custer as the Confederates fell back to defensive positions. With his command extricated from the pinch, Custer rode up to Sheridan, who inquired whether the Rebels had captured his flag. Custer pulled the banner from his coat and waved it wildly, shouting, "Not by a damned sight! There it is!"[50]

The brash young Custer was only twenty-five years old. Born in New Rumley, Ohio, on December 5, 1839, he was the son of a blacksmith and subsistence farmer. He spent much of his youth living with his half sister and brother-in-law in Monroe, Michigan, and briefly taught school before writing to Congressman John Bingham of Ohio in 1856 to request an appointment to the United States Military Academy. The appointment had already been filled, but Custer was successful in gaining admittance the following year.

With lackluster academic and disciplinary records at West Point, Custer's career showed little promise. The academy program was accelerated with the outbreak of the Civil War, and he graduated a year early, last among thirty-four cadets—the goat of the class of 1861. While serving as officer of the guard just days after graduation, he did not intervene in a fight between two cadets and was court-martialed for failure to do his duty. Only the need for junior officers in the rapidly expanding army saved him from severe punishment, and he reported to Company G, 2nd US Cavalry.

Custer was utterly fearless, and quickly gained the attention of senior officers. He served on McClellan's staff during the Peninsula Campaign and participated in the battles of Fredericksburg and Chancellorsville. He fought with distinction during the major cavalry engagements at Gettysburg and later at Yellow Tavern, rising rapidly to brigade and division command. By 1865, he had earned a reputation as a daring but impetuous cavalry commander, whose troops often suffered extremely high casualties.

The Rebel retreat from Trevilian Station left Sheridan in possession of the field, but the fighting had disrupted his mission to destroy railroad track. News that Hunter was not joining him but moving south toward Lexington further diminished the potential for the rest of the long-range raid. The Confederates dismounted and dug in during the night. Numerous attacks against the strong entrenchments were fruitless. Short on ammunition and with more than a thousand killed, wounded, and missing, Sheridan pulled back to rejoin Grant, reaching the main Union army on June 28. Confederate losses totaled more than eight hundred.

Although Sheridan fell short of his primary objectives—traffic was again rolling on the Virginia Central Railroad within two weeks—he had occupied the Confederate cavalry and prevented its detection of Grant's James River crossing. Sheridan went to his grave proclaiming that the Battle of Trevilian Station, one of the largest cavalry clashes of the Civil War, was a Union victory. Grant supported the assertion in his memoirs. However, at best the result was an inconclusive draw.

Within forty-eight hours of Sheridan's foray toward Trevilian Station, Maj. Gen. Benjamin F. Butler moved elements of his Union Army of the James, thirty-three thousand strong, against Petersburg. A month earlier, Butler had been ordered to advance up the James River on flatboats to Bermuda Hundred with instructions to march the fifteen miles up the small peninsula and attack either Richmond or Petersburg. When Butler arrived at Bermuda Hundred on May 5, he hesitated, squandering his initial opportunity to take Petersburg, then occupied by an ad hoc garrison of only two thousand Confederates under the command of Brig. Gen. Henry Wise, George Meade's brother-in-law and a former governor of Virginia. Within days, a Confederate force less than half the size of Butler's cut off his advance and bottled up the entire Army of the James at Bermuda Hundred.

Although many senior officers considered Butler unfit for command, political connections helped keep him in the field until January 1865. Butler did grasp the fact that his diversionary role, covering Grant's movement across the James, presented an opportunity for redemption. As the forces to his front were weakened, withdrawn northward to reinforce Lee before Richmond, Butler planned a raid on Petersburg, a three-pronged advance that was to begin on the evening of June 8. From the beginning, the operation was bungled. Its timetable was upset, preventing coordinated attacks, and two of the three commanders showed no initiative, waiting to launch attacks until the third force was in place.

Inside Petersburg, Wise welcomed the assistance of Brig. Gen. Raleigh Colston, who happened to be in the town. A less than stellar performance at Chancellorsville the previous year had left Colston without a command. Buoyed by the ineptitude of their adversaries, the unlikely tandem of Wise and Colston with the 46th Virginia, elements of the 23rd South Carolina, a few artillery pieces, and local militia consisting of old men and boys, managed to hold the vital town, shifting soldiers as needed. One of the militiamen loaded and fired his rifle using a pocketknife to cut the paper cartridges open because he had no teeth with which to tear them.

When a concerted Union effort was finally launched against the Petersburg defenses, several hours behind schedule, the three attacking forces lacked communication and did not coordinate their effort. Despite their problems, one column of attacking Federals came within 150 yards of the heart of Petersburg at midday. However, the other two Union commands had already withdrawn.

Grant, meanwhile, was carrying out his plan to cross the James and force Lee's hand. He wrote to his friend Congressman Elihu Washburne on June 9, "Everything is progressing favorably but slowly. All the fight except defensively and behind breast works is taken out of Lee's army. Unless my next move brings on a battle the balance of the campaign will settle down to a siege."[51]

Grant held the initiative and knew that Lee would be obliged to react to the movements of the 115,000-man Army of the Potomac. He had gone to great lengths to deceive Lee as to his next move, and the effort paid off. Lee remained uncertain of exactly what was happening as Grant ordered Meade to start his army across the James on the evening of June 12. General Warren's V Corps and cavalry under Gen. James H. Wilson crossed the Chickahominy and exercised their role in the deception capably.

Lee remained preoccupied with Warren's demonstrations against his flank and fought off the Federal feint at Richmond. He ordered an attack against Warren, but on the morning of June 9 the enemy was nowhere to be found. Warren had slipped away during the night to join the James crossing.

The commander of the Army of Northern Virginia nevertheless recognized the possibility of a Union advance to the south across the James. However, he was also required to defend Richmond while weakening his force before the Confederate capital, sending Hampton and Fitzhugh Lee against Sheridan and moving reinforcements to Petersburg to bolster Wise and Colston. As he waited for Grant to advance, Lee observed "The best course for us to pursue, in my opinion, would be to move down and attack him with our whole force, provided we could catch him in the act of crossing."

Grant's crossing of the James was virtually flawless, and two days into the operation Lee was still uncertain of his adversary's intent. On June 14, he telegraphed Confederate President Jefferson Davis in Richmond, "As I informed you last evening I intended to move troops nearer the exterior lines of defences around Richmond, but from the movements of the enemy's cavalry and the reports that have reached me this morning, his plans do not appear settled. Unless therefore I hear something more satisfactory, they will remain where they are."[52]

Lee did not fully realize that Grant's major offensive movement was underway for several days, possibly as late as June 18. In discussions with Gen. Jubal Early, who had replaced Ewell in command of the II Corps, Lee urged, "We must destroy this army of Grant's before he gets to the James River. If he gets there, it will become a siege, and then it will be a mere question of time."[53]

Lee hesitated uncharacteristically. He believed that Richmond remained the primary Union objective and that it would be impossible for such a large body of troops as the Army of the Potomac to cross the James River unnoticed. General Pierre Gustave Toutant Beauregard, who had assumed command of the Petersburg defenses, was under no illusions. He believed firmly that Petersburg was Grant's target and prepared for the worst with only about two thousand troops to man the defenses, formidable as they were.

Since early in the war, the Confederate military establishment realized that control of Petersburg was vital, and in 1862 Capt. Charles H. Dimmock of the engineers supervised the construction of a U-shaped trench line that stretched ten miles and anchored both east and west on the Appomattox River. The Dimmock Line, as it was called, included numerous triangular earthen strongpoints, or redans, with berms up to forty feet high and emplacements for fifty-five artillery batteries. The line was studded with *abatis* and *chevaux-de-frise*, logs with their sharpened tips pointed toward the enemy's avenue of approach, and deep ditches that would impede the progress of an assault.

Beauregard remained gravely concerned. His ranks were so thin that men were often spaced more than ten feet apart. Protecting the Norfolk & Petersburg Railroad was imperative, and most of the defenders were positioned in the eastern section of the defenses between Redan No. 1 along the Appomattox River and Redan No. 23 guarding the rail line.

Grant was anxious to take Petersburg and traveled by steamer on June 14 to confer with Butler at Bermuda Hundred. He had bolstered the Army of the James with the XVIII Corps under the command of Gen. William F. "Baldy" Smith and ordered an attack on the city for the morning of June 15. Doubting that Grant had moved at all, Lee dispatched an infantry division under Maj. Gen. Robert Hoke to augment Beauregard's command. Concurrently, about sixteen thousand Union infantry and cavalry under Baldy Smith and generals Edward Hinks and August V. Kautz started toward Petersburg.

The Union attack of June 15 went forward without enthusiasm and sputtered to a halt by afternoon. Just as he had done a few days earlier, Kautz hesitated, reluctant to press his attack on a handful of Confederate defenders, no more than six hundred dismounted cavalrymen, at Redan No. 20. Baldy Smith's corps had been mauled at Cold Harbor two weeks earlier, and his attack amounted to little more than a series of reconnaissances. Beauregard, who had commanded the Confederate defenses of Charleston when the first shots of the war were fired at Fort Sumter three years earlier and taken command of the Confederate army during the defeat at Shiloh in April 1862, after the death of Gen. Albert Sidney Johnston, used interior lines to transfer troops as needed and conducted a brilliant defense.

As darkness gathered, Smith finally ordered his command forward with overwhelming force. Approximately fourteen thousand Union troops opened a mile-wide gap in the Petersburg defenses, and soldiers of Brig. Gen. Edward W. Hinks's 3rd Division, XVIII Corps captured seven Confederate cannon. There were no immediate Rebel reinforcements to stem the tide, and Beauregard was resigned to the fact that Petersburg was lost. Smith, however, declined to move any further toward the town.

The lackluster Federal performance on June 15 became even more embarrassing in retrospect. That morning Grant had ordered Hancock's II Corps of the Army of the Potomac to march to

Petersburg, but apparently Hancock was never given specific orders beyond crossing the James once again and waiting for provisions to come up to feed his hungry troops. Hancock was further ill-served when instructed to halt at a place that did not exist on any available map. He arrived before Petersburg just as Smith's attack moved forward in the gathering darkness. Although he was senior, Hancock deferred continuing control of the operation to Smith, who had been on the scene all day. Smith merely requested that II Corps troops relieve some of his own men in their current positions.

Both senior commanders and foot soldiers in the ranks soon realized the magnitude of the lost opportunity of June 15, and Smith attempted to blame Hancock for the decision to forego further attacks that night. It was his last major assertion as a field commander in the Army of the Potomac. Smith was relieved of command the following month.

Years later, as he penned his memoirs while dying of throat cancer, Grant lamented the day that Petersburg might have fallen into his hand like a ripe plum. "I believed then, and still believe, that Petersburg could have been easily captured at that time," he wrote.[54]

Apparently, Lee remained uncertain of Grant's intent into the early morning hours of June 16. At approximately 2:00 a.m., he was awakened with a dispatch from Beauregard that the Confederate troops holding the "neck" at Bermuda Hundred and impeding the progress of Butler's army there were being withdrawn to the defenses of Petersburg. In itself, this news alarmed Lee. Beauregard would not order such a move without real concern that Petersburg might fall to the Federals.

Beauregard, whose judgment had been correct all along, implored Lee to send more assistance from the lines at Richmond. "I have abandoned my lines of Bermuda Neck to concentrate all my force here: skirmishers and pickets will leave there at daylight. Cannot these lines be occupied by your troops? The safety of our communications requires it. Five thousand or 6,000 men may do."[55]

Lee responded by sending two divisions of Lt. Gen. Richard Anderson's corps, Anderson's old division and that of General George Pickett, to the Bermuda Hundred line. Pickett's division left the vicinity of Frayser's Farm and crossed the James at Drewry's Bluff. Lee moved his headquarters south of the James and worried that his army near Richmond had been reduced to only about twenty-four thousand infantrymen of A. P. Hill's III

Corps and the 3rd Division of Anderson's corps. While he might be better able to direct the operations at Bermuda Hundred, Lee had to rely on the telegraph and a series of couriers to maintain contact with Richmond and with Beauregard at Petersburg.

During the remaining hours of June 15, Beauregard received reinforcements that raised the number of Petersburg's defenders to about fourteen thousand men. He also supervised the digging of new entrenchments to strengthen the line, since Union troops had managed to overrun several of the redans before the town earlier in the day.

On the morning of June 16, an already overwhelming show of Union strength was increased with the arrival of Burnside's IX Corps at Petersburg. Grant accompanied these troops, approved the disposition of forces Hancock made with his own II Corps in the center, Burnside's IX on the left, and Smith's XVIII on the right, and ordered another attack at 6:00 p.m. Hancock, the ranking Union commander on the scene until either Grant or Meade arrived, was still suffering periodically from a serious wound to the groin he had sustained on Cemetery Ridge at Gettysburg a year earlier and eventually had to be relieved as the number of Union troops in the Petersburg vicinity swelled to more than fifty thousand.

The II Corps stepped off ahead of schedule that evening and captured one redan before the effort waned. Meade came upon the scene as the attack faltered and along with Hancock spurred a renewal of the assault. Brigadier General Francis Barlow waved his hat enthusiastically and led a charge against three redans. Almost immediately the Federals came under heavy Confederate artillery fire. The attackers fought their way into the defenses, but at heavy cost.

Colonel Patrick Kelly, commander of the famed Irish Brigade, was among those cut down. Born in Galway, Ireland, Kelly was a seasoned veteran, leading something of a charmed life through the battles of Fair Oaks, Antietam, Fredericksburg, Chancellorsville, Gettysburg, and Cold Harbor. He led the 88th New York Volunteers before rising to brigade command and was eulogized in the history of the Irish Brigade as "Gentle, brave, and unassuming, no truer man nor braver officer fell during the war."[56]

A manpower shortage in the ranks of the Army of the Potomac had resulted in the decision to take the soldiers of heavy artillery units that protected Washington, DC, and repurpose them as infantry. The 7th New York Heavy Artillery was one of these units, and in the melee at Redan Nos. 13, 14, and 15, the regiment lost its colors. Among its dead was twenty-four-year-old Cpl. William Harrison Lamoureaux, who had enlisted in the army two years earlier in his hometown of Westerlo, New York. He was described as a farmer with gray eyes and dark hair, the son of Joshua and Eliza W. Lamoreaux."[57]

The death of Lamoreaux was, in itself, not remarkable. However, it was indicative of many deaths, Union and Confederate, at Petersburg and elsewhere during the Civil War.

The Federals gained some ground, but large numbers of Union prisoners were taken as the sun went down. The 44th Tennessee Regiment captured more than two hundred Federals inside the works. Hancock passed the word to dig in for the night.

Lee was still in the dark as to Grant's whereabouts. However, a telegram he received from Beauregard that evening provided troubling information. "There has been some fighting today without result. Have selected a new line of defences around city, which will be occupied tomorrow, and hope to make it stronger than the first. The only objection is its proximity to city. No satisfactory information received of Grant's crossing James River. Hancock's and Smith's corps are however in our front."[58] The knowledge that more than two corps of the enemy were attacking Beauregard at Petersburg weighed heavily on Lee. Still, he could not imperil Richmond further by transferring his army south of the James without conclusive evidence of Grant's intent.

Meanwhile, to Grant's lasting frustration, the opportunity to capture Petersburg slowly ebbed. Attacks on June 17 failed to achieve a sustainable advantage despite the gains made by two IX Corps brigades under Brig. Gen. Robert Potter. From a distance of only one hundred yards, Potter led his men at dawn on the seventeenth into the Confederate works and surprised the occupants, taking six hundred prisoners, five battle flags, and four artillery pieces. Potter ordered a renewed advance, but a second line of Rebel entrenchments stopped them.

Beauregard telegraphed Lee late that afternoon, "Prisoners just taken represent themselves as belonging to Second, Ninth, and Eighteenth corps. They state that Fifth and Sixth corps are behind coming on. Those from Second and Eighteenth came here yesterday, and arrived first. Others marched night and day from

Gaines' Mill, and arrived yesterday evening. The Ninth crossed at Turkey Bend, where they have a pontoon-bridge. They say Grant commanded on the field yesterday. All are positive that they passed him on the road seven miles from here."[59]

The resourceful Beauregard put his engineers to work during the night constructing yet another defensive line about a mile behind the Dimmock Line and instructed his troops to move to the new positions just after midnight. He also instructed his commanders to have their men light campfires to deceive the Federals into thinking the Confederate defenders remained in their former positions.

"The firing lasted on the 17th, until a little after 11 o'clock P.M.," Beauregard continued. "Just before that time I had ordered all the camp-fires to be brightly lighted, with sentinels well thrown forward and as near as possible to the enemy's. . . . The digging of trenches was begun by the men as soon as they reached their new position. Axes, as well as spades; bayonets and knives, as well as axes, —in fact, every utensil that could be found—were used. And when all was over, or nearly so, with much anxiety still, but with comparative relief, nevertheless, I hurried off this telegram to General Lee [18th 12:40 A.M.]: 'All quiet at present. I expect renewal of attack in morning. My troops are becoming much exhausted. Without immediate and strong reënforcements, results may be unfavorable. Prisoners report Grant on the field with his whole army.'"[60]

Although he had received some reinforcements from Lee's Army of Northern Virginia, Beauregard did not anticipate further assistance. "I had failed to convince its distinguished commander of the fact that I was fighting Grant's whole army," he wrote years later.[61]

Finally, however, reports from Rooney Lee's cavalry confirmed the presence of the pontoon bridge across the James and that Grant was indeed south of the river. By 3:30 a.m. on the eighteenth, Lee had his army in motion toward Petersburg. While Lee was on the march, Beauregard's weary soldiers were digging for their lives along the new defensive line. As dawn streaked the sky, they observed a most welcome sight, Gen. Joseph B. Kershaw's division marching through a ravine and into the trench line. Throughout the day, more Confederate troops arrived from Richmond.

Lee reached Petersburg at about 11:00 a.m., and rode the line with Beauregard, who was still full of fight and wanted to attack immediately. Lee declined to issue such an order. The men were exhausted.

The four days of the Battle of Petersburg concluded on June 18 with a disjointed series of attacks mounted primarily on the instructions of Union corps commanders. The II Corps, now under the command of Maj. Gen. David B. Birney as Hancock was incapacitated, and the XVIII Corps advanced against the left of Beauregard's abandoned line and bowled into his new defenses at first light, but Burnside's IX Corps and Warren's V Corps that had recently arrived and swelled the Union ranks to sixty-seven thousand troops did not move forward until the middle of the day. By that time, the II Corps had sustained heavy casualties.

"I shall never forget the hurricane of shot and shell which struck us as we emerged from the belt of trees. The sound of the whizzing bullets and exploding shells, blending in awful volume, seemed like the terrific hissing of some gigantic furnace. Men, torn and bleeding, fell headlong from the ranks as the murderous hail swept through the line. The shrieks of the wounded mingled with the shouts of defiance which greeted us as we neared the rebel works," remembered Capt. A. C. Brown of Company H, 4th New York Heavy Artillery.[62]

For the rest of the day, Union troops threw themselves against the Petersburg defenses. One brigade in Gen. Orlando Willcox's division of the IX Corps lost three commanding officers and half its strength. In less than an hour, the 1st Maine Heavy Artillery suffered 632 casualties. During four days of combat before Petersburg, the Army of the Potomac had lost more than 10,000 men. The anguish at such a high casualty toll was trebled by the knowledge that Petersburg might have been taken with little more than a skirmish just a few days earlier.

Grant regretted the missed opportunities, particularly the breakdown in communication that prevented Hancock from moving swiftly against the town. "I do not think there is any doubt that Petersburg itself could have been carried without much loss; or, at least, if protected by inner detached works, that a line could have been established very much in rear of the one then occupied by the enemy," he explained later. "This would have given us control of both the Weldon and South Side railroads. This would also have saved an immense amount of hard fighting which had to be done from the 15th to the 18th, and would have given us greatly the advantage in the long siege which ensued. . . . Thus began the siege of Petersburg."[63]

Among the wounded on June 18 was Col. Joshua Lawrence Chamberlain, a brigade commander who had distinguished himself a year earlier at Gettysburg in command of the 20th Maine Regiment. The 20th Maine held the extreme left of the Union line at Gettysburg and fended off repeated assaults against Little Round Top. On this day at Petersburg, Chamberlain's command took heavy fire while attacking a Confederate strongpoint called Rives' Salient. When a nearby color bearer was shot dead, the colonel, a professor of theology at Bowdoin College in Maine before the war, grasped the flag and continued the advance.

Moments later, Chamberlain was struck by a bullet that passed through both of his hips, severing vital arteries, and grievously injuring his bladder and urinary tract. Bleeding profusely, he steadied himself by jamming his sword into the ground and continued to issue orders until he collapsed. The wound appeared mortal, but Chamberlain's brother, Maj. Thomas Chamberlain, would not give up. He found two surgeons, M. W. Townsend of the 44th New York and Abner Shaw of the 20th Maine, who did the best they could to save the colonel's life under difficult conditions.

Still, it was doubtful that Chamberlain would survive. Grant, believing Chamberlain's death was inevitable, issued a battlefield promotion and wrote later, "He had several times been recommended for a brigadier-generalcy for gallant and meritorious conduct. On this occasion, however, I promoted him on the spot, and forwarded a copy of my order to the War Department."[64]

For several weeks, Chamberlain's life hung in the balance. He wrote to his wife, Fanny, on June 19, "My darling wife I am lying mortally wounded the doctors think, but my mind & heart are at peace Jesus Christ is my all-sufficient savior. I go to him. God bless & keep & comfort you, precious one. You have been a precious wife to me. To know & love you makes life & death beautiful. Cherish the darlings & give my love to all the dear ones. Do not grieve too much for me. . . . Ever yours, Lawrence."[65]

The terrible wound was one of six Chamberlain suffered during his service in the Civil War. He was also hospitalized with malaria for an extended period. Miraculously, five months after that terrible day at Petersburg, he returned to service.

By the end of June, the opposing armies were exhausted. Lee's Army of Northern Virginia numbered about thirty-six thousand at Petersburg, while slightly more than twenty thousand remained in defense of Richmond. The Army of the Potomac numbered about seventy thousand before Petersburg, while Butler's Army of the

James included about forty thousand more opposite Richmond at Bermuda Hundred and Deep Bottom on the north bank of the James. Although Lee had never wanted a lapse into siege warfare, he knew that the only equalizer of force was the continuing construction of earthworks and fortifications.

Grant, on the other hand, did not relish a siege either. However, his previous experience, forty-seven days at Vicksburg, had ended in victory, and he was nevertheless confident of a similar outcome at Petersburg although the enemy in Virginia was much stronger and perhaps more resolute than the one encountered in Mississippi the previous year. Grant was obliged to dig in at Petersburg due to the threat of a Confederate attack. Unless his own line was secure, he could not contemplate any offensive action that might bring the siege to an early and favorable conclusion.

The opposing trench lines at Petersburg eventually extended from the Appomattox River to the Jerusalem Plank Road, sometimes only two hundred yards apart. When Federal bands struck up a tune, the Rebel soldiers enjoyed their music. Commands shouted on either side could easily be heard on the other. At Elliott's Salient in the Confederate line, the distance to the Union works was only about five hundred feet. Pickets sometimes fraternized and traded goods before returning to their deadly business.[66]

By the spring of 1865, Lee's thin ranks were defending a line of trenches and fortifications that extended an astounding fifty-three miles. Soldiers on both sides rose before the sun to take up picks and shovels rather than rifles, digging through the heat of the day with scant breaks. No appreciable rain fell during the month of June, and the digging raised great clouds of choking dust.

The trench lines at Petersburg incorporated complexes of covered redans and strongpoints, sometimes reinforced with logs. Front-line trenches stretched in front of secondary lines that were dug parallel and connected to roads that had been burrowed into the earth so deeply that wagons could deliver supplies or infantrymen could change positions without detection. Communications and supply trenches ran in zigzag patterns from the front to the rear echelons. Traversing these was often a deadly business.

In mid-June, the 4th Alabama Regiment moved into position along the breastworks. Its captain, Alexander C. Murray, was a Pennsylvanian who had become a successful merchant in Alabama prior to the war. With his men in position, Murray, who had received his promotion to captain just a day earlier, started toward the rear along a zigzag trench. As he passed another soldier, the officer briefly exposed his head above the parapet. In a flash, the report of a sharpshooter's rifle was heard and the young officer lay dead.

Standard field artillery was often ineffective against stout entrenchments, and both sides brought up heavy siege guns and mortars that could deliver plunging fire at high trajectory. These weapons tore gaps in the opposing lines, their flying shrapnel capable of killing at great distances. One gargantuan weapon, a thirteen-inch seacoast mortar nicknamed the "Dictator," was placed on a railcar at City Point by Union troops and brought to the Petersburg front during the summer. The Dictator weighed 17,120 pounds, and artillerymen of Company G, 1st Connecticut Heavy Artillery, loaded it with a shell that weighed 218 pounds and a 20-pound gunpowder charge. Its range was well over four thousand yards.

Confederate engineer W. W. Blackford survived numerous mortar barrages. "These mortar shells were the most disgusting, low-lived things imaginable," he recalled. "There was not a particle of the sense of honor about them; they would go rolling about and prying into the most private places in a sneaking sort of way."

A Union soldier of the 35th Massachusetts Regiment remembered, "In the daytime the burst of smoke from the Confederate mortars could be seen; a black speck would dart into the sky, hang a moment, increasing in size, rolling over and over lazily, and the revolving fuze [would begin] to whisper audibly, as it darted towards us, at first, softly, 'I'm a-coming, I'm a-coming'; then louder and more angrily, 'I'm coming! I'm coming!;' and, at last, with an explosion to crack the drum of the ear, 'I'm HERE!'"[67]

The summer of 1864 was one of the hottest in memory with temperatures soaring above one hundred degrees Farenheit, and historian Douglas Southall Freeman wrote, "Heat, flies, and the stench of the latrines made the existence torture."[68] James C. Reid of the 115th New York Infantry recalled legions of lice, nicknamed "graybacks" by the soldiers. "The trenches were literally alive with them, therefore it was impossible to get rid of them and perform all the duties required of us. The days that we were at the rear gave us an opportunity to thoroughly rid our clothes of them, but the banks of the little streams where we did our laundry work rivaled the trenches as abiding ground of the obnoxious pest."[69]

With the autumn and winter came rain, mud, and even greater squalor. One Union soldier wrote home to his wife that rain had fallen for four straight days, making roads virtually impassable. In the same letter he implored her to send him a good, rich raisin cake. A Confederate soldier of A. P. Hill's corps wrote, "With slender rations of corn bread and rancid bacon, with scanty clothes, worn out shoes (some were shoeless) and an inadequate supply of fuel, the outlook for the winter was gloomy in the trenches. Trenches became wet, filthy, and squalid. Life was a combination of monotony and misery, with occasional intrusions of terror from artillery and mortar fire."[70]

A North Carolina soldier described his regiment's winter in the Petersburg trenches saying, "It lived in the ground, walked in wet trenches, ate its cold rations in ditches, slept in dirt-covered pits."[71]

The specter of starvation stalked the Army of Northern Virginia throughout the siege. Continuous Union cavalry raids disrupted rail lines, and with inclement weather the situation often became desperate. On February 8, 1865, Lee telegraphed President Davis in Richmond.

> SIR: All the disposable force of the right wing of the army has been operating against the enemy beyond Hatcher's Run since Sunday. Yesterday, the most inclement day of the winter, they had to be retained in line of battle, been in the same condition the two previous days and nights. I regret to be obliged to state that under these circumstances, heightened by assaults and fire of the enemy, some of the men had been without meat for three days, and all were suffering from reduced rations and scant clothing, exposed to battle, cold, hail, and sleet. I have directed Colonel Cole, chief commissary, who reports that he has not a pound of meat at his disposal, to visit Richmond and see if nothing can be done. If some change is not made and the commissary department reorganized, I apprehend dire results. The physical strength of the men, if their courage survives, must fail under this treatment. Our cavalry has to be dispersed for want of forage.

After reviewing the communication, Davis noted, "This is too sad to be patiently considered, and cannot have occurred without criminal neglect or gross incapacity. Let supplies be had by purchase, or borrowing or other possible mode."[72]

For Lee and Davis, the procurement of supplies was only half the problem. Getting them to the starving soldiers of the Army of Northern Virginia became increasingly difficult as Grant tightened his siege.

CHAPTER 4

FAILURE AT FIVE FORKS

All was never really quiet on the Richmond-Petersburg front. Long periods of monotony were punctuated by sharp clashes of arms and heavy bombardment by siege guns. Grant maintained his stranglehold, even tightening it where possible, from season to season. To keep Lee and the Army of Northern Virginia off balance, he also struck directly at Petersburg from time to time.

Perhaps the most bizarre action of the war occurred six weeks after the initial investment of Petersburg. The Battle of the Crater, several weeks in the making, took place on June 30, 1864, and unraveled into a tour de force for the ineptitude of Federal command.

Colonel Henry Pleasants of the 48th Pennsylvania was justifiably proud of the fact that his four-hundred-man regiment had advanced farther toward the Confederate breastworks at Petersburg than any other unit during the fighting of June 18. Many of his Pennsylvanians were experienced miners, digging anthracite coal out of the ground for a living prior to the war. Since no one relished the prospect of an extended siege, Pleasants conceived an incredible scheme.

With the support of General Burnside, the IX Corps commander, but only casual indifference from Meade and Grant, Pleasants set his men to digging a 510-foot tunnel that would extend underneath the Confederate fortifications at a critical point called Elliott's Salient, east of the Jerusalem Plank Road. When the tunnel was finished, it would be packed with four tons of black powder and detonated. The resulting explosion would undoubtedly blow a sizable breach in the Confederate line. Union soldiers would immediately secure the trenches on either side of what was left of Elliott's Salient, plunge through the gap, and drive on to capture Petersburg.

Pleasants calculated the necessary length of the tunnel and devised an ingenious method of providing fresh air to the soldier-miners digging at its head. The colonel estimated that his men moved eighteen thousand cubic feet of dirt and rock. The Confederates became suspicious, digging tunnels of their own to listen for such activity approaching their lines. However, no real concern was raised, and the rumor that something was afoot generated jokes and laughter among the Rebels.

After a month of digging, Pleasants was authorized to load the tunnel with explosives. The effort took six hours, and 320 barrels of black powder were placed forward in eight chambers. Standing in the main chamber, Pleasants lit a ninety-eight-foot fuse at 3:15 a.m. on July 30. When nothing happened, a pair of volunteers crept inside the tunnel and discovered that the fuse had gone out. It was relit, and at 4:40 a.m., a tremendous explosion roiled up, killing nearly three hundred men of the 18th and 22nd South Carolina regiments and an artillery battery. The eruption left a crater two hundred feet long, fifty feet wide, and up to thirty feet deep.

"It was a magnificent spectacle, and as the mass of earth went up into the air, carrying with it men, guns, carriages, and timbers, and spread out like an immense cloud as it reached its altitude, so close were the Union lines that the mass appeared as if it would descend immediately upon the troops waiting to make the charge," recalled Union Maj. William H. Powell.[73]

The detonation itself was the high point of the operation from the Union perspective. The Union troops in the vicinity were nearly as stunned as the Confederates, and their advance was doomed from the start. Their positions had not been opened for the assault, and the men had to climb out of their own trenches before charging across open ground and being confronted by a newly created twelve-foot berm that stretched from the crater's rim. The South Carolina troops on either side of the crater regained their composure and quickly moved to contain the oncoming Union soldiers.

Initially, Burnside had selected a division of US Colored Troops under the command of Brig. Gen. Edward Ferrero to lead the assault at the crater. However, concerns about repercussions in the event of heavy loss of life among these untried black soldiers prompted both Meade and Grant to veto Burnside's choice.

Burnside settled the matter among his other division commanders, brigadier generals James Ledlie, Orlando Willcox, and Robert Potter by having them draw straws. Ledlie got the assignment and failed miserably. Cowering in a bunker toward the rear, he drank heavily from a bottle of rum and did not accompany his men in the attack. When Ferrero's division was committed to the fighting, he joined Ledlie in the bunker rather than lead his troops. After the debacle, both were censured by a court of inquiry.

A Confederate counterattack sealed the fate of the Federals, and in the frenzied fight men of both sides tumbled forward and backward into the abyss. Some attempted to climb out of the hole, only to be shot in the back from the other side of its rim. As the day wore on, Confederate soldiers were firing directly into the crater at the hapless enemy. The fighting ended around two p.m., with 4,000 Union soldiers dead, wounded, or captured. The Confederates lost approximately 1,500.

Grant called the Battle of the Crater a "stupendous failure."[74]

Meade vented to his wife, "Our men crouched in the crater and could not be got forward. . . . The affair was very badly managed by Burnside, and has produced a great deal of irritation and bad feeling. . . . I am afraid our failure will have a most unfavorable influence on the public mind, prone as it is to despondency."[75]

At least half a dozen times from June through the following March, Union cavalry or combined cavalry and infantry formations mounted substantial raids against rail lines, roads, or strongpoints in the Confederate lines at Petersburg or against Richmond. Offensive moves to the south and west of Petersburg failed to take control of the Weldon Railroad south of the city by the end of July. However, Union troops managed to cut the Jerusalem Plank Road in late June, and the extension of the siege line to the west further strained the Confederates.

For three days in late August, Warren's V Corps battled A. P. Hill's corps, wresting control of several miles of the Weldon Railroad. At the end of the month, Hill struck back at Reams Station, stopping the Union foray and preventing further destruction of the railroad tracks. Lee's lifeline from the Carolinas subsequently became an even more difficult route. His trains had to unload at Stony Creek Station, about sixteen miles from Petersburg. From there, the provisions were loaded on wagons and transported across rough roads to the vicinity of Dinwiddie Court House, then along the Boydton Plank Road to the Rebels in the besieged town.

All the derring-do of the Confederate cavalry did not perish with Jeb Stuart at Yellow Tavern. As Lee's men grew hungrier and meat became a scarce commodity, Wade Hampton got wind of an opportunity that he could not let pass. Since Union forces did not completely encircle Petersburg, its rear areas, including the vast supply base at City Point, were vulnerable to Rebel raiding parties. Lee urged Hampton to come up with something.

Early in July, Grant had sent a message to Meade regarding a substantial herd of beef cattle. "Please detail 150 men as an additional guard for the general herd of cattle, now numbering some 3,000, and being grazed or directed to be grazed on the James River, near Coggins Point. Direct the detail to report to Captain W. R. Murphy, commissary of subsistence, in charge of herd," Grant wrote.[76]

On September 5, one of Hampton's scouts, Sgt. George Shadburne of the Jeff Davis Legion, reported from his camp at the Blackwater River, "I have just returned from City Point. . . . At Coggins' Point are 3,000 beeves, attended by 120 men, and 30 civilians without arms."[77]

Hampton inquired about troop strength near Coggins' Point, on the James River about five miles below City Point, and whether Grant might be away from his command in the coming days. Shadburne responded that only a handful of Union cavalry, 250 at most, were

The bustling Union supply depot at City Point, Virginia, served as the distribution point for the men and materiel that defeated the Army of Northern Virginia in the spring of 1865. This image, taken by photographer Andrew J. Russell, depicts the City Point railroad station and a view of the wharf near the confluence of the James and Appomattox rivers. The historic meeting between President Abraham Lincoln and Generals Ulysses S. Grant and William T. Sherman took place at City Point in late March 1865. *Library of Congress*

located within a reasonable ride of the targeted herd. Further, Grant was expected to be away from the Petersburg front, conferring with Sheridan in the Shenandoah Valley, on September 14.

On the morning of the fourteenth, Hampton led Rooney Lee's cavalry division along with the brigades of Brig. Gen. James Dearing and Brig. Gen. Thomas Rosser south along the Boydton Plank Road and then southeast to a bridge across Rowanty Creek. The following morning, the raiders reached the Blackwater River. After midnight on the sixteenth, they were within ten miles of Coggins' Point, and Hampton detailed Dearing to assume a blocking position at Cocke's Mill while Lee dispersed any enemy soldiers nearby, and Rosser, along with a battalion commanded by Col. Lovick P. Miller, took the herd.

The attack began about 5:00 a.m., and within the hour the raiders had control of the cattle. The few Union troopers of the 1st District of Columbia and 13th Pennsylvania Cavalry regiments were scattered. Retracing their route, the Confederates were seriously threatened only once, by a 2,100-man cavalry contingent under Brig. Gen. Henry Davies Jr., but Rosser held the Union horsemen at bay.

On September 17, Hampton rode triumphantly back into the Confederate lines. Afterward, he wrote, "The command returned to their old quarters after an absence of three days, during which they had marched upward of 100 miles, defeating the enemy in two fights, and bringing from his lines in safety a large amount of captured property, together with 304 prisoners. Of the 2,486 cattle captured 2,468 have been brought in, and I hope [to] get the few remaining ones. Three guidons were taken and eleven wagons brought in safely, several others having been destroyed. Three camps of the enemy were burned, after securing from them some very valuable stores, including quite a number of blankets. My loss was 10 killed, 47 wounded, and 4 missing."[78]

At the time of the Great Beefsteak Raid, only a fifteen-day supply of meat was available in Richmond. Although it boosted morale in the besieged lines, the Confederate supply situation remained critical. After Grant was informed of the raid, he was asked when he thought his troops might starve Lee out of Richmond. He responded, "Never, if our armies continue to supply him with beef cattle."[79]

As summer turned to autumn, Grant focused on the two remaining supply lines into Petersburg, the Boydton Plank Road and the South Side Railroad. While Butler's Army of the James threatened Richmond at New Market Heights, forcing Lee to weaken the Petersburg defenses by shifting troops north of the James River to protect the capital, Confederate resistance at Peebles' Farm and along the Boydton Plank Road was substantial enough to stop the Union effort short of its objectives. The Union line, however, was extended westward again.

Winter weather did not deter Union operations west of Petersburg. It only made them more miserable. Early in December, Warren's V Corps initiated a heavy raid on the Weldon Railroad south of Stony Creek Station. Snow, sleet, and Wade Hampton's cavalry hampered the effort to tear up more track, and three days of sporadic fighting convinced Warren to backtrack from the Meherrin River to the Federal lines at Petersburg.

On January 29, 1865, a flag of truce was waved at Petersburg, and a trio of high-ranking Confederate officials passed safely through the lines to City Point and then Hampton Roads on February 3, for peace talks aboard the *River Queen* with President Lincoln and Secretary of State William Seward. The Confederates, Vice President Alexander Stephens, Senator Robert M. T. Hunter of Virginia, and Assistant Secretary of War John A. Campbell, quickly learned that the restoration of the Union was a condition of peace. Seward was also reported to have shown them a copy of the Thirteenth Amendment to the Constitution that abolished slavery while hinting that if the Southern states were to rejoin the Union its ratification might be delayed or prevented. No agreement was reached beyond that of prisoner exchanges.

The possibility of a negotiated peace did not distract Grant from the business at hand. His object during the winter of 1864–1865 was threefold—to capture Petersburg, to capture Richmond, and principally to destroy the Army of Northern Virginia as an effective fighting force. Grant was firm in the conviction that Lee could not sit behind his entrenchments indefinitely while his army's strength continued to erode. Lee was pinned, but the prospect of a Confederate breakout troubled Grant.

"One of the most anxious periods of my experience during the rebellion was the last few weeks before Petersburg," Grant wrote in his memoirs. "I felt that the situation of the Confederate Army was such that they would try to make an escape at the earliest practicable moment, and I was afraid, every morning, that I would awake from my sleep to hear that Lee had gone, and that nothing was left but a picket line. . . . I knew he could move much more lightly and more rapidly than I, and that, if he got the start, he would leave me behind so that we would have the same army to fight again farther south—and the war might be prolonged another year."[80]

To maintain his grip on the Army of Northern Virginia, Grant, even while conducting the Confederate peace commissioners to Hampton Roads, was putting together another offensive movement against the Boydton Plank Road and the South Side Railroad. On February 5, a division of cavalry under Col. J. Irvin Gregg forayed several miles south of the Confederate line, cutting the Boydton

Plank Road near Dinwiddie Court House and putting twenty-five wagonloads of supplies to the torch.

Warren's V Corps came up from the east in support, while the II Corps, now under Maj. Gen. Andrew A. Humphreys, headed for Hatcher's Run, a small stream where the Confederates had established a seven-mile defensive line the previous October, crossing the Boydton Plank Road to defend the South Side Railroad.

Born in Philadelphia, the fifty-four-year-old Humphreys was the grandson of Joshua Humphreys, a renowned shipbuilder appointed by Congress in 1794 as "naval constructor." His six subsequent frigate designs formed the backbone of the fledgling United States Navy during the War of 1812. They included the famed *Constitution, President, United States, Chesapeake, Constellation,* and *Congress.*

Andrew Humphreys graduated from West Point in 1831 and fought as an artillery officer during the Seminole Wars, contracting an extended illness. A talented engineer, he returned to that branch of the army and surveyed extensively along the Mississippi River. During the 1850s, he worked closely with then-Secretary of War Jefferson Davis surveying a potential route for the first transcontinental railroad.

With the coming of the Civil War, Humphreys served first as chief topographical engineer of the Army of the Potomac. His lack of an early field command in the Union army has been attributed to distrust due to his previously close relationship with Davis. The situation changed quickly. By September, Humphreys commanded a V Corps division at Antietam. During the slaughter at Fredericksburg, his division made the furthest advance against the entrenched Confederates on Marye's Heights, while two horses were killed under him and bullets tore his clothing. He commanded divisions at Chancellorsville and in the Peach Orchard at Gettysburg and served as Meade's chief of staff during the Overland Campaign. When Winfield Scott Hancock relinquished command of II Corps at Petersburg in November 1864 due to a wound sustained at Gettysburg that refused to heal, Humphreys assumed the post.

Lee was alarmed by the stirring of so many Federal troops and sent two divisions, under Maj. Gen. Henry Heth and Brig. Gen. Clement A. Evans, to reinforce A. P. Hill's corps on his right. Late in the afternoon of the fifth, the Confederates attacked and were thrown back by well-entrenched soldiers of Brig. Gen. Thomas A.

Smyth's division of II Corps. Meade and Warren both sent fresh divisions toward Hatcher's Run.

The following day, Gen. John Pegram's Confederate division attacked Gregg's cavalry and Maj. Gen. Samuel Crawford's division in the brambles and thickets near Dabney's Mill. Soon, Lee ordered another division into the fight. At first, the Union troops stood fast, but the weight of the Confederate reinforcements began to tell. For many of the Union soldiers, it was their first taste of combat. As their cartridge boxes emptied, they fled the field in disorder. The timely arrival of Brig. Gen. Charles Griffin's V Corps troops turned the tables and put the advancing Rebels to flight.

During one of the day's last exchanges of rifle fire, General Pegram was shot and killed. Major Henry Kyd Douglas, who had served as aide to the legendary Thomas J. "Stonewall" Jackson earlier in the war, remembered, "General Pegram was shot through the body near the heart. I jumped from my horse and caught him as he fell and with assistance took him from his horse. He died in my arms, almost as soon as he touched the ground."[81]

On January 19, days before his death, the thirty-three-year-old Pegram had married the beautiful Hetty Cary at Saint Paul's Church in Richmond. Among those present at the ceremony were President Jefferson Davis and his wife, Varina. The young general's funeral took place in the same church. The bullet that killed him had narrowly missed a locket that hung around his neck with a portrait of his wife inside.

The Battle of Hatcher's Run was tactically inconclusive. The Confederates suffered about a thousand casualties, and Union losses were twice as high. The Federals did extend their line roughly another three miles, and their continuing effort to cut Lee's supply line was having the desired effect.

Two days after the Hatcher's Run fight, Lee sent his poignant plea of February 8 to Richmond describing the wretched condition of his army and the possibility of a "calamity." Lee had run out of options, and just as Grant had predicted, he entertained the evacuation of the Petersburg line. However, evacuating Petersburg meant abandoning Richmond to the Federals. Out of desperation, Lee's forlorn hope was born. He intended to find a vulnerable location in the Union line, smash through it, then detach forces to join Johnston's army in North Carolina. Once the two Rebel forces were united there, they would defeat Sherman and then return to Virginia to renew the fight with the Army of the Potomac.

It was a pipe dream. But it was all Lee could do—short of capitulation.

Lee's Army of Northern Virginia was wracked by hunger and disease, its ranks thinned by desertion and death, and he knew its offensive capability was rapidly waning. From February 18 to March 15, the army lost 2,934 soldiers to desertion, approximately 8 percent of its fighting strength.[82]

In early March, Lee summoned Maj. Gen. John B. Gordon, commander of the remnants of the Army of Northern Virginia's II Corps since December 1864, requesting that he locate the most promising location to break through Grant's Petersburg line. Lee had just returned from a conference with President Davis in Richmond. He told Gordon that Davis believed, despite the fact that only the South Side Railroad remained open, the capital could still be held.

Gordon later wrote that he asked Lee, "'What, then, is to be done, general?' He replied that there seemed to be but one thing that we could do—fight. To stand still was death. It could only be death if we fought and failed."[83]

At thirty-two, Gordon was one of a relative few senior commanders in either army who proved themselves capable on the battlefield but were not West Point graduates. A Georgian, he was born February 6, 1832, and attended the University of Georgia. He practiced law in Atlanta and entered the coal business with his father in northern Georgia and Tennessee. When war broke out, he was elected captain of a volunteer company called the "Raccoon Roughs." In the spring of 1862, he fought at the Battle of Seven Pines as colonel of the 6th Alabama Regiment. He was wounded while commanding a brigade at Malvern Hill during the Peninsula Campaign.

While leading his Alabama troops in defense of the Sunken Road at Antietam in September 1862, Gordon was wounded five times in a single day. The last bullet struck him in the face, pierced his left cheek, and exited through his jaw. Falling with his face buried in his hat, he would likely have drowned in his own blood had it not drained through a bullet hole in the hat. Promoted to brigadier general in November 1862, he led brigades at Chancellorsville, Gettysburg, and the Wilderness, and commanded a division at Spotsylvania.

On June 12, 1864, Lee had instructed Lt. Gen. Jubal Early to take II Corps on an extended campaign in the Shenandoah Valley with the mission of clearing the valley of enemy troops, relieving some of the pressure on the defenders of Richmond, and possibly threatening Washington, DC. Gordon commanded a division in Early's corps, and the foray raised great concern in the Union capital. Early drove to within six miles of downtown Washington, with the Capitol dome plainly visible. He crossed into Maryland and then Pennsylvania, burning much of the city of Chambersburg. Eventually, Grant sent Sheridan with the Army of the Shenandoah to end the threat. Sheridan's victory at Cedar Creek compelled the Confederates to return to Petersburg.

Three weeks after his meeting with Lee, Gordon returned to his commander with a plan. After going over "every rod of the Federal entrenchments, every fort and parapet on the opposing line of breastworks and on the commanding hills in rear of them," he suggested Fort Stedman as the target for the desperate Confederate assault.[84]

Located a scant 150 yards from the Confederate lines, Fort Stedman was a strong earthwork, studded with *chevaux-de-frise* and strongly defended by infantry and cannon. Behind Fort Stedman were three smaller redoubts, from which enemy troops could sweep the fields and ditches with deadly fire. Gordon advised that the Confederate attack could step off from nearby Colquitt's Salient. To deal with the log obstructions, he proposed to recruit fifty volunteers armed with sharp axes to chop through them, clearing the way for the attackers. Independent parties of one hundred soldiers each would neutralize the three redoubts to the rear of Fort Stedman, not by direct assault but from the rear, led to their objectives by soldiers whose homes were in the area and were familiar with the lay of the land. With the capture of Fort Stedman and the three redoubts, a gap would be opened, and Confederate cavalry would charge through, racing to outflank the Federal trenches on either side, cutting supply and communications lines, and throwing the entire Union left wing into chaos.

Lee peppered Gordon with questions and then assented to the operation, offering to find the three soldiers with local ties that could guide the hundred-man assault teams in taking the redoubts and giving Gordon control of more than four divisions of infantry, about half the Confederate strength at Petersburg, with the promise of more if required.

"The tremendous possibility was the disintegration of the whole left wing of the Federal army, or at least the dealing of such a staggering blow upon it as would disable it temporarily, enabling us to withdraw from Petersburg in safety and join Johnston in North Carolina. The capture of the fort was only the breasting of the first in the ocean of difficulties to be encountered," Gordon remembered.[85]

At 4:00 a.m. in the darkness of March 25, a single rifle shot signaled the Confederate advance. The ax men moved forward, and surprised Union pickets were subdued. The Confederates punched through the line just north of Fort Stedman between Battery No. 9 and Battery No. 10. Confusion reigned among the Federals, and the commander of Fort Stedman found himself issuing orders to soldiers he believed to be his own. Instead, they were Confederates who quickly took him prisoner.

Rapidly, the defenders of Fort Stedman were killed, captured, or fled to other nearby positions at Batteries No. 11 and 12. North Carolina troops reached the Federal works around Battery No. 9 and hit the 57th Massachusetts. Major William H. Hodgkins of the 36th Massachusetts observed the ensuing fight.

"The enemy's left column turned to our right down the works toward Battery Nine, striking the flank of the Fifty-seventh Massachusetts, capturing a portion and driving out the remainder, who retired out of reach of the fire," Hodgkins wrote. "The Second Michigan was next encountered, but as this regiment had received warning it was able to fight the enemy on this flank in a most spirited manner from their bomb-proofs and traverses. The artillery in Battery Nine opened a heavy fire on the enemy's flank, and Colonel Ely hurried the First Michigan Sharp-shooters from his right and formed it at right angles with the line of entrenchments, where they fought with such success as to prevent any farther advance of the enemy."[86]

During the opening minutes of the assault, Gordon sent word to Lee that good progress was being made. However, the Confederate advantage rapidly melted away. The three hundred-man detachments lost their way and never did find the redoubts they were supposed to attack, and Union commanders were roused to action.

Meanwhile, Gordon concentrated his attack on the Union left, driving toward nearby Fort Haskell under a cascade of artillery from Confederate and captured Union guns. Their flag shot away, the defenders at Fort Haskell managed to put the Stars and Stripes back up, but not before their own artillery had lobbed shells into the fort, thinking it had fallen to the Rebels.

Major General John G. Parke, commanding the IX Corps after Grant had finally relieved the ineffective Burnside following the debacle at the Crater, was the senior officer of the Army of the Potomac present during the fight. Meade was away at City Point during the attack, which happened to fall upon Parke's seven-mile section of the Union line. Grasping the situation quickly, Parke ordered Willcox and Potter to contain the Confederate breakthrough with their divisions. The reserve division of Gen. John Hartranft also came up.

The Confederate breach was pushed back onto Fort Stedman itself, and by daylight it was clear that Gordon's gamble had failed. A new peril confronted the Rebel troops that had made the deepest penetration.

"It was impossible for me to make further headway with my isolated corps," commented Gordon, "and General Lee directed me to withdraw. This was not easily accomplished. . . . A consuming fire on both flanks and front during this withdrawal caused a heavy loss to my command. I myself was wounded, but not seriously, in recrossing the space over which we had charged in the darkness."[87]

Some Confederate soldiers disobeyed orders to withdraw and surrendered where they were. Gordon's losses totaled about 3,500 men, with more than half of these taken prisoner. Union losses totaled about 1,000.

After the defeat at Fort Stedman, it was apparent to all that the Army of Northern Virginia could not lift the siege of Petersburg by direct assault. Lee's thrust had been turned aside by a single corps of Union troops. As Lincoln arrived at City Point on March 24, Grant was piecing together the details of his own renewed offensive, striking once again around the Confederate right flank. The probability of more action in the vicinity of Fort Stedman was so remote that it was deemed safe enough for the president to visit the scene of the fighting.

Long convinced that Lee's only option for survival was a junction with Johnston in North Carolina, Grant took steps to prevent the Army of Northern Virginia from escaping. On the day of the fight at Fort Stedman, Sheridan returned from the Shenandoah Valley, where he had defeated Early four times, the last of these at Waynesboro, and devastated the "breadbasket" of the Confederacy. Sheridan brought with him nearly six thousand veteran cavalrymen in two divisions commanded by Brig. Gen. George Custer and Brig. Gen. Thomas Devin and resumed command of the Army of the Potomac's Cavalry Corps, numbering eleven thousand troops.

Although diminutive in stature, Sheridan was full of fight. Born in Albany, New York, the son of Irish immigrants, he was pugnacious and driven. When he was a boy, he moved to Somerset, Ohio, and worked around the town as a clerk in several of the local stores. Congressman Thomas Ritchey was a sometime visitor to one of the stores, and Sheridan petitioned him for an appointment to the US Military Academy at West Point. Sheridan graduated in 1853, standing thirty-fourth in a class of fifty-two, but not before he was suspended a year for threatening to run a fellow cadet through with a bayonet for an insult on the parade ground.

After the Civil War broke out, Sheridan held a succession of quartermaster and clerical posts and gained the attention of Maj. Gen. Henry W. Halleck, then the senior military commander in the Western Theater and future general-in-chief of the Union armies. He served at the Battle of Pea Ridge in Arkansas and in the siege of Corinth, Mississippi. In the spring of 1862, he was appointed to command the 2nd Michigan Cavalry, and two months later at Booneville, Mississippi, his skillful handling of a brigade resulted in promotion to brigadier general.

While commanding a division at the Battle of Stones River in December 1862, Sheridan led a heroic stand against repeated Rebel assaults, buying precious time for the rest of the Army of the Cumberland to rally. His exploits earned him a promotion to major general. Grant was with Sheridan at Chattanooga in November 1863, when his division was among those assaulting Missionary Ridge, routing the Rebels from the high ground and restoring a measure of the honor of the Army of the Cumberland that had been lost in its defeat at Chickamauga.

When Grant moved eastward, he summoned Sheridan to command the Cavalry Corps, and he had discharged his duties ably during the Overland Campaign.

Sheridan believed the defeat of the Army of Northern Virginia was imminent, and as his command rode toward Grant at Petersburg, the troopers continued tearing up the tracks of the Virginia Central Railroad and disabled the James River Canal. He remembered years later, "I was master of the whole country north of the James as far down as Goochland; hence the destruction of these arteries of supply could be easily encompassed, and feeling that the war was nearing its end, I desired my cavalry to be in at the death."[88]

Grant intended that his latest offensive, set for the end of the month, would force Lee from his strong defenses around Petersburg and into a decisive battle, with the Union armies' overwhelming numerical superiority prevailing. On the other hand, should Lee continue to shelter at Petersburg, Grant's successful flanking movement would hold the Rebels in place while the South Side and Danville railroads, Lee's only rapid lines of supply or escape, were cut. Sheridan would indeed have his opportunity to be in on the endgame. His cavalrymen were assigned a prominent role in the coming operation.

A complex series of troop movements began at 3:00 a.m. on March 29. Detached from General Ord's command north of the James River, the XXIV Corps, under Maj. Gen. John Gibbon, and a division of cavalry commanded by Brig. Gen. Ranald Mackenzie, relieved the II and V Corps, thirty-five thousand strong under Humphreys and Warren, to advance beyond the Confederate right flank. After marching about five miles, the infantry columns were to pivot north toward the Rebel lines and menace the flank without attacking it. Sheridan was instructed to drive his cavalry west toward Dinwiddie Court House and then north to the crossroads of Five Forks.

At 9:00 a.m., Grant and his staff said goodbye to President Lincoln at City Point and rode the rickety railroad to the front. "As the train was about to start, we all raised our hats respectfully," wrote Horace Porter. "The salute was returned by the President, and he said in a voice broken by an emotion he could ill conceal: 'Good-by gentlemen. God bless you all! Remember, your success is my success.' The signal was given to start; the train moved off; Grant's last campaign had begun."[89]

As the train chugged along, Grant told Porter, "The President is one of the few visitors I have had who has not attempted to extract from me a knowledge of my plans. He not only never asked them, but says it is better he should not know them, and then he can be certain to keep the secret. He will be the most anxious man in the country to hear the news from us, his heart is so wrapped up in our success, but I think we can send him some good news in a day or two."[90]

In turn, Porter observed, "I never knew the general to be more sanguine of victory than in starting out on this campaign."[91]

By the morning of the twenty-ninth, Lee was well aware that something was afoot, and as the details of the Federal movement became clear he understood its implication. The nearest counter-measure available was Gen. George Pickett's infantry division, initially directed from General Longstreet's I Corps to support the attack on Fort Stedman but too late to take part. Now, Pickett was in position to support the understrength corps of Gen. Richard Anderson. Lee also dispatched Fitzhugh Lee with all the cavalry north of the James except one brigade to join the two cavalry divisions under Rooney Lee and Thomas Rosser, already to the south, and take command of this force.

Rain began to fall, and as the day wore on pleasant weather turned beastly. Clouds gathered, and soon rain was pouring in torrents. In the afternoon, a Union column was spotted moving northward along the Quaker Road. Anderson pushed forward Maj. Gen. Bushrod Johnson's division to identify the enemy force, and soon a brisk fight was underway with Brig. Gen. Charles Griffin's division, the vanguard of Warren's V Corps.

In command of Griffin's lead brigade was Brig. Gen. Joshua Lawrence Chamberlain, still in great pain from his near-mortal wound suffered at Petersburg the previous summer. As Chamberlain's horse reared, a bullet passed through its neck and into the officer's chest, where it was deflected by a mirror encased in leather in his coat pocket. The bullet then creased his ribcage and exited through the back of his coat, finally knocking another officer from his horse.

Chamberlain was momentarily rendered unconscious. "My dear general, you are gone," said Griffin, who had come up to his side. Chamberlain responded, "Yes, general, I am." In moments, though, he was back on his horse and resumed directing his troops before the skirmish died down.[92]

Sheridan was somewhat dismayed by part of Grant's original order—to tear up the tracks of the South Side and Danville railroads and, if the situation should dictate, turn south to join Sherman in North Carolina. He rode into Dinwiddie Court House on the afternoon of the twenty-ninth and moved into the ramshackle tavern with his staff just as a heavy rain began to fall. There were no tents available, and the wagon with his mess equipment was stuck in the mud some distance to the rear. Two young ladies made coffee, and a couple of officers produced bottles of wine. One of the women played the piano, while a few of the soldiers joined in song, lifting the spirits of the company a little.

"The dreary night brought me one great comfort," remembered Sheridan. "For General Grant sent me instructions to abandon all idea of the contemplated raid, and directed me to act in concert with the infantry under his immediate command, to turn, if possible, the right flank of Lee's army. The dispatch made my mind easy with respect to the objectionable feature of my original instructions."[93]

Grant told Sheridan, "In the morning push around the enemy, if you can, and get on his right rear. We will act together as one army until it is seen what can be done. I feel now like ending the matter, if it is possible to do so, before going back."[94]

Heavy rain continued during the night and into the next day as Sheridan sent Maj. Gen. Wesley Merritt, nominal commander of the Army of the Shenandoah, along with Devin's cavalry division forward to seize the crossroads at Five Forks, cutting Lee's most likely route of withdrawal. Fitzhugh Lee's cavalry had already occupied the vital junction. Skirmishing, steady rain, and mud as thick as molasses slowed the advance.

Sheridan said, "The rain that had been falling all night gave no sign of stopping, but kept pouring down all day long, and the swamps and quicksands mired the horses, whether they marched in the roads or across the adjacent fields."[95] Nevertheless, he had his command on the move. However, around noon Grant issued orders to suspend operations.

The deluge did not prevent the energetic Sheridan from riding to Grant's camp in an old cornfield south of the Vaughn Road near Gravelly Run. Sheridan was in no mood to halt his progress, difficult though it might be. Astride a gray pacing horse he had named Breckinridge after its capture from the command of Gen. John C. Breckinridge, former Vice President of the United States, during the Battle of Missionary Ridge, Sheridan was excited.

"Instead of striking a pacing gait now, it [the horse] was at every step driving its legs knee-deep into the quicksand with the regularity of a pile-driver," recalled Horace Porter. "He [Sheridan] said, 'I can drive in the whole cavalry force of the enemy with ease, and if an infantry force is added to my command, I can strike out for Lee's right, and either crush it or force him to so weaken his intrenched lines that our troops in front of them can break through and march into Petersburg.'"[96]

Sheridan proclaimed, "'I tell you, I'm ready to strike out tomorrow and go to smashing things,'" wrote Porter, "and, pacing up and down, he chafed like a hound on a leash."[97]

Grant listened to Sheridan and agreed to allow the cavalry to struggle forward. When he returned to Dinwiddie Court House, Sheridan ordered a reconnaissance in force and received the news that Pickett's division had occupied Five Forks, intending to stand and fight. Robert E. Lee himself had ridden to the vicinity of Five Forks on the morning of the thirtieth and ordered Pickett there to support Fitzhugh Lee's cavalry. Lee added two brigades from Anderson's division to Pickett's command, hoping that Pickett could hold the critical junction while troops under Anderson and A. P. Hill mounted an attack against the exposed Federal flank.

Sheridan notified Grant that the Confederates held Five Forks and repeated a request for infantry support. He wanted Gen. Horatio Wright's VI Corps, which had fought with him during the Valley Campaign, but such a transfer was impractical. Warren's V Corps was nearby.

Major General Gouverneur Kemble Warren had served the Union cause heroically, particularly at Gettysburg. However, as the war dragged on, his behavior had become somewhat erratic. His demeanor changed abruptly at times, and his temper had grown short. Both Grant and Sheridan were aware of the change in Warren, and Sheridan was not inclined to involve his command in the coming operation. Nevertheless, V Corps was the appropriate choice. If issues arose, Sheridan would have to cope, and Grant gave him the leeway to relieve Warren if he felt it necessary.

On the morning of March 31, Sheridan was intent on fixing his enemy and bringing on a general engagement. However, Pickett struck first, sending infantry against the Federal front and driving the Union troops back across the road to Dinwiddie Court House. Pickett then pivoted south and headed for the town itself. Stubborn resistance from dismounted Union cavalry slowed their progress, but the Confederates were moving steadily. Sheridan recalled two cavalry brigades, one of them Custer's, which had been escorting Union supply wagons, and patched together a line on a small rise. Custer's men threw back two Rebel charges, and darkness ended the fighting.

George Pickett was forty years old. A native Virginian, he graduated from the US Military Academy fifty-ninth and last in the class of 1846, which produced twenty generals, both Union and Confederate, who served in the Civil War. Among these were Stonewall Jackson, George McClellan, A. P. Hill, Darius Couch, George Stoneman, and Cadmus Wilcox. The zenith of Pickett's military career had occurred on July 3, 1863, when he led the ill-fated charge against Union positions on Cemetery Ridge at Gettysburg. Forever known as Pickett's Charge, the attack failed, and it has lived in history as the "High Water Mark of the Confederacy." Pickett's division was shattered, and he blamed Lee for ordering the charge. Pickett remained bitter for the rest of his life.

On March 31, 1865, Pickett was aggressive and skillful, but his force advanced within half a mile of the courthouse building and could go no further. Unbeaten on the day, Lee realized that the situation was precarious. The enemy was on his right and possibly in his rear, threatening the railroads and the Five Forks escape route. Without doubt, fighting would erupt again the next morning. Lee wrote a plainspoken, even curt directive to Pickett, whose men were already falling back some distance from rather exposed positions near Dinwiddie Court House. "Hold Five Forks at all hazards," he demanded. "Protect road to Ford's Depot and prevent Union forces from striking the South Side Railroad. Regret exceedingly your forced withdrawal, and your inability to hold the advantage you had gained."[98]

Meanwhile, the events and orders of March 31 were conspiring against Warren. When Warren sent his vanguard down the White Oak Road in an attempt to cut Pickett off from the rest of Lee's army, it ran headlong into Anderson's flank attack that Lee had ordered in conjunction with Pickett's advance.

Alabama and Virginia troops threw the New Yorkers of Brig. Gen. Frederic Winthrop into headlong retreat, and it fell to Griffin's division to restore order. As the retreating Union troops streamed through their ranks, Griffin steadied his line and stopped the Confederate advance. Late in the morning, Warren himself rode to one of Griffin's brigade commanders, Joshua Lawrence Chamberlain, wounded but still in command. Chamberlain led a spectacular charge toward the White Oak Road, drove the Rebels back, and stabilized the line.

If the stress of leading troops in combat had begun to tell with Warren, the next few hours exacerbated the situation. Warren exercised sound judgment in sending a brigade to aid Sheridan at Dinwiddie Court House; however, an avalanche of orders, some of them conflicting, came rolling in from all quarters—Grant, Meade, and Sheridan. Send more troops to aid Sheridan's cavalry, withdraw V Corps from its advanced position, and more.

Instead, on the evening of the thirty-first, Warren asked permission to move west and attack the Confederates on one flank while Sheridan continued to press the Rebels from the other. Although Sheridan was threatened with being cut off, Pickett was as well. Grant had ordered Colonel Porter forward to assess the situation, and Sheridan told him bluntly that Pickett's force was "in more danger than I am. If I am cut off from the Army of the Potomac, it is cut off from Lee's army, and not a man in it ought ever be allowed to get back to Lee. We at last have drawn the enemy's infantry out of its fortifications, and this is our chance to attack it."[99]

Grant agreed, but bad weather, faulty maps, and a bridge that had been temporarily put out of commission over Gravelly Run on the Boydton Plank Road hampered Warren's progress. Warren was not in position to make his attack until early the next morning, and by then Pickett had begun to withdraw from his rather exposed position, back to his former entrenchments at Five Forks. The opportunity to grip Pickett in a vise had slipped away, and Sheridan was livid.

The tactical situation was obvious. Pickett expected a renewed effort to turn his flank and arrayed his troops to prevent such an attack on left that might cut him off from the rest of the Army of Northern Virginia. He turned that portion of his line at a right angle to the rest of his positions. Sheridan did plan to send Warren's three divisions against the angled Confederate entrenchments, and he met with Warren at midday on April 1, hardly able to contain his frustration that the corps commander was getting his troops into position without any sense of urgency.

Later in the day, Sheridan rode up to Warren's column and noted its slow progress. "I was disappointed that more of the corps was not already up, and as the precious minutes went by without any apparent effort to hurry the troops on to the field, this disappointment grew to disgust," he wrote in his memoirs. "Warren did not seem to me to be at all solicitous; his manner exhibited decided apathy, and he remarked with indifference that 'Bobby Lee was always getting people into trouble.'"[100]

The encounter was the beginning of the end of Warren's military career.

Pickett was satisfied with his deployment and confident that if Federal cavalry were the only opposition, the horsemen would be dealt with easily. He expressed little or no concern about the probable presence of strong Union infantry formations, and if Lee's terse communication had shaken him at all, it was not readily apparent. Tired and no doubt hungry, Pickett and Fitzhugh Lee welcomed an invitation from Rosser to join him on the banks of the Nottoway River for a shad bake. The fish were running in the springtime, and Rosser had found a net and managed to catch a few of them. An afternoon of food and rest was too tempting to decline.

Just as Fitzhugh Lee was departing, one of his division commanders, Brig. Gen. Thomas Munford, rode up with news that Sheridan's cavalry had already moved in force and probably reached the White Oak Road, cutting communications with the main Confederate lines. Before riding off with Pickett toward Rosser and the shad bake, Lee brushed the information aside saying, "Well, Munford, I wish you would go over in person at once and see what this means and, if necessary, order up your division and let me hear from you."[101]

Apparently none of Pickett's or Fitzhugh Lee's subordinate officers knew where their commanders were going. The next few hours were spent in leisure, and as the lounging officers picked the bones of their shad meals, two of Rosser's pickets came up to report that the enemy was advancing. Still, little concern was roused among the generals, whose troops were already fighting. No sound of battle drifted their way.

At 4:00 p.m., Pickett asked for a courier to send a message to his command at Five Forks. Rosser's standard practice was to send two, one riding some distance behind the other. Within minutes, rifles discharged, and the startled Confederate officers looked up to see the first courier being captured by Union infantrymen just across the river. Pickett quickly jumped on his horse, doffed his hat, and splashed back across Hatcher's Run with enemy infantrymen only about a hundred yards away.

Early on the afternoon of April 1, Sheridan's cavalry made a feint toward the Confederate right. Warren eventually stepped off to the north against the Confederate left. Munford sent numerous couriers to find Pickett and Fitzhugh Lee and advise them that a fight was taking shape. The generals were nowhere to be found.

Munford later advised, "All this time Warren's swarming blue lines were plainly visible from the road, forming into line and preparing to assault Pickett's left."[102]

When the storm broke, the result was a disaster for the Army of Northern Virginia. Although the weight of the opening thrust was mistakenly directed several hundred yards from the intended point of attack, Maj. Gen. Romeyn B. Ayres' division hit Brig. Gen. Matthew

Ransom's brigade of North Carolina troops, hurling them back on Brig. Gen. William H. Wallace's brigade of South Carolinians.

Horace Porter was awed as he watched Sheridan inspire the wave of Union soldiers. "He put spurs to his horse and dashed along the front of the line of battle from left to right," wrote Porter, "shouting words of encouragement, and having something cheery to say to every regiment. 'Come on, men,' he cried; 'go at 'em with a will! Move on at a clean jump, or you'll not catch one of 'em. They're all getting ready to run now, and if you don't get on them in five minutes they'll every one get away from you! Now go for them!'"[103]

The pace of the battle quickened, and a few yards from Sheridan a soldier was struck in the neck. "The blood spurted as if the jugular vein had been cut," remembered Porter. "'I'm killed!' he cried, and dropped to the ground. 'You're not hurt a bit!' cried Sheridan. 'Pick up your gun, man, and move right on to the front.' Such was the electric effect of his words that the poor fellow snatched up his musket, and rushed forward a dozen paces before he fell, never to rise again."[104]

General Winthrop was mortally wounded by a bullet through his lungs as he led his New York brigade over the angled Rebel entrenchments, and Capt. Henry Chambers of the 49th North Carolina recalled the piteous cries of wounded men asking to be carried to safety "and all this time the Yankee column in the rear was bearing down upon us."[105]

When Pickett arrived on the scene, he found his position thoroughly flanked. His left had given way. Crawford had cut the Ford's Depot Road, the only route of withdrawal to the north, and efforts to halt his advance were thwarted. At the height of the battle, twenty-three-year-old Col. William Johnson Pegram, with his adjutant, Capt. Gordon McCabe, at his side, directed his Virginia artillery with total disregard for his personal safety.

Historian Douglas Southall Freeman wrote of Pegram, "'Fire your canister low,' he said to his men. A moment after he reeled and fell from his horse. 'Oh Gordon,' he cried to his companion, 'I'm mortally wounded; take me off the field.'"[106] Young Pegram died the following morning, just days after his older brother, John, had perished at Hatcher's Run.

Pickett made a desperate stand. When Warren received word that his advance was beginning to falter, he rode personally to the front, waved the V Corps banner, and sparked a renewed effort. His horse was killed under him, and a bullet that would surely have wounded Warren grievously was instead taken by Lt. Col. Hollon Richardson of the 7th Wisconsin Regiment, who bravely moved forward to shield the general.

Soon enough, the Battle of Five Forks was over. The Confederates were driven from the crossroads, and V Corps alone collected 3,244 prisoners and eleven battle flags. Altogether, more than 5,000 Rebel soldiers were captured, while the dead and wounded numbered more than 600. Union casualties totaled 803 killed and wounded.

Captain Chambers wrote in his diary, "Day of evil omen! All Fools Day! And surely it has been an evil day for us—for our whole company. My heart sickens as I contemplate recording the days [*sic*] disasters."[107]

Despite the victory, Sheridan wanted no more of Warren, dismissing him from command of V Corps and appointing Griffin to take charge immediately. Warren rode to Sheridan's headquarters and pleaded for reconsideration. None was forthcoming. Subsequently, Warren petitioned for a court of inquiry. Fourteen years later, he was exonerated. However, he died of a heart ailment on August 8, 1882, and did not live to hear the court's decision, which came three months later.

As darkness began to shroud the countryside, Porter rode back toward Grant's headquarters with news of the victory. "General Grant was sitting, with most of the staff about him, before a blazing camp-fire," the colonel remembered. "He wore his blue cavalry overcoat, and the ever-present cigar was in his mouth. I began shouting the good news as soon as I got in sight, and in a moment all but the imperturbable commander-in-chief were on their feet giving vent to boisterous demonstrations of joy. For some minutes there was a bewildering state of excitement, and officers fell to grasping hands, shouting, and hugging each other like school-boys. The news meant the beginning of the end, the reaching of the 'last ditch.' It pointed to peace and home."[108]

Grant inquired about the number of prisoners taken, walked to his tent, and by the light of a flickering candle wrote several dispatches. He then returned to the group gathered at the camp-fire, and Porter was amazed at his demeanor, writing later that Grant "said as coolly as if remarking upon the state of the weather: 'I have ordered a general assault along the lines.'"[109]

PART III

COME RETRIBUTION

CHAPTER 5

RICHMOND IN RUINS

On Sunday, April 2, 1865, Jefferson Davis, president of the Confederacy, sat in his family pew, number sixty-three, halfway down the center aisle on the right-hand side at Saint Paul's Episcopal Church at the corner of Ninth and Grace Streets in Richmond. Dressed in gray trousers and a frock coat, he rested his wide-brimmed hat in the pew beside him.

In a few minutes, the German-born rector, Rev. Charles G. Minnigerode, speaking with a thick accent, began the service in the Anglican tradition. It was the first Sunday of the month, and Holy Communion had been prepared. After the sermon on the topic of the Last Supper began, William Irving, the church sexton, stepped forward and handed President Davis a note.

The text was brief. It read:

> His Excellency President Davis, Richmond, Va.: I think it is abso-
> lutely necessary that we should abandon our position to-night. I
> have given all the necessary orders on the subject to the troops,
> and the operation, though difficult, I hope will be performed suc-
> cessfully. I have directed General Stevens to send an officer to Your

Excellency to explain the routes to you by which the troops will be moved to Amelia Court House, and furnish you with a guide and any assistance that you may require for yourself. R.E. Lee.[110]

Davis was already well aware that the military situation was dire. At 10:40 a.m., the War Department had received the third in a series of morning messages from Lee, and the president had been informed of its content while walking to church with Col. Francis R. Lubbock, former governor of Texas and a member of Davis's staff. Earlier communication had already broken the news that Lee's line was shattered.

This third telegram from the commander of the Army of Northern Virginia was addressed to Secretary of War John C. Breckinridge. It warned, "I advise that all preparation be made for leaving Richmond tonight. I will advise you later according to circumstances."[111]

For more than three years, the Army of Northern Virginia had defended the capital. The citizens of Richmond were firm in their unshakable trust that Robert E. Lee would never allow Union soldiers to set foot in the city. On this day, though, the unthinkable was happening.

When he received the communication from Lee, Davis rose and walked from the church with an unsteady gait. From his office at the War Department a block away, he issued the directives that initiated the evacuation of Richmond. He had already disposed of his furniture and other belongings at auction. His wife, Varina, had parted with jewelry and other personal effects that fetched more than twenty-eight thousand dollars. During the last week of March, Davis had sent Varina and their children by train to Charlotte, North Carolina, where she rented a house and endured seemingly endless days waiting for a word here and there from her husband.

The congregation at Saint Paul's began to shuffle. Irving went back and forth down the aisle three more times. With the last, "all restraint of place and occasion yielded, and the vast congregation rose en masse and rushed towards the doors," remembered Dallas Tucker, a young boy who attended church with his parents. "I sat still for a moment, wondering and withal listening to the preacher's earnest appeal to the people to remember where they were and be still. Good Dr. Minnigerode, he might just as well have tried to turn back the waters of Niagara Falls."[112]

While Minnigerode tried to calm his congregation and finish his sermon, other ministers abruptly ended their services. Reverend

Moses Hoge of the Second Presbyterian Church stopped in the middle of his sermon as rumors began to circulate. He intoned, "Brethren, trying times are before us . . . but remember that God is with us in the storm as well as in calm. . . . We may never meet again. Go quietly to our homes, and whatever may be in store for us, let us not forget that we are Christian men and women, and may the protection of the Father, the Son, and the Holy Ghost be with you all."[113]

Politician Jefferson Davis, a Kentuckian by birth, was also a military man. He graduated from West Point twenty-third of thirty-three in the class of 1828. He served in the US Army during the Black Hawk War and was conspicuously brave at the Battle of Buena Vista during the Mexican War. In August 1861, his family moved into the mansion at the corner of Marshall and Governor Streets, and after serving as provisional president, Davis was inaugurated on February 22, 1862, to serve a six-year term as President of the Confederacy.

Davis was a former US senator and secretary of war. His first wife, Sarah, had died in 1835 at the age of twenty-one. His second wife, Varina, was seventeen years his junior. She bore six children in twelve years. Just as Abraham and Mary Todd Lincoln grieved the loss of their son Willie, who died in the White House in 1862, Jefferson and Varina Davis mourned their five-year-old son Joseph, who fell to his death from a balcony at their Richmond home in 1864.

Varina remembered the tragic accident vividly and wrote in her memoirs, "I left my children quite well, playing in my room, and had just uncovered my basket in [Jefferson's] office when a servant came in for me. The most beautiful and brightest of my children, Joseph Emory, had in play climbed over the connecting angle of the banister and fallen to the brick pavement below. He died a few minutes after we reached his side."[114]

It was after dark on April 1 when Lee received enough news to fully grasp the magnitude of the defeat at Five Forks. A part of the line in the bend of Hatcher's Run was abandoned, and in some places single soldiers stood nearly twenty feet apart. South of the James River, Lee had barely 16,000 troops—and only 11,000 between Hatcher's Run and the Appomattox River. He sent a message to Longstreet to send Gen. C. W. Field's division of 4,600 men to shore up the battered Confederate right. Then, Lee went to bed at his headquarters, the Turnbull House on Edge Hill just west of Petersburg. Thoughts of the desperate situation robbed him of sleep, and he felt ill, probably suffering from a recurring bout of rheumatism.

At about 4:00 a.m., Longstreet arrived, finding Lee still in bed but not sleeping. A. P. Hill was already there. Longstreet took a seat at the foot of the bed, and the ensuing council of war was indeed somber. A few minutes later, Col. Charles Venable, a member of Lee's staff, interrupted the conference. Union troops were advancing down the Cox Road. In the faint light of early dawn, Lee walked to the front door of the Turnbull House and looked into the distance. A line of infantry was moving up from the southwest. Their uniforms were blue. Hill's line had been broken. Field's division had not yet arrived and could not intervene. The only alternative was to rally the available Confederate troops in the vicinity of Fort Gregg on the far right.

Lee turned to speak to Hill, but the general had already galloped off toward his command. With Hill were his chief courier, Sgt. George W. Tucker, and another courier, William H. Jenkins. Hill's abrupt departure worried Lee, particularly since Hill had been suffering from extended periods of poor health. Lee sent Venable after the III Corps commander, bearing a message to use caution.

Venable closed the gap with the trio and remembered telling Hill, "The general requests that you not expose yourself." Hill responded, "I thank General Lee for his consideration. I am only trying to get in communication with the right."[115]

Lieutenant General Ambrose Powell Hill was thirty-nine years old. Born the youngest of seven children in Culpeper, Virginia, on November 9, 1825, he learned to ride at an early age and was easy in the saddle. He doted on his hypochondriac mother. In 1842, Powell, as he was known to his friends, received an appointment to the US Military Academy at West Point. Originally a member of the class of 1846, which produced twenty Civil War–era generals, he enjoyed life, particularly the company of young ladies. He contracted gonorrhea during a furlough, and the disease caused him to miss so many classes that he was required to repeat his third year and graduated fifteenth of thirty-eight in the class of 1847. Among his close friends were Ambrose Burnside and Henry Heth, a future Confederate division commander.

Prior to the Civil War, Hill served in the Mexican War and the Seminole Wars. When Virginia left the Union in 1861, he resigned his commission in the US Army. In February 1862, he was promoted to brigadier general, and while in command of his famed "Light Division" during Lee's first invasion of the North that autumn, his timely arrival from Harpers Ferry saved the day for the Army of Northern Virginia at the Battle of Antietam. When Stonewall

Jackson died in May 1863, Hill was elevated to corps command and was present at Gettysburg and beyond. He was fond of wearing a bright red shirt when he led soldiers into battle. Modern historians have often praised Hill as a stalwart division commander while labeling him something of a disappointment at the corps level.

On the morning of April 2, 1865, as Hill hurried toward his command he was probably unaware that he was crossing the right rear of Maj. Gen. Horatio G. Wright's Union VI Corps, rushing forward after breaking the Confederate line. Enemy pickets were being thrown out liberally. Hill noticed an idle artillery battalion and ordered Venable to position the guns. About two hundred yards further along, the riders encountered two Federal stragglers and ordered them to surrender at gunpoint. Hill told Jenkins to take the prisoners to General Lee.

Tucker grew more nervous by the minute, particularly after he and Hill passed a group of Union soldiers scrounging around the former winter camp of a Confederate division. Hill did not appear concerned. When Tucker asked, "Please excuse me, general, but where are we going?" the response was, "Sergeant, I must go to the right as quickly as possible."[116]

Hill and Tucker emerged from thick woods and into an open field opposite the line held by Confederates under the command of his old friend Henry Heth. As they rode toward a clump of woods, Tucker pushed ahead and saw two Federal soldiers slip away from a group of at least half a dozen. They ran behind a large tree and, one above the other, pointed their rifles at the two Confederates.

Hill caught up with Tucker, drew his revolver, and said, "We must take them." As they approached within twenty yards of the enemy soldiers, Tucker yelled, "If you fire, you'll be swept to hell! Our men are here! Surrender!" Hill held the reins of his horse, Champ, and bellowed, "Surrender!"[117]

The two Union men were twenty-nine-year-old Cpl. John W. Mauk, a carpenter by trade from Bedford County, Pennsylvania, and Pvt. Daniel Wolford, both of Company F, 138th Pennsylvania Infantry.

Rather than surrender, they chose to fire. Wolford missed Tucker, but Mauk's bullet tore off Hill's thumb inside its heavy glove, pierced his heart, and exited through his back. Hill was dead before he landed motionless on the ground. Tucker escaped with Champ in tow.

Nearly three decades later, the *Baltimore American* newspaper published an interview with Mauk, who remembered whispering to Wolford after the surrender demand. "I said, 'I could not see it,' and said to comrade Wolford, 'Let us shoot them.' Comrade Wolford and myself shortly after this joined our regiment, and nothing more was thought of the affair until summoned to brigade and corps headquarters to answer questions. After I had given a statement of the affair General Wright asked me if I knew whom I had killed. I told him that I did not. He said: 'You have killed General A.P. Hill of the Confederate army.'"[118]

The commander of the Army of Northern Virginia was dressed minutes after Longstreet and Hill departed, in full uniform with his sword at his waist. It was no longer safe to remain at the Turnbull House. The Union soldiers Lee had seen were the leading elements of Wright's VI Corps, which had shattered the Rebel right flank. Their advance had been so rapid that these particular men had outrun the rest of their regiments. Lee rode down the slight prominence of Edge Hill and across the road. He saw several men approaching on horseback, but the man riding Hill's dapple gray, Champ, was Sergeant Tucker. After Hill was fatally shot, Tucker switched to the faster horse and sent his own horse, riderless, back toward Hill's headquarters.

Tucker told Lee the story of the fatal encounter, and the general replied, "He is at rest now, and we who are left are the ones to suffer."[119]

Soldiers of the 5th Alabama Battalion serving as the headquarters guard and members of Hill's staff recovered the general's body within half an hour of his death. Hill was buried first in Chesterfield County, Virginia, and two years later reinterred in Richmond's Hollywood Cemetery. During the 1880s, friends of Hill began raising money for a monument to his memory. When the monument was dedicated in Richmond on May 30, 1892, his body was laid to rest for the final time at its base.

The Union troops in the trenches before Petersburg prepared for battle throughout the night of April 1, and before the sun was up artillery boomed from one end of their line to the other. The weight of four Union corps was thrown at the beleaguered Confederates.

Two divisions of Parke's IX Corps, under Brig. Gen. Robert Potter and Brig. Gen. John Hartranft, were the first to hit the Confederates on April 2, striking Gordon's depleted II Corps toward the Rebel left at Fort Mahone. Three Confederate batteries were quickly captured as the Union soldiers braved a hail of shot and shell. Many of their number fell wounded in a flooded ditch, and some drowned. Just after 7:00 a.m., Rebel resistance stiffened, and the attack bogged down. At the height of the battle, Lt. Col. John C. Goodgame of the 12th Alabama exhorted his men while standing exposed atop a crossing point in the trenches. "Alabamians! Stand up!" he railed. "Aim low and fight like men!"[120]

At 3:00 p.m., Gordon launched a counterattack that reclaimed all of Fort Mahone. Reinforcements from the Army of the Potomac Provost Brigade and a brigade of VI Corps helped Parke retain a foothold in the Rebel lines. One Confederate officer remembered that the "open space inside Fort Mahone was literally covered with blue-coated corpses," while a Confederate soldier, his face blackened with gunpowder from opening cartridges with his teeth and the numerous discharges of his rifle, asked another man how many times he had fired his weapon. The reply came, "I know from the number of times I have replenished my supply of cartridges that I have fired more than two hundred rounds."[121]

The IX Corps lost 1,700 soldiers killed, wounded, and missing in the fight at Fort Mahone, and the dismal earthen structure became known among the Union troops as Fort Damnation.

Elsewhere, the situation was different. To the west, Wright's VI Corps assault achieved some degree of surprise as the advancing infantrymen, their canteens and other equipment left behind, leaned forward with fixed bayonets. A low fog hung in the early gloom, and Wright waited for it to lift before sending his troops into battle. The opening bombardment had been so deafening that the sound of the signal gun fired at 4:40 a.m. from Fort Fisher, one of the Union fortifications, was drowned out.

As they surged across open ground toward the six brigades of Heth's and Maj. Gen. Cadmus Wilcox's divisions of Hill's corps, the Federals began taking heavy rifle fire. Men with axes to chop away the *abatis* and *chevaux-de-frise* led the way toward the Confederates. Among the first to reach the enemy was Capt. Charles Gould of the 5th Vermont. Leaping into a trench held by one of six North Carolina regiments directly in the path of the assault, Gould was bayoneted through his cheek and mouth. He hacked the Rebel to death with his saber and fired his revolver at others approaching. Clubbed by a rifle butt and bayoneted in the back, he kept fighting. A color sergeant rushed up swinging his own rifle at the attackers. Grabbing Gould by the collar, he lifted the young officer out of the trench and pointed him toward the rear.

The Union onslaught was irresistible, and the Confederates were too few to make a stand. Gould's Vermonters breached the line, and waves of VI Corps infantry swept through. One New York soldier remembered that the surge "carried the works with a yell that would have alarmed the 'seven sleepers.' The rebels fled, pell-mell, over the country, with our good boys charging after them, capturing them, or killing them if they would not halt or surrender." Writing to his parents after the battle, another soldier from New York related, "We got in the rear of the forts and mowed the Johnies down like grass. The Johns were panic stricken and run like sheep."[122]

Twenty-three-year-old Maj. Hazard Stevens of the 79th New York observed that the Rebels were "swept away like chaff before a tornado." Nearly thirty years later, Stevens received the Medal of Honor for gallantry during the Battle of Fort Huger in 1863. Along with a partner, he was the first to make a documented climb of Mount Rainier in Washington on August 17, 1870.

Flush with victory, Wright's troops crossed the Boydton Plank Road and the South Side Railroad, then wheeled and swept down the Confederate line to Hatcher's Run and a junction with Maj. Gen. John Gibbon's XXIV Corps from Ord's Army of the James, which had also broken through the thin Rebel defenses.

"When Wright reached Hatcher's Run," Grant wrote, "he sent a regiment to destroy the South Side Railroad just outside of the city [Petersburg]. My headquarters were still at Dabney's saw-mills. As soon as I received news of Wright's success, I sent dispatches announcing the fact to all points around the line, including the troops at Bermuda Hundred and those on the north side of the James, and to the President at City Point. Finding at length that they were all in, I mounted my horse to join the troops who were inside the works. When I arrived there I rode my horse over the parapet just as Wright's three thousand prisoners were coming out."[123]

In the midst of a growing disaster, Lee put together a plan to withdraw his army through Petersburg, across the three bridges that spanned the Appomattox River, one of which might already have been damaged, and then march toward Burkeville and a general rendezvous point at Amelia Court House, forty miles west of Petersburg and on the Richmond & Danville Railroad. When darkness fell, the abandonment of Petersburg was to begin. Artillery had to be removed from the fortifications by 8:00 p.m. and across the

Appomattox by 3:00 a.m. Longstreet was to take the left fork in the Hickory Road and Gordon the right as they slipped away.

But Lee needed time. He had to hold Petersburg through the night. Wright's rapid pace might carry the Federals into the town, where they could take the vital bridges and trap what was left of the Army of Northern Virginia. Longstreet's troops were moving into the innermost line of defenses, stretching from the Boydton Plank Road to the Appomattox River only a mile from the city, but it would be midafternoon at the earliest before they were in the trenches to oppose the oncoming Federals.

By 11:00 a.m., Wright's VI Corps was winded and somewhat disorganized from its headlong advance, but it was still coming toward Longstreet's new line. Gibbon's XXIV Corps and elements of Humphreys's II Corps, which had moved forward between Hatcher's Run and the White Oak Road against Henry Heth's retiring division, were coming up as well. Two hours later, Grant was watching from a nearby hill. He saw Longstreet's soldiers arriving and ordered an attack. Two divisions of Gibbon's corps, commanded by Brig. Gen. Robert Foster and Brig. Gen. John W. Turner, went forward.

A pair of detached strongpoints, Fort Gregg and Battery Whitworth, had to be taken prior to assaulting the inner line of defenses. Inside the fortifications, Wilcox commanded a vastly outnumbered but stubborn handful of veterans, most of them from Mississippi. Private Frank Foote of the 48th Mississippi wrote, "Each defender had two or more rifles at hand, and while the rear rank loaded them, the front rank handled them with most deadly execution."[124]

At first heavy Rebel fire rocked the attackers backward. Foster's men fought their way to a broad ditch in front of Fort Gregg and found themselves mired in mud that was up to the waists of some of the soldiers. Turner's troops piled into those of Foster, and some Union soldiers tried to move behind the earthen fort to enter through its rear. They were thrown back by a line of Rebel riflemen firing through loopholes in a makeshift palisade.

The fighting at Fort Gregg was described by eyewitnesses as some of the most desperate of the entire war. Captain John C. Gorman of the 2nd North Carolina Regiment watched from the main line. He recalled that as the Federals rushed forward "cannoneers and infantry simultaneously fire on the confident assaulters, who stagger, reel under their death-dealing volley, and in a moment the Federal lines are broken and they retreat in masses under cover. A loud and wild cheer succeeds the breathless stillness that prevailed amongst us, and is answered exultingly by the heroic little garrison in Fort Gregg. But reinforcements have come to the help of the assaulters."[125]

When the Union troops regrouped and came on again, Gorman witnessed a bitter struggle:

> The Federals have reached the ditch. They climb up the sides of the works, and, as the foremost reach the top, we can see them reel and fall headlong on their comrades below. Once, twice and thrice have they reached the top, only to be repulsed, and yet they persevere, and the artillery in the embrasures continues to fire in rapid succession. But, at last, all is hushed! The artillery once more, and for the last time, fire a parting shot, and we can see the Federals as with impunity they mount the works and begin a rapid fire on the defenders within. Their ammunition is exhausted, and, unwilling to surrender, they are using their bayonets and clubbing their guns in an unequal struggle. At last one loud huzza proclaims the fort lost . . . .[126]

The defenders of Fort Gregg and Battery Whitworth sacrificed themselves heroically. When the battle was over, only 30 of the original 214 Confederates inside Fort Gregg were uninjured; 56 were dead and 129 wounded. Gibbon's corps suffered 122 killed and 592 wounded.

While his men were moving into the trench line, Longstreet watched the fighting at Fort Gregg through his field glasses. He saw his old friend Gibbon at a distance and raised his hat as a greeting. However, Gibbon was absorbed with the deadly business at hand and did not notice. Longstreet also saw Grant, chewing a cigar, dispensing orders, and calmly whittling.

Just as the fighting began to slow at Fort Gregg, Gordon launched his afternoon counterattack at Fort Mahone. Unsatisfied with its results, he was preparing for another when he received the news that Wright's VI Corps had broken through Hill's lines on his right. Another assault would be meaningless, only yielding more dead and wounded. Gordon began preparing to evacuate his troops.

Late in the afternoon, Maj. Gen. Nelson Miles's division of II Corps, detached initially to support Sheridan's cavalry and then to deal with Heth as II Corps turned north toward Petersburg, caught Heth's division at Sutherland Station on the South Side Railroad. Brigadier General John R. Cooke's brigade fought a valiant rear-guard action while the other Rebel troops withdrew to the west, away from the rest of the Army of Northern Virginia.

Miles's soldiers mounted two charges against the Confederate line, both of which were beaten back. He then called up reinforcements, outflanked the defenders near Ocran Church, and forced them to fall back, bagging large numbers of Confederate prisoners in the process. Soon, Sutherland Station was in Union hands, cutting the South Side Railroad, Lee's last supply line into Petersburg.

The vast Union armies had fought hard the entire day, and as evening approached the men in the ranks were exhausted. Despite their fatigue, the Federal soldiers understood to a man the implications of their achievement. Private William Hopkins of the 7th Rhode Island Regiment wrote, "Our flags were floating on the rebel works, and, as daylight faded into darkness, we hopefully watched them, clinging closer and closer to their eagle-peaked staffs until they were lost in the gloom. Thus closed that wild, stormy Sabbath, a day of blood, carnage, and victory."[127]

Grant reflected on the day's accomplishments and recounted them in a dispatch to City Point. He later wrote, "During the night of April 2d our line was intrenched from the river above to the river below. I ordered a bombardment to be commenced the next morning at five A.M., to be followed by an assault at six o'clock; but the enemy evacuated Petersburg early in the morning."[128]

Lee and his tattered army ebbed away in the darkness.

The citizens of Richmond were no strangers to the privations of war. The newspapers published casualty lists routinely. Rumors of Union armies coming toward the Confederate capital were frequent. As they moved about the streets, the people sometimes heard the rumble of artillery just a few miles from their homes. The Union's naval blockade had choked off shipments of supplies, weapons, medicine, and staples such as coffee or tea. Blockade runners plied their trade, delivering wartime luxuries that were once readily available.

By the winter of 1862, prices were steadily climbing, and a smallpox epidemic brought added discontent. Coal and wood were precious commodities. The street lamps were turned off every day until 4:00 p.m. to save diminishing supplies of gas. Beef was nowhere to be found. Flour was $200.00 a barrel, while salt was $2.00 a pound, turkeys were $30.00, and hams were sold to those who could afford as much as $350.00. Just the previous spring, bacon was running 36 cents a pound, butter $1.20, flour $7.12, and corn 85 cents. By April 1864, a pound of bacon sold for $7.42, butter $9.50, flour $250.00, and corn $45.00.[129]

A thriving black market and the continuous requirements of the military meant constant shortages. When shoppers ventured to the First Market at Seventeenth and Main Streets, one of the oldest farmer's markets in the country, they often found little to purchase. One woman observed, "By 1865 food was so scarce, and the currency so inflated, that when you went to market, it was said that 'you carried your money in your market basket, and brought your provisions home in your purse.'"[130]

Word of the evacuation order roared through Richmond like an ill wind. Some gathered their families together and set off. Others decided to stay. At 4:00 p.m., the official announcement was posted. Frank Lawley, a correspondent for the *London Times*, wrote, "The scene that followed baffles description. During the long afternoon and throughout the feverish night, on horseback, in every description of cart, carriage, and vehicle, in every hurried train that left the city, on canal barges, skiffs, and boats, the exodus of officials and prominent citizens was unintermitted."[131]

Amid the chaos, the driver of a single ambulance was attempting to enter the city of Richmond rather than flee. Accompanying the driver were G. Powell Hill and Henry Hill, cousins of the slain A. P. Hill. The general's body was not embalmed, and there was no casket readily available outside the city.

The mournful ride through the burning and looted business district was etched in G. Powell Hill's memory.

> Time was pressing us closely, as we were expecting the entrance of the Federal troops into the city at any moment. The stores on Twelfth, Thirteenth, Main, and Cary streets had been broken into, and in many instances sacked and fired. Belvin's furniture store had been opened at both ends (the rear being then on Twelfth street), and my cousin and myself entered the rear door, hoping to find a representative to whom we could apply for a coffin. After making repeated calls and receiving no answer, we secured a coffin and took it to a vacant office (which had been occupied by General P. T. Moore, about where the St. James' Hotel

now stands). We removed the body from the ambulance into the office, where we washed his face and removed his gauntlets, and examined his body to discover where the fatal ball had entered.[132]

The two men set about their task as quickly as they could, wrapping the body in the general's overcoat and then departing. G. Powell Hill concluded, "We hastily placed the body in the coffin (which was rather small), and putting it in the ambulance, left the city by way of Fourteenth street and Mayo's bridge, slowly and sadly wending our way through Manchester and up the river to my father's refugee home."[133]

Orders were given to prepare a train to Danville for President Davis and members of his cabinet. Documents and currency, both US and Confederate, were burned. The archives were packed. For a while, Davis seemed to deny the facts, sending a telegram to Lee that complained a departure from Richmond that night would "involve the loss of many valuables, both for the want of time to pack and of transportation." When he received the message, Lee momentarily lost his temper and tore the note to pieces. The general blurted, "I am sure I gave him sufficient notice." Then he regained his composure and replied to Davis that the evacuation was "absolutely necessary."[134]

The president gathered up his personal belongings and rode through the chaotic streets to the Danville Depot, arriving just prior to 8:00 p.m., the appointed departure time. The rest of the passengers were not as punctual. The train did not pull away until three hours later. From its rickety boxcars hung banners reading "War Department," "Treasury Department," and other identifiers of a fleeing government. Among those aboard were Secretary of State Judah P. Benjamin, Secretary of the Navy Stephen Mallory, Secretary of the Treasury George Trenholm and his wife, the only woman with the group, Postmaster General John H. Reagan, and Attorney General George Davis.

Rear Admiral Rafael Semmes, commander of the James River Squadron, had survived the sinking of his commerce raider CSS *Alabama* by the sloop of war USS *Kearsarge* off the coast of Cherbourg, France, on June 19, 1864. He was startled to receive orders to destroy the navy yard and burn his ironclads and other vessels moored along the James waterfront. A detail of naval cadets, their training ship put to the torch, escorted the

Confederate treasury, a hoard of nearly $530,000 in gold and silver bars, silver coins from Mexico, and double eagle gold coins, on the train to Danville. The Union prisoners of war at Libby Prison were marched to the riverbank for transport.

Lieutenant General Richard S. Ewell, commanding the Confederate troops in Richmond, issued orders for those in the city and the fortified positions to the east to begin withdrawing toward the town of Manchester, south of the James River, burning bridges as they crossed. Ewell also advised Mayor Joseph Mayo that the government food warehouses should be opened to keep the citizenry occupied while the army continued its evacuation.

One Richmond resident, Nellie Grey, remembered hesitating to avail herself of the opportunity to take the government food "in spite of my loathing for dried apples and peas, and a lively objection to starvation." After discussions with other ladies, she heard one of them say that she was "bound to have a whole barrel of flour, and she was going for it. . . We put on our bonnets— hand-made straw trimmed with chicken feathers—and started. Such a crowd as we found ourselves in! . . . A starveling mob! I got frightened sick."[135]

As darkness fell and many of the soldiers and civil officials departed, anarchy reigned. Mobs of thugs, drunks, army deserters, and prostitutes roamed the streets. The guards at the state penitentiary evacuated, leaving the prisoners to walk out.

To prevent the liquor supplies throughout Richmond from fueling the orgy of looting and devastation, the city council ordered the destruction of every barrel and bottle. A few minutes after midnight, casks were being hacked open in the streets and bottles emptied into the gutters. The safety measure backfired in a most malevolent way. Already drinking to excess, ruffians scooped the alcohol up from puddles, using pots, pans, and china cups. Rags were soaked in whiskey and used to light torches.

In its April 4 edition, the *Richmond Whig* reported, "The gutters ran with a liquor freshet and the fumes filled and impregnated the air. Fine cases of bottled liquors were tossed into the street from third story windows, and wrecked into a thousand pieces."[136]

After arguing for more than an hour, Mayo and several other city officials failed to dissuade the retreating soldiers from following Ewell's orders to destroy any goods that might be of value to the enemy. The troops set fire to at least four major tobacco and cotton warehouses located in an area known as "the Basin" and probably to several others in the vicinity. The Shockoe Warehouse at Thirteenth and Cary Streets held ten thousand hogsheads of tobacco. Flames leaped into the sky and cast lurid shadows across the masses of people, some milling aimlessly, others screaming, and still others carrying away all they could manage. Bags of flour were thrown from the windows of the blazing Gallego Mills.

A strong breeze blew from the south, and the flames spread in a flash. The raging fire hissed and boiled to the northeast, belching smoke and consuming the Petersburg and Danville railroad depots, numerous businesses and shops, and several banks. Before it was brought under control, the fire had destroyed or heavily damaged fifty-four city blocks and more than six hundred buildings. Just before dawn, the arsenal and its stock of black powder erupted in a monstrous explosion, a pillar of smoke and flame billowing into the sky.

As morning neared, Mayo's Bridge at the foot of Fourteenth Street was the last span standing across the James River. Captain Clement Sulivane of South Carolina was commanding two hundred militiamen, and Ewell ordered him to guard the bridge with pine logs, tar, kerosene, and brush at the ready when the last Confederate troops were across.

"Every now and then, as a magazine exploded, a column of white smoke rose up as high as the eye could reach, instantaneously followed by a deafening sound," Sulivane recalled. "The earth seemed to rock and tremble as with the shock of an earthquake, and immediately afterwards hundreds of shells would explode in air and send their iron spray down far below the bridge."[137]

Secretary of War Breckinridge reached Mayo's Bridge, and Brig. Gen. E. Porter Alexander, commander of Longstreet's I Corps artillery, rode up and waited for the last of his batteries. A handful of soldiers from a Georgia regiment showed up. All crossed safely. Sulivane's men scattered a mob that had surrounded a supply train, and the wagons rolled across.

Among the last of the military men to cross the bridge was Lt. Col. Walter H. Taylor, a trusted aide-de-camp of General Lee. Earlier in the day Taylor had asked the general for permission to go to Richmond. Lee was incredulous. Then the twenty-six-year-old Taylor explained that he wanted to marry his fiancée, Elizabeth Seldon Saunders. Lee relented, but Taylor missed the last train to the chaotic capital. He took a locomotive from Dunlop Station and caught up with the passenger train. A few minutes after midnight, Reverend Minnigerode married the couple in the parlor of the Crenshaw House, where the bride was living. Duty called, and Taylor returned to Lee, crossing Mayo's Bridge amid the "lurid glare of the fire."[138]

A cavalry brigade under Brig. Gen. Martin W. Gary thundered to the other side of the river. Gary halted momentarily as his last company of horsemen clattered past. "My rear guard," he shouted to Sulivane, tipping his hat and adding, "All over, goodbye; blow her to hell."[139]

Sulivane and his men set Mayo's Bridge on fire and skittered to the far side, some with flames licking at their feet.

Richmond was ablaze. The capital of the Confederacy had become the nation's funeral pyre.

CHAPTER 6

A VISIT TO THE OTHER WHITE HOUSE

Daylight in Richmond revealed a ravaged city. Fires still burned, and in their paths were blackened chimneys, stark reminders of the previous night's upheaval.

Some buildings were abandoned, their windows shattered and their doors creaking ajar. Broken glass, heaps of discarded belongings, toppled trunks, and forgotten furniture were everywhere. A slight breeze blew tattered papers along the streets. Here and there lay a body, drunk or dead. Not everyone had fled Richmond in the chaotic night, but those who remained in the city were reluctant to venture outside.

Even as Clement Sulivane and his militiamen crossed Mayo's Bridge, Union cavalrymen were not far behind. Their scouts were already in the city. While the majority of Grant's armies had been in action during the past four tumultuous days, the XXV Corps of the Army of the James had been idle before the Richmond defenses north of the river. Commanded by Maj. Gen. Godfrey Weitzel, the corps had just been organized the previous December, incorporating many of the black troops previously assigned to IX, X, and XVIII Corps.

Weitzel was cautious by nature, and as Union soldiers began creeping into Richmond in the predawn hours, he chose to wait for the sun to come up before sending troops into the city. Weitzel told his subordinate commanders to make sure their soldiers ate breakfast in the event that they had to fight. At 5:30 a.m., he detailed Maj. Eugene Graves and Maj. Atherton Stevens to take two companies, about forty troopers, of the 4th Massachusetts Cavalry forward to find someone with at least the implied authority to surrender the city to the Union army.

One of the cavalrymen, William B. Arnold, remembered the exhilarating ride through the deserted Confederate trench line and toward a man waving a flag of truce. Arnold wrote:

> In the distance were mounted men and carriages. We halted and Major Stevens and his officers went forward and conferred with the party, who proved to be the Mayor of Richmond accompanied by Judge Meredith and other prominent people of Richmond. The city was formally surrendered to Major Stevens and we then went forward at a rapid pace, and coming round a turn in the roadway at the Rockets, came in full view of Richmond.
>
> We halted for a moment to contemplate the scene. A portion of the city toward the James river was on fire . . . We gave three cheers and went on and were soon in the streets of Richmond passing Libby Prison; and we clattered up the paved street on the gallop to the Capitol, and were soon in the space in front of the Capitol building.[140]

Stevens and a few other officers hurried inside, up the stairs to the roof, and ran the guidons of Companies E and H of the 4th Massachusetts up the flagstaff. The escorting cavalrymen encircled the equestrian statue of George Washington a few yards away on Capitol Square near Grace Street and cheered wildly.

From December 1862 through the end of the war, Phoebe Yates Pember worked as a nurse and chief matron at Chimborazo Hospital, a sprawling complex in Richmond that treated more than seventy-five thousand patients during the conflict. A member of a prominent Jewish family of Charleston, South Carolina, she had come to the Confederate capital after the death of her husband, Thomas Pember of Boston.

On the morning of April 3, 1865, Phoebe looked out on Main Street and saw two carriages rolling along. She recognized the passengers as

Richmond's mayor, Joseph Mayo, and other local dignitaries. She correctly deduced that they were en route to surrender the city.

A half hour later, Phoebe glanced eastward toward the sunrise and was immediately impressed by what she saw. She wrote in her memoir:

> [A] single Federal blue-jacket rose above the hill, standing transfixed with astonishment at what he saw. Another and another sprang up as if out of the earth, but still all remained quiet. About seven o'clock, there fell upon the ear the steady clatter of horses' hoofs, and winding around Rocketts, close under Chimborazo hill, came a small and compact body of Federal cavalrymen, on horses in splendid condition, riding closely and steadily along. They were well mounted, well accoutered, well fed—a rare sight in Southern streets—the advance of that vaunted army that for four years had so hopelessly knocked at the gates of the Southern Confederacy.[141]

Weitzel and his staff rode into Capitol Square around 8:15 and set the Union cavalrymen and infantry that followed to extinguishing fires, restoring order, and calming the nervous populace. A pair of Richmond's horse-drawn fire engines was dragged out and hitched to race off toward the worst of the conflagration. Anyone on the street—stragglers, drunks, former prisoners—was pressed into service in a bucket brigade, chopping away brush, and removing anything that could feed the fires. Buildings that were directly in the path of advancing flames were toppled to fashion firebreaks.

At 707 Franklin Street, the residents had decided to remain in Richmond. With her ancestral home at Arlington confiscated by the Federal authorities, Mary Anna Custis Lee, the wife of the embattled commander of the Army of Northern Virginia, was with her daughters in the house, doors and windows bolted. Suffering from rheumatoid arthritis, Mrs. Lee was an invalid.

Sometime during the morning, the flames reached Eighth and Franklin streets. The house next door caught fire, and one of the Lee daughters sought help to move her mother to safety. A Union officer responded, but Mrs. Lee refused his pleas to leave the house. Fortunately, the wind shifted, and the structure was saved. Afterward, a guard was placed at the front door to protect the women.

By 1:00 p.m., after five arduous hours, the fires were under control. Weitzel noted the irony that resided with the destruction.

Just west of the Virginia state capitol building, the famous equestrian statue of George Washington dominates Capitol Square in Richmond. The square was a focal point for Union troops who occupied the Confederate capital city on April 3, 1865. To the left of the statue is the prominent steeple of Saint Paul's Episcopal Church, where Confederate President Jefferson Davis received communication from Gen. Robert E. Lee advising that the city be evacuated. *Library of Congress*

"The rebel capitol, fired by men placed in it to defend it, was saved from total destruction by soldiers of the United States, who had taken possession."[142]

Among the prominent citizens who had chosen to leave the capital were several of the city's pro-Confederate newspaper editors. A dispatch from Secretary of War Edwin M. Stanton in Washington noted that the *Richmond Whig* had resumed publication on April 4 as a Union newspaper with the name of the former owner on its masthead.

The *Whig* reported, "Mr. Isaac Davenport, an old citizen, was instantly killed by the falling of a portion of the wall of the American Hotel. The body was recovered. Mr. William Royster was seriously wounded by the explosion of a shell in one of the burning buildings. It is believed that at least several other persons were buried under falling ruins, who are as yet unknown."[143]

The devastation was remarkable, but it would have been considerably worse without the intervention of the Federal soldiers. They cared for the injured, gave food to those who were hungry, and patrolled the streets. "The order of the city has been excellent since the occupation by the Federal forces," noted the *Whig*. "We have not heard a single complaint on the part of the citizens against the soldiers, and we are glad to record that the soldiers have found no reason to complain of the conduct of the citizens. We trust this gratifying state of affairs will continue."[144]

After parting company with Grant at City Point on March 29, President Lincoln spent hours at the telegraph operator's tent, anxiously waiting for news on the progress of the Union offensive that later became known as the Appomattox Campaign. He sent and received messages regularly over the next few days, asking about the progress of the Union armies and relaying information to Washington from time to time.

On the 29th, Lincoln inquired of General Weitzel east of Richmond, "What, if any thing, have you observed on your front today?" Weitzel responded that he had only heard reports of Fitzhugh Lee's cavalry passing through Richmond the previous day and on toward Petersburg that morning "at a fast gait."[145]

Grant appreciated the president's anxiety and did all he could to keep Lincoln informed. The general sent Lincoln three wires by late afternoon, but the president wanted more. "Your three despatches received. From what direction did the enemy come that attacked Griffin? How do things look now?"[146]

About 10:15 that night, Lincoln was restless aboard the *River Queen*. He heard the low rumble of artillery and the sharp reports of rifles from the direction of Petersburg and concluded that a major engagement was underway. He cabled Secretary of War Stanton on the morning of March 30, almost poking fun at himself. "It seemed to me a great battle, but the older hands here scarcely noticed it, and, sure enough, this morning it was found that very little had been done."[147]

Lincoln also became concerned about his extended absence from the White House, telling Stanton, "I begin to feel that I ought to be at home, and yet I dislike to leave without seeing nearer to the end of General Grant's present movement."

Stanton responded, "I hope you will stay to see it out, or for a few days at least. I have strong faith that your presence will have great influence in inducing exertions that will bring Richmond; compared to that no other duty can weigh a feather. There is . . . nothing to be done here but petty private ends that you should not be annoyed with. A pause by the army now would do harm; if you are on the ground there will be no pause. All well here."[148]

Washington policeman William Crook, who had been assigned as a White House guard two months earlier, recalled the president's growing sense of depression with the prospect of another major battle. It was something that Lincoln had hoped to avoid; however, he remembered that both Grant and Sherman had said during their discussions that such an engagement was inevitable.

On the evening of March 31, Grant notified the president of heavy fighting. "Our troops after being driven back on to Boydton plank road turned & drove the Enemy in turn & took the White Oak Road which we now have. This gives us the ground occupied by the Enemy this morning. I will send you a rebel flag captured by our troops in driving the Enemy back. There has [sic] been four (4) flags captured today. The one I send you was taken from a Va regiment of Hunter's Brigade.[149]

While Sheridan wrested control of Five Forks from the Confederates on April 1, Lincoln waited for news of the renewed fighting. He knew that Sheridan was attacking and that Warren's V Corps had marched in support, but little progress had been noted in messages from Grant. Just before 1:00 p.m., the president sent a telegram to Stanton saying as much and then requesting that the secretary of war instruct coachman Alfonso Donn to meet Mrs. Lincoln at the Arsenal wharf on her return to Washington the following morning.

The decisive action at Five Forks was not underway until after 4:00 p.m., and did not conclude until three hours later. Just after 5:00 p.m., Grant forwarded a dispatch from Horace Porter to the president that noted, "Our men have never fought better. All are in excellent spirits and anxious to go in. The enemy is said by all the officers to be fighting badly giving away constantly before our dismounted Cavy. The enemy's loss yesterday was very heavy many of their dead are lying in the woods. I [saw?] several old men with heads perfectly bald. The enemy threw away many arms in their retreat & seem to have been pretty much demoralized."[150]

Lincoln left the telegraph operator's tent and paced the deck of the *River Queen* late into the night unable to rest amid the continuing rumble of artillery around Petersburg and then likely robbed of a fitful sleep by the troubling dream of his own assassination.

Late on the afternoon of Sunday, April 2, the president wired Mrs. Lincoln, "At 4:30 p.m. to-day General Grant telegraphs that he has Petersburg completely enveloped from river below to river above, and has captured, since he started last Wednesday, about 12,000 prisoners and 50 guns. He suggests that I shall go out and see him in the morning, which I think I will do. Tad and I are both well."[151] That night, he sent heartfelt congratulations to Grant, on the brink of victory at Petersburg.

Eager to talk with his highest ranking general and to see the ground where the most recent fighting had occurred, a few minutes after 8:00 a.m. on Monday President Lincoln boarded a train with Tad on the US Military Railroad and headed for Hancock Station, where his son Robert was waiting to accompany them into Petersburg. Some accounts assert that the train took the presidential party to Patrick Station, about a mile from the city. However, based on other information and the location of Patrick Station, west of Hancock Station where Robert was waiting, this appears unlikely.

The stop at Hancock Station was also adjacent to the Jerusalem Plank Road, which ran directly into Petersburg. While some accounts relate that the president and Tad took an ambulance from Hancock Station to Petersburg, others report that horses were waiting. They did proceed down the Jerusalem Plank Road, and their brief pause along the way at Fort Mahone is well-documented.

As Lincoln prepared to travel, he sent a telegram to Stanton saying, "This morning Gen. Grant reports Petersburg evacuated; and he is confident Richmond also is. He is pushing forward to cut off if possible, the retreating army. I start to him in a few minutes."[152]

Stanton was astounded that Lincoln would venture so soon into a city that was recently occupied by hostile troops. He responded, "I congratulate you and the nation on the glorious news in your telegram just recd. Allow me respectfully to ask you to consider whether you ought to expose the nation to the consequence of any disaster to yourself in the pursuit of a treacherous and dangerous enemy like the rebel army. If it was a question concerning yourself only I should not presume to say a word. Commanding Generals are in the line of their duty in running such risks. But is the political head of a nation in the same condition."[153]

Riding north along the Jerusalem Plank Road, the president paused to survey the detritus of the previous day's fighting at Fort Mahone. Burial details had not reached the area, and the dead were sprawled across the earthworks.

Among the Union casualties were members of the 114th Pennsylvania Regiment, commanded by Brig. Gen. Charles H. T. Collis. The soldiers of the 114th were known as Zouaves, wearing colorful uniforms patterned after those of French light infantry that had become famous during the Crimean War and the French colonization of North Africa. The 114th Pennsylvania was a familiar sight to the president during his stay at City Point, performing guard and escort duty. Ordered to the front line to participate in the assault on Fort Mahone, the regiment sustained heavy losses. Among them were three notable officers, Maj. Henry M. Eddy, Capt. Andrew J. Cunningham, and Lt. Edward T. Marion. A trooper of the cavalry escort remembered that tears ran down Lincoln's cheeks.

The Union army was in motion before sunrise on April 3. Grant remembered entering Petersburg and allowing Confederate stragglers in plain sight to shuffle away unmolested. "I had not the heart to turn the artillery upon such a mass of defeated and fleeing men." He did not intend for his troops to tarry in Petersburg and reasoned that these haggard enemy soldiers would be taken soon enough. "I was sure Lee was trying to make his escape and I wanted to push immediately in pursuit. I hoped to capture them soon."[154]

Grant added in his memoirs, "I had started all the troops out early in the morning, so that after the National army left Petersburg there was not a soul to be seen, not even an animal in the streets. There was absolutely no one there, except my staff officers and, possibly, a small escort of cavalry. We had selected the piazza of a deserted house, and occupied it until the President arrived."[155]

Lincoln's countenance brightened significantly when he reached the fine, two-story Italianate home of local attorney Thomas Wallace and rushed through the gate about 11:00 a.m. to greet Grant, "his face beaming with delight."[156] Although Grant wrote in his 1885 memoirs that the house was deserted, other accounts contradict that assertion. A member of the Whig Party, Wallace had served in Congress and known Lincoln before the war. His wife was a cousin of A. P. Hill and had learned of the general's death only hours earlier. Although the family was in mourning, Lincoln was welcomed and met with his general for an hour and a half.[157]

Once again, accounts of the meeting vary. One relates that Lincoln and Grant were sequestered in the library for their conference. Another says that the two were situated in the home's vestibule, just inside the front door with a large chair brought over for Lincoln's comfort, his long legs extending out the door and onto the front porch. Yet another version recounts that Lincoln and Grant smoked cigars on the front porch and discussed recent events. When Thomas Wallace invited them inside, they elected to stay on the porch due to the cigar smoke. Wallace brought a high-backed wooden chair outside, and Lincoln sat at the edge of the porch, his legs dangling.[158]

Certainly, the conversation included the recent military successes and the prospect that news of the fall of Richmond would soon arrive. Grant had always been aware of the president's heightened anxiety concerning the progress of the war. He was selective when it came to providing information on future operations.

"I would have let him know what I contemplated doing, only while I felt a strong conviction that the move was going to be successful, yet it might not prove so; and then I would have only added another to the many disappointments he had been suffering for the past three years," Grant wrote. This day was different. Grant noted, "Our movements having been successful up to this point, I no longer had any object in concealing from the President all my movements, and the objects I had in view."[159]

Interestingly, after informing Lincoln of his intent to pursue the Army of Northern Virginia, Grant turned the conversation to a political concern. Strategic discussions had included a plan for the armies of Grant and Sherman to unite to finish off Lee. Buoyed by the recent victories and sensing that the end was near, Grant told the president that he was anxious for the "Eastern armies" alone to complete the task. Sherman's "Western armies" had been successful in their campaigns from the Mississippi River to North Carolina. He wrote:

> I said to him that if the Western armies should be even upon the field, operating against Richmond and Lee, the credit would be given to them for the capture by politicians and non-combatants from the section of country which those troops hailed from. It might lead to disagreeable bickerings between members of Congress of the East and those of the West in some of their debates. Western members might be throwing it up to the members of the East that in suppression of the rebellion they were not able to capture an army, or to accomplish much in the way of contributing toward that end, but had to wait until the Western armies had conquered all the territory south and west of them, and then come on to help them capture the only army they had been engaged with.[160]

The usually pragmatic Lincoln responded that in his strong desire to finish the war he had not considered such a turn of events. Grant closed the topic with, "Possibly I am the only one who thought of the liability of such a state of things in advance."[161]

The last meeting between Lincoln and Grant concluded about 12:30 p.m. The president mounted his horse, and the general turned to join his army, already in pursuit of Lee. Within a few minutes of Lincoln's departure, Grant received word from General Weitzel that Union troops were occupying Richmond.

After returning to City Point, Lincoln replied at 5:00 p.m. to Stanton's morning telegram—possibly with a chuckle, at least a smile. "Yours received. Thanks for your caution; but I have already been to Petersburg, staid with Gen. Grant an hour & a half and returned here. It is certain now that Richmond is in our hands, and I think I will go there to-morrow. I will take care of myself."[162]

For some time, Admiral Porter's James River naval force had been responsible for keeping the Confederate Navy iron-clads and warships bottled up around Richmond. At the same time, the Confederates did their best to eliminate the threat of a Union Navy flotilla venturing up the James. The Rebels sank old ships in the watercourse and distributed floating mines called "torpedoes" to impede the enemy's progress. In early April, the delicate process of clearing the torpedoes and other obstacles was ongoing.

On the morning of April 4, the president and his small entourage, including twelve-year-old Tad, took the *River Queen* to a rendezvous with Admiral Porter's flagship, the side-wheel steamer *Malvern*, for the trip up the James to Richmond. When the *Malvern* was unable to negotiate a series of obstructions in the river, the presidential party was transferred to a barge with a shallow draft and taken in tow by the tugboat *Glance*. The swift current forced the *Malvern* against a bridge pillar, and the *Glance* was ordered to pull the large vessel back into the channel. Twelve sailors were detailed and took to the oars, muscling the barge to its destination, a usually busy place called Rocketts at James River Landing about one hundred yards from Libby Prison. The proceedings amused Lincoln immensely.[163]

"I had never been to Richmond before by that route, and did not know where the landing was; neither did the coxswain, nor any of the barge's crew," remembered Porter. "We pulled on, hoping to see some one of whom we could inquire, but no one was in sight. The street along the river-front was as deserted as if this had been a city of the dead. The troops had been in possession some hours, but not a soldier was to be seen. The current was now rushing past us over and among rocks, on one of which we finally stuck. . . . So I backed out and pointed for the nearest landing."[164]

No welcoming party had gathered, and there was no substantial contingent of troops waiting ashore to provide protection for the president. A boat carrying a contingent of twenty-four marines who were supposed to serve as security had run aground. Twelve sailors, probably those who had rowed Lincoln to Rocketts, took up their rifles, fixed bayonets, and formed in front of and behind Admiral Porter and the president, who held Tad's right hand.

Porter saw a small house nearby. Outside were about a dozen black laborers. Their leader was a man about sixty years old. "He raised himself to an upright position as we landed, and put his hands up to his eyes," wrote Porter. "Then he dropped his spade and sprang forward. 'Bress de Lord,' he said. 'Dere is de great Messiah! I knowed him as soon as I seed him. He's been in my heart fo' long yeahs, an' he's cum at las' to free his chillum from deir bondage! Glory, Hallelujah!' And he fell upon his knees before the President and kissed his feet . . . and in a minute Mr. Lincoln was surrounded by these people."[165]

The crowd of former slaves grew, and soon the throng was pressing the president so closely that his impromptu bodyguard became alarmed. Finally, the president spoke, telling the growing crowd not to bow to him. "My poor friends, you are free—free as air," he told them.[166]

The day was warm and bright, and amid the smoke and ruins of Richmond, Lincoln removed his heavy overcoat but kept his stovepipe hat on, wiping sweat from his brow during the walk up to Main Street. A girl, about seventeen years old, stepped forward and handed him a bouquet of roses. Porter found a Union cavalryman, the first soldier he had seen in the few minutes since landing. He ordered the trooper to find a suitable escort for the president, and a few minutes later a number of horsemen arrived. They escorted the president to General Weitzel's headquarters, a walk of about two miles.

Thomas Thatcher Graves, an aide to General Weitzel who was then using the Confederate White House as his headquarters, had just started down Clay Street when he saw a crowd coming. He noted the president's long stride and remembered Lincoln asking whether it was far to Jefferson Davis's house. Graves guided the group the rest of the way.

"At the Davis house, he [Lincoln] was shown into the reception-room, with the remark that the housekeeper had said that the room was President Davis's office," remembered Graves. "As he seated himself, he remarked, 'This must have been President Davis's chair,' and, crossing his legs, he looked far off with a serious, dreamy expression. At length he asked me if the housekeeper was in the house. Upon learning that she had left, he jumped up and said with a boyish manner, 'Come, let's look at the house.'"[167]

Lincoln was actually seated in Davis's former study rather than his office on the second floor. Another observer remembered that the tired president exhibited "no triumph in his gesture or attitude" and that he asked, "I wonder if I could get a glass of water."[168]

As Lincoln and Thatcher, his spontaneous tour guide, descended the staircase, Weitzel arrived. Lunch was quickly prepared and consumed. While the president was still in the house, Weitzel and Gen. George Shepley, the newly appointed military governor of Richmond, advised him that a delegation of prominent Confederates wished to meet with him.

The *New York Herald* reported, "The President listened patiently, and indicated his sense of the magnitude of the proposition submitted for his consideration by great nervousness of manner, running his hands frequently through his hair and moving to and fro in the official chair of the late [*sic*] Jefferson Davis, in which he sat."[169]

Lincoln agreed to meet with Judge John A. Campbell and a Confederate army officer. Campbell, one of the delegates to the peace discussions at City Point in January, asked Lincoln for leniency toward the Confederate states. Lincoln was concerned about the return of Virginia to the Union and proposed another meeting for the following day.

On April 5, the president met with Campbell and Gustavus A. Myers, a Richmond attorney, aboard the *Malvern*, finally able to pass through the obstacles on the James. Lincoln told the men that he was considering allowing the Virginia legislature to meet if the body would vote to repeal the ordinance of secession. Campbell and Myers listened eagerly and responded that General Lee and all other Virginians would lay down their arms as soon as their state was restored to the Union. Lincoln said that he would make a decision on the issue after he returned to City Point.

By the time the president departed the Confederate White House, a large crowd of former slaves had gathered. They cheered loudly, and some threw their hats into the air. Some accounts of his departure say that Lincoln then rode in an open carriage drawn by four horses. Bodyguard William Crook remembered that an ambulance was provided and there was no room for him to squeeze inside. Crook, therefore, rode a horse and stationed himself to the side of the ambulance where the president sat.

Passing Saint Paul's Church, Lincoln stopped at the Virginia Statehouse. It was a shambles with desks and chairs overturned, documents scattered everywhere, and Confederate thousand-dollar bonds littering the floor. The president saw the damage caused by the rioting and upheaval during the evacuation and the fire that followed. Graves recalled accompanying the party to Libby Prison and Castle Thunder, another prison where Union soldiers had been confined.[170]

Weitzel remembered that during the tour he engaged the president in a lively discussion. "I had considerable conversation with him in regard to the treatment of the conquered people," wrote the general. "The pith of his answers was that he did not wish to give me any orders on that subject, but as he expressed it: 'If I were in your place, I'd let 'em up easy—let 'em up easy.'"[171]

Late in the afternoon, Lincoln returned to the *Malvern*. The day had been long and exhausting. There were concerns for his safety in the city that had until recently been the capital of the Confederacy. There were reports of a suspicious character, who had appeared in the second floor window of a nearby building wearing a Confederate uniform and possibly taken aim with a rifle. Two other men had come close to the *Malvern* asserting that they had messages to deliver to the president. They were not allowed to board the vessel.[172]

One vignette of President Lincoln's visit to Richmond involved an old friend. It may well have been embellished, and evidence as to its veracity is inconclusive.

While Maj. Gen. George Pickett and his shattered division struggled to escape the grip of the Federal armies west of Richmond, Pickett's lovely young wife, LaSalle Corbell "Sallie" Pickett, holding ten-month-old George Edward Pickett Jr., answered a knock on her door in a fashionable Richmond neighborhood. In her 1913 book *Pickett and His Men*, Sallie wrote her recollection of the encounter with the visitor:

With my baby on my arm, I answered the door, and looked up at a tall, gaunt, sad-faced man in ill-fitting clothes who, with the accent of the North asked:

"Is this George Pickett's place?"

"Yes sir," I answered, "but he is not here."

"I know that ma'am," he replied, "but I just wanted to see the place. I am Abraham Lincoln."

"The President," I gasped.

The stranger shook his head and said, "No, ma'am; no ma'am; just Abraham Lincoln, George's old friend."

Abraham Lincoln did, in fact, know George Pickett before the war. Lincoln's former law partner and comrade during the Black Hawk War, Congressman John Todd Stuart, had arranged Pickett's appointment to the US Military Academy. Lincoln had also apparently corresponded with Pickett during his four years at West Point.

Sallie went on to describe the touching scene as her baby stretched toward the president, who took young Pickett in his arms. A wet baby kiss followed. Lincoln handed the child back to his mother and turned to walk down the steps.

As they parted, the president remarked, "Tell your father, the rascal, that I forgive him for the sake of that kiss and those bright eyes."[173]

Sallie Pickett was an inventive woman. Although born in 1843, she was said to have changed her birth date to 1848 and billed herself as the "child bride of the Confederacy," twenty-three years younger than her husband. She was a prolific writer and became a popular speaker of the late nineteenth and early twentieth centuries. Numerous historians have concluded that a series of letters purported to have been written by General Pickett to his wife were actually penned by Sallie herself. She was also accused of plagiarizing extensive portions of *Pickett and His Men*.

Sallie's writings, lectures, and performances became prominent with the wave of Lost Cause sentiment during the postbellum period. She idealized the memory of her husband, with whom she fled to Canada for a year after the war. George sold insurance in Norfolk, Virginia, and died in 1875 at the age of fifty. Sallie outlived him by fifty-six years. She died in 1931, having made a substantial contribution to the myth of the Lost Cause.

The Pickett family requested that Sallie be buried with her husband in Richmond's Hollywood Cemetery. However, no woman had been interred in the soldiers' section of the cemetery, and the Hollywood Ladies Memorial Society refused to allow it.

Instead, Sallie was interred at Abbey Mausoleum near Arlington National Cemetery. In 1968, Abbey Mausoleum became insolvent. Years passed, and the facility fell into decline. In 1998, Sallie was finally buried beside her husband at the foot of the Pickett Monument in the Gettysburg Hill section of the Hollywood Cemetery in Richmond.

Whether President Lincoln's visit to the Pickett home actually took place may never be known. It remains, however, such a picturesque image of the time that many historians hope mightily that it did.

PART IV
BEYOND REBEL REACH

CHAPTER 7

FOR RATIONS AND RAIL

Shortly after Grant and Meade arrived in Petersburg on the morning of April 3, an individual representing himself as an engineer of the Army of Northern Virginia was brought to them. The man claimed that Lee had prepared yet another strong series of entrenchments and was drawing the troops out of Richmond to make a stand. Immediately, Meade's level of concern was heightened.

Meade strongly suggested crossing the Appomattox River, moving northward, and confronting the Rebels along this new line. Grant, however, overruled him. Even now men were on the move from Sutherland Station and other points, headed west where Grant believed Lee was taking the Army of Northern Virginia. Grant remembered:

> I had already given orders for the movement up the south side of the Appomattox for the purpose of heading off Lee . . . I knew that Lee was no fool, as he would have been to have put himself and his army between two formidable streams like the James and Appomattox rivers, and between two such armies as those of the Potomac and the James. Then these streams coming together as they did to the east of him, it would be only

necessary to close up in the west to have him thoroughly cut off from all supplies or possibility of reinforcement. It would only have been a question of days, and not many of them, if he had taken the position assigned to him by the so-called engineer, when he would have been obliged to surrender his army. Such is one of the ruses resorted to in war to deceive your antagonist.[174]

Grant was correct. He had been prepared to renew the battle for Petersburg that morning, but when word came of the Confederate evacuation he explained to Sheridan that the object of the Federal drive westward was not to follow the Army of Northern Virginia, but to move parallel with it, staying between Lee's army and North Carolina and then getting in front of the Rebels to cut off their advance. This would prevent a turn to the south to join Joseph Johnston's Confederate army. Sheridan's cavalry would provide the mobility to make it happen. The slower moving infantry of Griffin's V Corps, with Humphreys's II Corps and Wright's VI Corps close behind, were to follow.

In darkness and hours ahead of Grant's orders, the scattered Army of Northern Virginia had begun its last week of life as an organized fighting force with a desperate race to Amelia Court House on the Richmond & Danville Railroad thirty miles southwest of the ravaged Confederate capital. Traveling initially along five routes, the Confederates intended to concentrate at Amelia Court House, and Lee's hungry soldiers would finally be fed with rations sent by rail from Richmond. Estimates of the number of Confederate troops on the march vary from approximately thirty thousand to nearly sixty thousand.

The distance to the Roanoke River, the nearest point where Lee might affect a junction with Johnston, was 107 miles. Past Amelia Court House, the Army of Northern Virginia would swing southwest along the line of the Richmond & Danville Railroad through Jetersville and then Burkeville. The army had to cover 55 miles from Petersburg to Burkeville, and Grant's route toward the same objective from the vicinity of Sutherland Station was 36 miles. The Confederates, however, had almost a full day's head start. Time was either Lee's best ally or his worst enemy.[175]

Coordinating the complicated Confederate move west was no simple task. The troops were spread thinly across a front of more than thirty miles. The Appomattox and James rivers were still swollen from the recent heavy rains, and muddy roads made the trek difficult for men and horses. Ewell and Custis Lee were instructed to lead the former defenders of Richmond, now including a contingent of naval personnel whose ships had been blown up along the capital city's waterfront, to the south bank of the James and then on a northerly route, crossing the Appomattox at the Genito Bridge. In the center, Maj. Gen. William Mahone pulled his division from the fortifications of the Howlett Line across the neck of Bermuda Hundred. These troops were to use Goode's Bridge across the Appomattox and proceed through Chesterfield Court House.

The Confederate troops defending Petersburg, including Longstreet's I Corps, Gordon's II Corps, and the remnants of A. P. Hill's III Corps, now under the command of Henry Heth, marched through the town and crossed to the north side of the Appomattox River before wheeling to the west along multiple roads toward Bevil's Bridge about seven miles west of Amelia Court House. Once there they intended to cross the Appomattox again, approaching their destination from the northeast.

Further south of the Appomattox, Lt. Gen. Richard Anderson was in overall command of the Confederates that had been cut off after the defeat at Five Forks and the collapse of the right flank of the Petersburg defenses on April 2. These included Pickett's and Bushrod Johnson's depleted divisions, Fitzhugh Lee's cavalry, and Anderson's small IV Corps, formed the previous October. These troops had the shortest distance to cover, moving northwest to Amelia Court House, but several small streams and continual harassment from Sheridan's cavalry slowed them considerably.

Despite their hunger and hardship in the face of a superior enemy, some of the Confederate soldiers were actually relieved to be again on the march. Even Lee's spirits seemed to be lifted. Napier Bartlett, an officer of the Washington Artillery of New Orleans, described the feeling as "getting rid of some hideous dream in leaving behind the trenches, and once again moving in column on the road."[176]

The notable exception was among the troops to the south, who had been roughly handled during the recent fighting. Lieutenant James F. J. Caldwell of the 1st South Carolina Regiment, Pickett's division, noted that the regiment was "so crushed by the defeats of the last few days that it straggled along without strength and almost without thought. So we moved on in disorder, keeping no regular column, no regular pace. There were not many words spoken. An indescribable sadness weighed upon us."[177]

Lee watched the last of his tired troops march out of Petersburg and followed them for more than twenty miles. Judge James H. Cox, a prominent citizen and former lawmaker from Chesterfield County, heard that Lee was passing nearby and extended an invitation to dinner at his home, Clover Hill. Lee, Longstreet, and several staff officers, perhaps comforted by the perceived advantage of time their early westward movement had brought, accepted the invitation. Longstreet was still convalescing from his wound in the Wilderness and had difficulty cutting his meat.

In her book *My Confederate Girlhood*, Kate, the judge's daughter, remembered the rather somber officers and the meal. She wrote, "General Lee's time for being with us was short, but before dinner could be placed on the table, there was a brief interval. To me belonged the privilege of a short talk with General Lee, which incident is written on my memory never to be effaced. I said, 'General Lee, we shall still gain our cause; you will join General Johnston and together you will be victorious.' My poor little attempt at sympathy—breathing hope, was met with: 'Whatever happens, know this, that no men ever fought better than those who have stood by me.'"[178]

Complicating the run to Amelia Court House, Longstreet and Gordon were forced to detour northwest to Goode's Bridge across the Appomattox River when they learned that the swollen stream had washed out Bevil's Bridge. The Genito Bridge was shaky, and planking and supports that were supposed to arrive to shore it up were nowhere to be found. Ewell's soldiers were delayed when they were required to lay planks over the tracks at the Mattoax Railroad Bridge and cross the river there.

The only appreciable fighting of April 3 included several rear-guard actions of Anderson's command, whose rear-guard cavalry was required to halt and dismount a number of times to beat back Sheridan's cavalry. Union horsemen had been hot on Anderson's heels virtually from the beginning of his westward movement as Thomas Devin's division harassed Bushrod Johnson's infantry on the Namozine Road.

Two brigades of Rooney Lee's cavalry, under brigadier generals William Roberts and Rufus Barringer, were detailed as the rear guard of Fitzhugh Lee's column covering the route of march for Johnson's infantry. After daybreak, elements of Custer's leading cavalry brigade, under Col. William Wells, ran into Barringer's cavalry along Willicomack Creek, and chased the Rebels in a running skirmish toward the whitewashed-frame Namozine Presbyterian Church.

Meanwhile, at the ford on Namozine Creek about five miles from the church more of Wells's troopers were menacing Roberts's cavalry brigade and some accompanying infantry. Roberts recognized the threat and ordered the 16th North Carolina Cavalry Battalion and the 4th North Carolina Cavalry Regiment to dismount and dig in on the west side of Namozine Creek.

Custer appeared on the scene and ordered the 1st Vermont Cavalry to cross the creek at a distance where the Confederates were not likely to see the Union horsemen and proceed to outflank the entrenchments. He also brought artillery forward to fire on the Rebel line. However, before Custer could fix his quarry the Confederates spotted the Vermont cavalrymen and pulled out of their entrenchments, falling back toward the church with the Federals after them.

As he reached the Namozine Church, Barringer turned on his pursuers, launching the 1st, 2nd, and 5th North Carolina Cavalry Regiments against Wells's vanguard, the 8th New York Cavalry. Moments later, the 15th New York and the 1st Vermont joined the fray, pushing Barringer back.

"Soon the enemy appeared in force, with shouts of triumph and trumpets blowing," General Barringer remembered. "I ordered the whole [force] to fall back and skirmish in retreat. The 5th [North Carolina Cavalry] Regiment, which was dismounted, fought with . . . obstinacy and seemed slow to give up the contest. Before it retired under further orders, the enemy had gained the main road of retreat."[179]

As the 2nd North Carolina deployed behind makeshift entrenchments, Capt. Thomas Custer, an aide to his older brother George, urged his horse to jump a nearby obstacle. The horse was shot from under Thomas as he seized the colors of the 2nd North Carolina and forced three officers and eleven other Confederate soldiers to surrender. He received the Medal of Honor for his actions.

With the North Carolina cavalry holding the Federals back, Bushrod Johnson's infantry passed close to Namozine Church at about 8:00 a.m. and promptly took a wrong turn to the right at a fork in the road. When Johnson reached the rain-swollen Deep Creek and saw that the bridge across it had been washed away, he ordered his troops to countermarch. The hard-pressed

Confederate cavalry held the road open long enough for Johnson to retrace his steps and take the proper fork. Custer's tired cavalrymen had been fighting all morning and were compelled to retire with the approach of Johnson's infantry on its return march. The Confederates then crossed Deep Creek by the correct route.

About an hour after the skirmishing subsided, a Union cavalryman rode up to the Namozine Church, which was serving as a temporary hospital, and peered inside. "A Captain Goodrich I think of the 8th New York Cavalry lay in the little church, having been shot through the head. He soon died. There were some three or four men, most of them badly wounded, in the church."[180]

The dying officer was Capt. Asa L. Goodrich of the 8th New York Cavalry. He was probably buried in a temporary grave somewhere nearby. In 1866 Lt. Col. James Moore began surveying the Petersburg area for a suitable location to establish a national cemetery. He chose ground that had served as a bivouac for the 50th New York Engineers, who had constructed a Gothic-style church of pine logs in the area and named it Poplar Grove.

Over a three-year period, 6,718 burials were completed in Poplar Grove National Cemetery, the remains placed in simple wooden coffins. Captain Goodrich is one of 2,139 who were positively identified. At Blandford Cemetery in Petersburg, nearly 30,000 Confederate dead are buried, and all but 2,000 remain unknown.

Custer renewed his pursuit later in the day, but Johnson's infantry stood its ground at Sweathouse Creek and stopped the Federal advance. Wells harassed the Confederates throughout their crossing of Deep Creek. As the tumult of war passed by, Sheridan briefly used the Namozine Church as his headquarters. Built in 1847, the structure still stands.

The Union cavalry lost 95 killed and wounded in the fighting. The number of Confederate dead and wounded is unknown. Major J. D. Ferguson, Rooney Lee's adjutant, was taken prisoner after dark. However, the biggest catch among 350 Rebels captured at Namozine Church that day was Barringer.

Sheridan considered his intrepid scouts, commanded by Maj. Henry H. Young, some of the most valuable men in the Union Army. These fearless covert operators often dressed in Confederate uniforms and passed themselves off as Rebel soldiers. Sometimes, they masqueraded as local farmers and pretended to have recently lost their homes, moving with little notice through the lines. All the while, they were marching or riding among the enemy troops to gather information and create confusion. The Confederates were aware that these shadowy interlopers were operating and referred to them as "Jessie Scouts."

One scout dressed as a Confederate quartermaster major. He directed that every team of horses crossing a certain creek had to halt and be watered. The imposter held up an entire wagon train for hours and then slipped away unnoticed. A Confederate officer who was later captured saw the scout's familiar face as he conversed leisurely with other Union soldiers. Only then did the Rebel realize that the man had pulled off a masterly deception.

After the skirmish at Namozine Church was over, Young and a band of his scouts, clad in Confederate uniforms, encountered General Barringer and several members of his staff. Maj. Henry Edwin Tremain was one of the scouts. He wrote years later of the chance meeting:

> I saw a rebel officer riding a beautiful gray horse; along with him were his staff, and just then I heard the word "surrender;" looking back, Major Young was laughingly leveling an old antiquated double barreled shot gun on me. I said to him, "Look down the woods." He looked and half wheeled his horse. I said to him, "Don't go back; come up here quick." I, being on higher ground could see that nothing was behind Barringer and staff. . . . I said to him, "I will go down into the woods and talk with these fellows."
>
> I rode down and saw the Confederate was a Major General. I saluted and said, "What command, General?" "I am General Barringer of the North Carolina Brigade" "I belong to the 17th Virginia, Fitzhugh Lee's command," I replied. He asked me if there were any more of the men around. I told him half a dozen up on the road and would be down in a few minutes. When Young and his men came down, I introduced Young as Major Grandstaff, of the 17th Virginia, one of Fitzhugh Lee's regiments. After a few minutes talk, the signal was given, and we covered the General and his staff with revolvers and took them in. Barringer was very angry. When asked at headquarters that night what he thought of Sheridan's scouts, he said, "They are spies, spies; I would hang every one of them to the highest limb if I caught them." He was very quickly informed: not in this war.[181]

The aggressive Sheridan had quickly grasped Lee's intent. While two of his cavalry divisions, under Custer and Devin, were stalking Anderson, he ordered his third, under Maj. Gen. George Crook, to Jetersville, halfway between Amelia Court House and the vital rail junction at Burkeville, fifteen miles to the southwest on the Richmond & Danville Railroad.

"From the beginning it was apparent that Lee, in his retreat, was making for Amelia Court House, where his columns north and south of the Appomattox River could join, and where, no doubt, he expected supplies, so Crook was ordered early on April 4 to strike the Danville railroad, between Jettersville [sic] and Burkeville, Merritt [in charge of Custer's and Devin's cavalry divisions] to move toward Amelia Court House, and the Fifth Corps to Jettersville itself."[182]

Bone weary, the retreating soldiers of the Army of Northern Virginia covered an average of about twenty-one miles on April 3, some soldiers pitching from the ranks to lie down by the roadside while others stumbled along literally walking while they slept. During the evening, Lee was able to establish communications with all the commands streaming away from Petersburg. He rested for a short time at Hebron Church and then followed the last of Longstreet's troops across Goode's Bridge about 7:30 a.m. on April 4.

As the hungry soldiers marched on toward Amelia Court House, word circulated through the ranks that rations were waiting for them. The prospect of this newfound abundance of food spurred them on, even as the crackle of rifles and carbines told them that Union cavalry was not far away. Lee was aware that 350,000 rations had been collected in Richmond, and the provisions were vital to his effort to eventually turn south along the rail line to Danville and reach Johnston's army in North Carolina.

Around 8:30 a.m., Lee arrived at Amelia Court House, and his staff began looking for the promised provisions. Aboard the railcars at Amelia instead were 96 full artillery caissons, 200 boxes of shot and shell, and 164 boxes filled with harnesses for artillery horses. There was no food.[183]

Major John Esten Cooke, a staff officer, watched Lee lose his composure. "No face wore a heavier shadow than that of General Lee," he wrote. "The failure of the supply of rations completely paralyzed him. An anxious and haggard expression came to his face."[184]

Brigadier General E. Porter Alexander, commander of the I Corps artillery, said later, "We should have gotten rations here, but in all the crash we had come through many plans had been sure to miscarry, and the plan to have rations here for us had been one of them."[185]

Throughout the day, Confederate soldiers straggled into the vicinity of Amelia Court House. Longstreet's corps was in the town, while Heth brought in the ragged soldiers of Hill's former command. Gordon camped five miles to the east, and Mahone's division waited at Goode's Bridge until Ewell's troops were safely across the Appomattox. The number of hungry men increased. As more rain began to fall, orders were given to assemble some wagons for foraging, and the commander of the army wrote a heartfelt appeal to the local population.

To The Citizens of Amelia County, Virginia.

The Army of Northern Virginia arrived here today, expecting to find plenty of provisions, which had been ordered to be placed here by the railroad several days since, but to my surprise and regret I find not a pound of subsistence for man or horse. I must therefore appeal to your generosity and charity to supply as far as each one is able the wants of the brave soldiers who have battled for your liberty for four years. We require meat, beef, cattle, sheep, hogs, flour, meal, corn and provender in any quantity that can be spared. The quartermaster of the army will visit you and make arrangements to pay for what he receives or give the proper vouchers or certificates. I feel assured that all will give to the extent of their means.[186]

Lee had intended to remain at Amelia Court House only long enough to distribute rations and allow his soldiers a little time to eat. Now, he had no choice. Foraging would consume precious time, probably a full day. His advantage of time, measured only in hours, was rapidly dwindling. He knew that Federal cavalry was racing forward south of his position, and if the infantry caught up the Army of Northern Virginia might be overwhelmed. The enemy might also continue to the west and cut the railroad to Danville, where 1.5 million rations of meat were supposedly gathered. Lee ordered provisions up from there to Burkeville but harbored some doubt that they would get through. Another battle had become more likely since the army had traveled beyond the shield of the

Appomattox River, which had provided some measure of protection from the enemy for its long left flank.

The reason for the supply debacle at Amelia Court House has never been fully determined. However, the finger pointing that followed provides clear evidence that government officials, particularly those whose governments are crumbling, often seek to assign blame during and after their demise.

Many observers were quick to blame the ineptitude of the fleeing Confederate government, particularly Commissary General Isaac M. St. John. Rumors later surfaced that the train had been dispatched from Richmond and then recalled to provide food for government officials during the evacuation of Richmond. Major Cooke observed that the problem was due to "the rubbish of the departments."[187]

Jefferson Davis took umbrage to these assertions and defended the former Confederate government for years after the war. He offered a letter from St. John dated July 14, 1873, which read in part, "No calls, by letter or requisition, from the general commanding, or from any other source, official or unofficial, had been received by the Commissary-General or the Assistant Commissary-General; nor was any communication transmitted through the department channels to the bureau of subsistence, for the collection of supplies at Amelia Court-House."[188]

The most plausible explanation is that a communication breakdown occurred between Lee's staff and Richmond on the morning of April 2. During the hasty departure from the Turnbull House at Edge Hill, it is likely that no response was sent to an inquiry from the commissary general's office concerning the disposition of rations stockpiled at the capital.[189]

April 5 dawned with a drizzle. In the early mist the forage wagons came rolling back to Amelia Court House, mostly empty. Four years of war had taken their toll on the local citizenry. Stores of provisions were already depleted, and the people had little to feed themselves, let alone a starving army numbering in the thousands. Bands of hungry soldiers walked away on foot looking for food, and many of these simply did not return. Along with those men that Union troops killed or captured, desertion was steadily eroding the ranks of Lee's army.

The delay at Amelia Court House cost the Confederates nearly a full day, and there was nothing to show for it. Those soldiers who answered the order to assemble were disheartened. They were on the march again, with empty stomachs. This time, the objective was the rail junction at Burkeville. Lee intended for the Army of Northern Virginia to make its wide turn southward along the railroad, toward provisions and eventually Johnston's army in North Carolina.

Lee ordered the supply train that had trailed Ewell out of Richmond to take a northerly arc through Painesville, where the wagons would hopefully be safe from the long reach of Sheridan's marauding cavalry and to clear the road through Jetersville for the foot soldiers. Gary's cavalry brigade was detailed to escort the wagons, while Rooney Lee's cavalry division was sent ahead to scout the rail line. Longstreet's corps stepped off to lead the infantry column, and elements of Gordon's corps filed in as the rear guard.

The artillery limber chests were filled, and the excess ordnance was destroyed with a deafening roar, a dismal cacophony that punctuated the desperation of the day. Pickets and troops in outlying areas were startled by the sound and leaped to their weapons thinking they were under attack. When word was passed that the origin of the disturbing sounds was not belligerent, a few of the Rebel soldiers found humor in the event. "Suddenly the earth shook with a tremendous explosion," remembered Pvt. Carlton McCarthy, an artilleryman of the Richmond Howitzers, "and an immense column of smoke rushed up into the air to a great height. For a moment there was the greatest consternation. Whole regiments broke and fled in wild confusion. Cutshaw's men stood up, seized their muskets, and stood at attention till it was known that the ammunition had been purposely fired and no enemy was threatening the line. Then what laughter and hilarity prevailed, for a while, among these famishing men!"[190]

By late morning, the last of the infantry had set off down the road toward Burkeville. Around 1:00 p.m., Lee mounted Traveller, the sturdy gray American Saddlebred of sixteen hands that he had acquired in February 1862 and ridden during so many campaigns and battles. He looked to the west as Longstreet rode up, and the two generals started forward. Lee may have already known that Union cavalry was at Jetersville. Sometime during the morning a pair of enemy dispatch riders had been captured, and their presence indicated that an organized force of some strength was ahead.

The road to Burkeville ran close to the Richmond & Danville rail line, rising slightly beyond Jetersville, where a small stream flowed down to Flat Creek and for about a half mile the railroad ambled through heavy forest. Hearing rifle fire, Lee and Longstreet pressed ahead. About seven miles from Amelia Court House, they encountered Rooney Lee, who delivered disturbing news. His horsemen had encountered dismounted Union cavalry in position along a ridge beyond the screening woods. Rooney could not be sure, but he thought enemy infantry might also be present, and earthworks had been hastily thrown up from the edge of the woods to the left at North Buckskin Creek.[191] One thing was certain. Federal troops were directly in the path of the Army of Northern Virginia.

Never one to shrink from a fight, Lee wanted with every fiber of his being to strike the enemy there and then. E. Porter Alexander recalled the ride forward with the other officers. He later wrote, "We were not long in coming to where our skirmish line was already engaged. I never saw Gen. Lee seem so anxious to bring on a battle in my life as he seemed this afternoon; but a conference with General W.H.F. [Rooney] Lee in command of the cavalry in our front seemed to disappoint him greatly. [Rooney] Lee reported that Sheridan . . . was more than we could venture to attack."[192]

Lee left the gathering of officers that had quickly assembled and alone peered through his field glasses at the Union positions. He saw enemy battle flags fluttering in the light breeze and correctly concluded that Union infantry had reached Jetersville as well. The presence of the V Corps vanguard bolstering the lightly armed cavalrymen changed the game for the Confederate commander.

Lee knew little of the surrounding terrain and did not have a highly detailed map to consult. Available evidence suggested that the Federals had arrived south of Jetersville in force. Although the leading elements of his infantry had halted and deployed in line of battle, the majority of his army was still in column. If these troops were needed, deploying them into line of battle would take time. The men were tired and hungry. The skirmishing was enough. This was neither the place nor the time to lock with the enemy in a general engagement.

Lee returned to the other officers and told them the Federal positions to their front were formidable. He instructed his commanders to take a new route of march, turning from their southwest orientation to the north and then back to the west, around the flank of the enemy positions at Jetersville, toward Rice's Station, and then perhaps to Farmville, twenty-three miles away.

Both Rice's Station, seven miles northwest of Burkeville, and Farmville were on the South Side Railroad, and supplies could possibly reach the army from Lynchburg about forty miles to the west. Once the troops had received provisions, Lee could assess the situation anew, turning again to the south toward Danville and Johnston or heading west toward Lynchburg. In either case, he was obliged to remain close to a railroad, the Richmond & Danville or the South Side.

At this point, though, Lee abandoned the Richmond & Danville line as an avenue of resupply. If he could feed his army at Farmville, then he might turn south toward Johnston in North Carolina once again.

The hours spent at Amelia Court House had erased any advantage in time or distance the Confederates once held. There was no time to waste. Once again, the famished and weary Rebel soldiers were assembled to undertake another seemingly endless march. The route around the Federals at Jetersville was open to Deatonsville, but the bridge across Flat Creek near Amelia Springs was damaged. While the infantry forded the stream, wagons waited for repairs to be completed. The wreckage of Ewell's wagons destroyed by Davies clogged another road, and beyond Deatonsville multiple routes converged into a single path, slowing progress even further. The movement was fully underway by midafternoon and continued all night long. Heavy rain began to fall, compounding the soldiers' misery.

Crossing Flat Creek, the Army of Northern Virginia reached the resort enclave of Amelia Springs, a collection of about twenty buildings on more than 1,300 acres where visitors had come since 1825 to partake of the curative properties of its sulphur spring water. Lee and his family had visited Amelia Springs in happier times. During the forced march of April 5 and 6, he did receive some good news. The commissary general's office confirmed that eighty thousand rations were waiting on railcars at Farmville.

Still, the road was long. One famished officer recalled, "We stopped for what was supposed to be a midday meal. The midday was there, but the meal was not."[193]

Major William M. Owen of the Washington Artillery of New Orleans sensed what the detour around Jetersville meant for the Army of Northern Virginia. Marching long and hard in inclement weather—with little rest and no food—meant only one thing.

He wrote, "It is now a race for life or death."[194]

CHAPTER 8

THE RELENTLESS FEDERAL HOST

Irrepressible Phil Sheridan refused to be a bystander on April 4. Issuing orders to his cavalry commanders and to Griffin's V Corps to concentrate at Jetersville, he sent an optimistic message to Grant concerning the future of the Army of Northern Virginia. "If we press on we will no doubt get the whole army."[195]

Then Sheridan headed to Jetersville himself. Riding hard, with only his personal escort—the two hundred horsemen of the 1st United States Cavalry—in company, he arrived there late in the afternoon intent on blocking the path of the Army of Northern Virginia.

"I reached Jettersville [*sic*] some little time before the Fifth Corps, and having nothing else at hand I at once deployed this handful of men to cover the crossroads till the arrival of the corps," Sheridan remembered.[196] Some anxious moments passed before the leading elements of the V Corps came up at about 5:00 p.m. When the infantrymen arrived, they set to work, eventually extending the entrenchments to a length of four miles, with cavalry protecting both flanks. A soldier of the 155th Pennsylvania recalled, "The Fifth Corps immediately occupied the cavalry works, and in a short time with pick and shovel had them thick and high."[197]

Although Gen. Phil Sheridan was actually Ulysses S. Grant's second choice to command the Cavalry Corps of the Union Army of the Potomac, Sheridan proved more than equal to the task. During the pursuit of the Army of Northern Virginia, Sheridan skillfully led his cavalry, dogging the enemy relentlessly and positioning his horsemen to block the Confederate route of escape. *Library of Congress*

While Sheridan and his escorting cavalry were dismounting on the best defensive ground they could find, a ridgeline just southwest of Jetersville, a man riding a mule rode into the picket line. He was captured and hauled before the general. During a thorough search, two copies of a telegram signed by Lee's commissary general tumbled out of his boot. These were addressed to supply officers in Danville and Lynchburg, and Sheridan concluded that they were sent via courier because Crook's cavalry had cut the telegraph lines north of Burkeville.

Lee's telegram read, "The army is at Amelia Court House, short of provisions. Send 300,000 rations quickly to Burkeville Junction."[198]

Sheridan's troopers and the Federal infantrymen who were approaching had left their own wagon trains behind. They had grown hungry. Griffin, Humphreys, and Wright were in a bit of a quandary as well. There were no provisions at hand. Nevertheless, the troops were in high spirits.

Grant remembered their enthusiasm years later, writing, "The Army of the Potomac, officers and men, were so elated by the reflection that at last they were following up a victory to its end, that they preferred marching without rations to running a possible risk of letting the enemy elude them."[199]

In the captured Confederate communication, Sheridan saw opportunity. He summoned Young and instructed him to send scouts along the rail lines toward Lynchburg and Danville. As soon as they found telegraph stations, the scouts were to instruct the operators to send the messages to their destinations. When Lee's order was followed, any provisions coming from either depot would be intercepted to feed Sheridan's command instead. The general did not record the outcome of the ruse.

As the afternoon of April 5 wore on, Sheridan waited impatiently for Humphreys and Wright to reach Jetersville with the II and VI Corps infantry. Around 2:00 p.m. a heavily escorted ambulance carrying Meade rolled into Sheridan's camp. Meade had been ill for several days but intended to retain field command. In a letter to his wife, he described his ailment.

"Though late at night, I seize time to send you a few lines," Meade wrote. "I don't know when I last heard or wrote to you, for besides the battles and marches of the last ten days, I have been nearly all the time quite under the weather with a severe bilious catarrh, taking an intermittent form. Thanks to my powerful constitution, and the good care of my attending physician, together with the excitement of the scenes I have passed through, I have managed not to give up, but to be on hand each day."[200]

Finally, an hour after Meade arrived, the leading elements of II Corps appeared, and VI Corps followed. Due to his illness, Meade asked Sheridan to deploy his troops appropriately. As it turned out, Sheridan might secretly have wished that Meade's discomfort had kept him from accompanying the two corps of the Army of the Potomac. Meade planned to attack Lee at Amelia Court House but decided to wait until the morning of April 6 to do it. Meade wanted all of his troops on the field and planned an envelopment of the Confederates from the south and east, which would leave the door open for Lee to withdraw to the west yet again.

Since early on the morning of April 5, Sheridan's entrenched cavalry and V Corps infantry had brushed back probes from Rooney Lee's cavalry. To counter the Rebel horsemen and to gain some knowledge of whether Lee was advancing or fortifying his positions at Amelia Court House, Sheridan ordered Crook to send the cavalry brigade of Brig. Gen. Henry E. Davies on a reconnaissance around Lee's flank to Painesville, a crossroads town about five miles north of Jetersville.

Davies proceeded through the resort town of Amelia Springs and then turned his command north toward Painesville. About four miles from Jetersville, his horsemen from New York, New Jersey, and Pennsylvania found the wagon train that Lee had sent to the northwest and hopefully out of harm's way. The Union cavalrymen fell upon the train. Driving Gary's escorting brigade away, they wreaked havoc, torching 180 wagons and capturing 5 artillery pieces, draft animals, and a large number of prisoners, many of them teamsters who were now out of a job.

Confederate cavalry under Fitzhugh Lee and Thomas Rosser joined with Gary, who rallied his brigade, and set off in pursuit of Davies, chasing the Union raiders in a running three-mile skirmish with saber and pistol. The fight rolled through Amelia Springs and beyond Jetersville. Davies lost twenty killed and eighty-six wounded. He had decimated the wagon train and burned many of Lee's personal papers along with the official diary of the Army of Northern Virginia. He also brought valuable intelligence to Sheridan.

It was clear now to Little Phil that the Confederates were headed west from Amelia Court House and did not intend to stand and fight there. His frustration began to mount as the opportunity to attack in force was being squandered.

"It being plain that Lee would attempt to escape as soon as his trains were out of the way, I was most anxious to attack him when the Second Corps began to arrive," explained Sheridan years later, "for I felt certain that unless we did so he would succeed in passing by our left flank, and would once again make our pursuit a stern-chase; but General Meade, whose plan of attack was to advance his right flank on Amelia Court House, objected to assailing before all his troops were up."[201]

Sheridan could not sit idly by while Lee escaped, but Meade outranked him. Bursting with pent-up frustration, Sheridan breached protocol and scrawled a message directly to Grant, who was to the south with General Ord's Army of the James. On a piece of tissue paper, Sheridan wrote that he wished Grant were present himself to assess the situation and noted, "I feel confident of capturing the Army of Northern Virginia if we exert ourselves."[202]

The final lines of Sheridan's message indicated that he was placing all his cavalry, with the exception of Brig. Gen. Ranald Mackenzie's small division, to the left of his command, in position to move rapidly again to cut the Rebels off. He reiterated that he did not see any avenue of escape for Lee.

One of Young's scouts put on the uniform of a Confederate colonel. He folded the note and wrapped it in tin foil and then covered it with a generous wad of leaf tobacco. With the message in his mouth, he set out to find Grant.

In addition to the message, Sheridan also handed the scout a letter that had just been captured. He wanted Grant to take note of its poignant expression of the condition of the Army of Northern Virginia. It read,

Amelia C.H., April 5, 1865.

Dear Mamma:
Our army is ruined, I fear. We are all safe as yet. Shyron left us sick. John Taylor is well—saw him yesterday. We are in line of battle this morning. General Robert Lee is in the field near us. My trust is still in the justice of our cause, and that of God. General Hill is killed. I saw Murray a few minutes since. Bernard, Terry said, was taken prisoner, but may yet get out. I send this by a negro I see passing up the railroad to Mechlenburg. Love to all.

Your devoted son,
Wm. B. Taylor, Colonel.[203]

After dark, Grant halted at Nottoway Court House, a stop on the South Side Railroad, to confer with a group of officers. The Army of the James had already marched through Ford's Station, White's Station, Blacks and Whites, and then on to Nottoway Court House on its trek toward Burkeville.

A Northern newspaper reporter accompanying the Army of the James described what he found as the Union troops occupied the area where Grant held his war council.

The village of Nottoway Court House as it is usually called, is an old, dilapidated looking concern, composed of a few dozens of old unpainted frame houses, and two or three brick ones.

The courthouse and surrounding offices are substantial brick edifices, and stand in a pleasantly shaded square, about two hundred yards to the left of the main road going westward. Streets or street Nottoway has not . . . A few empty box cars were captured and a few dollars' worth of saddlery trimmings. Nearly all else of value has been removed . . .

In the clerk's office was found a large collection of records, dating back to 1787, embracing court proceedings, a book of wills, election returns, deeds and other legal papers, which would offer interesting material for months of investigation. But the march of an army makes too much history daily for the correspondents to devote much time to that of the past.

Some Union soldiers did ravage the clerk's office, tearing documents to shreds and throwing record books into a nearby horse trough. One soldiers scribbled in a volume, "Johney Reb you can thank me for saving Lawyer Jones books. I save them because I am a sort of a Yankee lawyer myself. Charles Cook, York. Pennsylvania."[204]

After his conference, Grant rode ahead a few miles toward Burkeville Station. About halfway there, at Crewe, a small town then known as Robertson's Switch, the lone Union scout dressed in Confederate uniform approached Grant, took the urgent message from Sheridan out of his mouth, and delivered it to the commanding general.

Immediately, Grant and seventeen others, staff members, couriers, and escort troops, started for Jetersville, riding for two and one-half hours through unfamiliar territory where stragglers and Confederate cavalry lurked. A sliver of moonlight helped guide the group through the darkness, and Grant reached Sheridan's pickets around 10:30 p.m. After convincing the nervous guards that he was indeed the commander of the Federal armies en route to a conference with high-ranking generals, he rode into Sheridan's camp at midnight.

Once Grant's identity was established, the fact that he was so close to the enemy lines became quite noteworthy. Whispers of his presence rippled through the ranks of the Federal soldiers, and one remarked, "Why, there's the old man. Boys this means business."[205]

From Sheridan's headquarters, Grant sent instructions to Ord to march to Burkeville, bivouac there for the night, and then proceed west to cut the roads leading to Farmville. Grant ate a quick meal and sat down to discuss the situation with Sheridan.

Little could be done until daylight, but Sheridan presented a compelling argument for his conclusions about Lee's plans. Within a few minutes, Grant and Sheridan went to see Meade. Grant repeated his desire to cut off the Confederate route of retreat and expressed his displeasure with Meade's intended course of action.

"I explained to Meade that we did not want to follow the enemy; we wanted to get ahead of him, and that his orders would allow the enemy to escape, and besides that, I had no doubt that Lee was moving right then," Grant affirmed. "Meade changed his orders at once. They were now given for an advance on Amelia Court House [direct assault rather than envelopment], at an early hour in the morning, as the army then lay; that is, the infantry being across the railroad, most of it to the west of the road, with the cavalry swung out still farther to the left."[206]

Meade asked for and received the return of the V Corps to the Army of the Potomac from Sheridan's Army of the Shenandoah. "I made no objections," Sheridan remembered, "and it was ordered to report to him."[207]

After meeting with Confederate envoys Campbell and Myers, Abraham Lincoln, fatigued by his whirlwind tour of beleaguered Richmond, returned to City Point aboard the *Malvern*. Along the way, he strolled the deck of the steamer and noticed a nearby barge carrying a full load of Rebel prisoners. The captives recognized the president and offered three hearty cheers, and he acknowledged their apparent goodwill.

Upon his arrival, Lincoln received several visitors and shuffled through papers that had accumulated during his excursion. Stanton sent notification that Secretary of State William Seward had suffered serious injuries in a carriage accident. The president briefly considered returning to Washington, particularly since Seward had previously asked about tending to several matters of state and offered to bring documents to the president at City Point. Later communication from Stanton indicated that Seward's injuries, though severe, were not life threatening.

Another telegram may have conjured up mixed emotions. Mrs. Lincoln, apparently recovered from her extended bout of paranoia and childish behavior, was coming back to City Point. At 11:00 that morning, she boarded the steamer *Monohasset* with an entourage that included the Marquis de Chambrun, a French aristocrat; antislavery Radical Republican Senator Charles Sumner of Massachusetts; Republican senator James Harlan of Illinois, soon to take office as secretary of the interior; and former Kentucky legislator and US Attorney General James Speed. The party arrived the following day.

On the evening of April 5, General Collis, the commander of the Pennsylvania Zouaves who had fought so bravely at Fort Mahone and now the commandant at City Point, sat with the president in the tent of Lt. Col. Theodore Bowers, Grant's adjutant general, who had stayed behind to monitor communications when the senior commander moved out.

Collis had met General Barringer, recently taken prisoner at Namozine Church, and along with his wife, Septima, had entertained the general and other high-ranking Confederate officers at dinner. Collis found Barringer "a polished, scholarly, and urbane gentleman, scrupulously regarding the parole I had exacted from him, and deeply sensitive and appreciative of my poor efforts to make him comfortable."[208]

Barringer heard that the president was at City Point and "begged" Collis to arrange a meeting. Later, while chatting with the president in Bowers's tent, Collis casually mentioned the incident. He recalled the president's reaction. "Mr. Lincoln immediately asked me to present his compliments to the general, and to say he would like very much to see him, whispering to me in his quaint and jocose way: 'Do you know I have never seen a live rebel general in full uniform.'"[209]

Collis dutifully arranged the meeting, convincing Barringer that he was not overstepping the bounds of protocol and helping the prisoner to clean up a bit. He wrote:

We walked over to headquarters, where we found the President in high feather, listening to the cheerful messages from Grant at the front. I formally presented General Barringer, of North Carolina, to the President of the United States, and Mr. Lincoln extended his hand, warmly welcomed him, and bade him be seated. There was, however, only one chair vacant when the President arose, and this the Southerner very politely declined to take. This left the two men facing each other in the centre of the tent, the tall form of Mr. Lincoln almost reaching the ridge pole. He slowly removed his eyeglasses, looked the General over from head to foot, and then in a slow, meditative, and puzzled manner inquired: "Barringer? Barringer? from North Carolina? Barringer of North Carolina? General, were you ever in Congress?"[210]

The general explained that the former congressman was his brother Daniel, and Lincoln beamed. Collis observed, "'Well! well!' said he; 'do you know that that brother of yours was my chum in Congress. Yes, sir, we sat at the same desk and ate at the same table. He was a Whig and so was I. He was my chum, and I was very fond of him. And you are his brother, eh? Well! well! shake again.'"[211]

After a lengthy and pleasant conversation, General Barringer feared that he had overstayed his welcome and rose to leave. Collis remembered, "Mr. Lincoln once more took him by the hand almost affectionately, placed another hand upon his shoulder, and inquired quite seriously: 'Do you think I can be of any service to you?'

"Not until we had all finished a hearty laugh at this quaint remark did the President realize the innocent simplicity of his inquiry, and when General Barringer was able to reply that 'If anybody can be of service to a poor devil in my situation, I presume you are the man,' Mr. Lincoln drew a blank card from his vest pocket, adjusted his glasses, turned up the wick of the lamp, and sat down at General Bowers' desk."[212]

Lincoln wrote a short note to Stanton. It read,

This is General Barringer, of the Southern army. He is the brother of a very dear friend of mine. Can you do any thing to make his detention in Washington as comfortable as possible under the circumstances? A. LINCOLN.

A significant section of the business district of Richmond was looted
and burned during the chaos of April 2, 1865, as government officials,
military personnel, and ordinary citizens fled the Confederate capital
city. This photograph by Andrew J. Russell shows Union soldiers amid
the ruins of the devastated area. When the first Union troops entered
Richmond, many of them were put to work fighting the fires and restoring order. *Library of Congress*

Collis concluded, "A few years afterwards I met the General socially in Philadelphia, and we went over this episode in his life, as I have narrated it, and then, for the third time, his eyes filled as he told me how he had wept and wept at 'the deep damnation of his taking off.'"[213]

By the time of his capture, Barringer, a former member of the North Carolina House of Delegates, was fortunate to have survived his wartime experiences. He was said to have fought in seventy-six engagements and was wounded three times, the most serious at the Battle of Brandy Station when a bullet entered his right cheek and exited his mouth, requiring five months of convalescence.

General Barringer was confined at Fort Delaware on Pea Patch Island in the Delaware River and held until August 1865, much longer than most Confederate prisoners. It seems that his meeting with Lincoln and the existence of the note became well known. After the president's assassination just days later, both brought suspicion and extensive questioning during the hunt for conspirators.

When he was released, Barringer returned to North Carolina, practiced law in Charlotte, and was instrumental in the repair and growth of the state's railroad system. He ran unsuccessfully for governor in 1880, retired four years later, and died in 1895.

The train bound for the temporary haven of Danville, close to the North Carolina line near rail and water transportation and symbolically still in the state of Virginia, clickety-clacked out of chaotic Richmond sometime after 11:00 p.m. on April 2. The gas lights along the city streets faded from view, and for a while longer the passengers could see the eerie flicker of fires already beginning to burn.

Jefferson Davis stared out a window as the train rolled into Clover Station, not quite three-quarters of the way to Danville and several hours behind schedule. There was no sleep. A small crowd gathered and gave a cheer, and the exhausted leader of a government on rails acknowledged the goodwill. Soon, the train was underway again, crossing the appropriately named Difficult Creek. The railroad was in disrepair, and the locomotive could hardly manage twenty miles per hour. The rail line itself was in poor condition, and there were numerous delays. One horrific incident that stalled the presidential train occurred about thirty miles from its destination when the floor of a dilapidated boxcar on a train some distance ahead fell through, spilling several soldiers under the rolling wheels.[214]

Lieutenant John Sergeant Wise, the s.
Wise, who had temporarily commanded the c.
and was leading a brigade in Gordon's II Corps.
bearing Davis and the fugitive departments tha.
rolled through Clover Station. "It was a marvelous
debris of the wreck of the Confederate capital," h.
"There were very few women on these trains, but am
the long procession were trains bearing indiscriminat.
men and things. In one car was a cage with an African p.
box of tame squirrels, and a hunchback!"[215]

The 140 mile journey from Richmond to Danville, u
four-hour trip, was accomplished in sixteen. A crowd ga
when the train pulled into the station at Danville around 3:00
on April 3, and the dignitaries were shown to quarters in hon.
boarding houses, and other buildings. Clerks tried to establi.
some order and routine, restoring the semblance of a functioning
government as they could.

Davis inspected the earthworks intended to protect Danville
against a possible Union attack and ordered improvements.
He knew nothing of Lee's immediate situation or the necessary
changes in the Army of Northern Virginia's route of march.
The following morning, he called a meeting of his cabinet and
told the ministers that he would compose a statement informing the population of the current military and political situation.
Davis wrote:

To the People of the Confederate States of America,

The General-in-Chief found it necessary to make such movements as to uncover the capital. It would be unwise to conceal
the moral and material injury to our cause resulting from its
occupation by the enemy. It is equally unwise and unworthy of us
to allow our energies to falter and our efforts to become relaxed
under reverses, however calamitous they may be . . . We have
now entered upon a new phase of the struggle. Relieved from the
necessity of guarding particular points, our army will be free to
move from point to point to strike the enemy far from his base.
Let us but will it, and we are free . . . Let us, then, not despond,
my countrymen, but, relying on God, meet the foe with fresh defiance and with unconquered and unconquerable hearts.[216]

The proclamation, delusional though it may have been, was printed in the April 5 edition of the *Danville Register* and distributed across the telegraphic network as it existed, interrupted by the advancing Federal armies at several locations.

John Wise remained on duty at Clover Station. He observed that the little whistle stop was now the "Northern outpost of the Confederacy," and was caught up in the general anxiety since no word had been received concerning the Army of Northern Virginia. "All day Tuesday, and until midday Wednesday, we waited," he later wrote, "expecting to hear of the arrival of our army at Burkeville, or some tidings of its whereabouts. But the railroad stretching northward was as silent as the grave."[217]

On the morning of the fourth, a telegram related that the battered Army of Northern Virginia had reached Amelia Court House. By the next day, the telegraph office there had gone silent. A communication from Burkeville noted that the wires were cut at Jetersville.

Davis remained in the dark throughout April 5, and his frustration was steadily growing. He wrote to Varina in Charlotte, "I have sought in vain to get into communication with Genl. Lee. I do not wish to leave Virginia, but cannot decide on my movements until those of the army are developed."[218]

Davis sent numerous messages to Clover Station requesting information on the whereabouts of the Army of Northern Virginia and then asking for a reliable man willing to risk his life in boarding a locomotive toward Burkeville and gathering what information he could on the military situation. Eighteen-year-old John Wise volunteered. He was told that the Federals might already be in Burkeville. The reason—several suspicious telegrams had come through requesting that provisions be sent there. These messages were likely sent by Sheridan's scouts attempting to divert rations for their own use.

Wise was instructed to proceed with caution and, if the enemy was indeed at Burkeville, to retreat to Meherrin Station, send the engine back to Danville, and take a horse to the west to locate Lee's army. With foresight, Davis had provided a signed order for a courier at Clover Station, leaving the name of the individual blank. Wise's name was penciled in, and he was off, carrying only a Colt navy revolver, a few rounds in his haversack, and the signed order buttoned inside his overcoat.

The train rolled off into the chilly, overcast night with a single baggage car behind. Wise rode in the baggage car and tried to sleep, but he remembered the train, chugging on worn track, as the noisiest he had ever heard. He watched deserted stations fall away and at a water stop joined the engineer in the locomotive, ordering the baggage car cut loose on a siding. Stopping at Meherrin Station, twelve miles from Burkeville, he found the building empty.

Wise knocked loudly on the door of a nearby house, rousing the owner and asking if he had seen Lee's army. The reply was negative. He asked, "Where is Grant's army?" This time, the bleary-eyed man responded, "Gord knows. It 'pears to me like it's everywhar."[219]

Moving on, the train passed the deserted station at Green Bay, eight miles from Burkeville. A few minutes later, Wise caught the glow of fires in the distance. He had no idea who was ahead and thought about stopping the train and going forward on foot to investigate. Discounting that idea since it would take too much time, he instructed the engineer to move ahead at normal speed and to be prepared for a rapid reversal if these men were the enemy.

"Ain't you afraid they are Yankees? If they are, we're goners," blurted the engineer. Wise was insistent, and in a moment the train was nearly on top of Federal troops that appeared to be destroying track but were actually changing the gauge to accommodate Union supply and troop trains. "The enemy was not only in Burkeville, but he had been there all day, and was thus following up his occupation of the place," Wise wrote.[220]

The approach of the engine startled the Union soldiers, who dropped their picks and axes and reached for their rifles. Wise yelled to the engineer, "'Reverse the engine!' He seemed paralyzed. I drew my pistol. 'It's no use, lieutenant. They'll kill us before we get under away,' and he fumbled with his lever. 'Reverse, or you're a dead man!' I shouted, clapping the muzzle of my pistol behind his ear. He heaved at the lever; the engine began to move, but how slowly!"[221]

A shot shattered the window above Wise's head, and he remembered the narrow escape with a bit of humor. "When we were well out of harm's way, the engineer, with whom I had been on very friendly terms till this last episode, turned to me and asked, with a grieved look, 'Lieutenant, would you have blowed my brains out sure 'nuff, if I hadn't done what you tole me?' 'I would that,' I replied not much disposed to talk; for I was thinking, and thinking hard, what next to do. 'Well,' said he, with a sigh, as with a greasy rag he gave a fresh rub to a piece of machinery, 'all I've got to say is I don't want to travel with you no mo'.'"[222]

A short while later, Wise granted the engineer's wish, stepping off the train as it retraced the line to Meherrin Station and scribbling a note for the commander at Clover Station that he was going west to look for Lee in the vicinity of High Bridge. Wise walked off into the darkness and covered about four miles by daylight. Providence, he believed, smiled on him at that point. A fresh mare, saddled and ready, was tied in front of a small house. After a knock, Wise was invited in for breakfast. The owner of the house was too old for military service, but the horse's owner turned out to be a cavalryman, Sergeant Wilkins of the Black Walnut Troop from Halifax County. Wilkins had been on furlough to replace his broken-down horse with a fresh mount and was on his way back to his unit.

Wise explained the situation over his first decent meal in quite a while, and Wilkins laughed loudly. He then flatly refused to give up his horse. Wise produced the order signed by President Davis, convinced Wilkins that it was genuine, and finally persuaded the cavalryman to give up the horse for the good of his country.

Riding swiftly away, Wise dodged two columns of Federal cavalry, probably the vanguard of Sheridan's horsemen riding close on Lee's flank. Wise praised the spirit and the speed of his little mare. Then, as his pace slowed momentarily, a man stepped up from behind, just ten feet away, and leveled a cavalry carbine.

Thinking the jig was up, when Wise was asked to identify himself, he told the truth. Believing his captor was one of Sheridan's Jessie Scouts, Wise was relieved when the man led him into the woods, mounted his own horse, and identified himself as Curtis, one of Rooney Lee's scouts. Curtis rode ahead to a crossing of Flat Creek and motioned for Wise to follow. Just then, a Federal cavalry column thundered toward him as the mare struggled through the water. Confederate pickets provided covering fire, and another narrow escape was accomplished.

Curtis advised Wise to head toward Farmville and then ride eastward, where he should find Lee. Soaked, the young courier moved on, the mare shaking off as much water as she could while the rider shivered.[223]

During the extended march on the evening of April 5, Lee rode with Longstreet, whose I Corps took the lead with the remnants of A. P. Hill's old command under Henry Heth, followed by the corps wagons. Next came Anderson's corps and Pickett's division, a shadow of its former self after near annihilation at Five Forks. Ewell and his corps of veteran infantry regiments, sailors who were now soldiers, and garrison troops from Richmond were ahead of a second wagon train, and Gordon's II Corps brought up the rear.

Lee's starving army stumbled through the sunset and into darkness and driving rain. Men and animals passed the point of endurance, falling out of the ranks or dropping into the mud where they were. Blankets, haversacks, rifles, and other equipment littered the roadside in the wake of the Rebel retreat, their owners too weak to carry them. Stragglers offered little or no resistance to Union cavalrymen attempting to round them up.

One North Carolina soldier wandered away alone, looking for food. He was spotted by a group of Union soldiers. They approached him cautiously and yelled, "Surrender! Surrender! We've got you!" As they closed in, he responded, "Yes, you've got me, and a hell of a git you got."[224]

PART V

FAMISHED, FATIGUED, AND FIGHTING

CHAPTER 9

DEBACLE AT SAILOR'S CREEK

Crowded, muddy roads, tormenting hunger, and a multitude of Federals on the flank and in the rear of the Army of Northern Virginia threatened the undoing of Robert E. Lee's effort to reach Danville and subsequently unite with Joseph E. Johnston's Army of Tennessee.

The desperate Confederate march through Rice's Station to Farmville had to be accomplished in a hurry, and time was only one thing of which Lee had precious little. He knew that the Federal infantry would follow in the early morning of April 6 and that the slashing enemy cavalry would be in full vigor, striking at targets of opportunity and rushing to cut off his long, pitiful column strung out across miles of the Virginia countryside.

At 4:00 a.m., the bivouacs of the three powerful corps of the Army of the Potomac began to stir. The soldiers brewed coffee, ate rations by the light of their fires, and then formed in ranks. At daylight Meade ordered his infantry forward to Amelia Court House.

Sheridan wrote scornfully, "He found, as predicted, that Lee was gone . . . Satisfied that this would be the case, I did not permit the cavalry to participate in Meade's useless advance, but shifted it out toward the left to the road running from Deatonville to Rice's station."[225]

Soon, Crook's horsemen spotted Confederate wagons on the road. They were strongly guarded, and Sheridan chose not to attack them directly. He divided his cavalry, moving the majority to the left in a cross-country route parallel with the Rebel line of march.

Meade's columns had covered about four miles toward Amelia Court House when he received a report that large numbers of enemy troops were seen marching to the west. Union pickets had spotted the tail end of Gordon's corps heading past Amelia Springs. Finally convinced that Lee was on the move, Meade reoriented his command to pursue along the same route. The maneuver was time consuming, but by 8:30 a.m. troops of Maj. Gen. Gershom Mott's division of Humphreys's II Corps were skirmishing with Gordon's rear guard.

"It was about nine o'clock in the morning when our division caught up with the rearguard of the enemy near Salt Sulphur Spring [Amelia Springs]," wrote Brig. Gen. Régis de Trobriand, one of Mott's brigade commanders. "General Mott communicated his instructions to me while my regiments were rapidly advancing. Ten minutes after, we were engaged with the enemy. The Twentieth Indiana, deployed as skirmishers and supported by the One Hundred and Twenty-fourth New York, had rapidly ascended a hill, and begun to drive the Rebels, who fell back along the Deatonsville [sic] road.

"We advanced firing, with a rapid step," continued de Trobriand. "Mott ventured forward to assess the progress of the assault, urging the men to push toward some nearby Confederate wagons. He had hardly stepped back four paces, when the sound of a ball striking leather made me turn my head. I remarked a hurried movement among the staff officers. Several leaped from their horses, and, in the midst of a group, I saw the general stretched on the ground. A ball had gone through his leg, passing between the two bones below the knee."[226]

De Trobriand, a French aristocrat who had emigrated to the United States in 1841 and become popular among the social elite of New York City, assumed command of Mott's division. With additional infantry committed, the Union troops continued to drive the Rebels back until artillery fire brought their advance to a halt. Union guns were unlimbered and began to reply. Humphreys came forward amid steady Rebel rifle fire, and de Trobriand remembered that he paid it no attention. The two officers conferred, and then ordered a renewal of the advance.

"In a few minutes, six regiments are ready to charge: the Seventy-third and Eighty-sixth New York, the One Hundred and Fifth and the One Hundred and Tenth Pennsylvania, the First and the Seventeenth Maine," wrote de Trobriand. "At the command all dash forward at once. The strife is to see who will pass ahead of the others and first plant the colors on the enemy's intrenchments [*sic*]. No one remains behind. The wounded fall; they will be picked up afterward. The first thing was to strike the enemy. It was a beautiful sight. The six flags advanced in line as though carried by six human waves."[227]

The charging Union soldiers emptied their cartridge boxes, scooped up about three hundred prisoners, and maintained the chase. There was no respite for the Rebel rear guard. The fighting continued into the afternoon, and a soldier of the 17th Maine remembered, "After firing a few moments, the Rebels were discovered to be giving way on our left. Major Mattocks, with the colors, and with as many of the regiment as could keep up, charged with a yell, rushed over the breastworks, and captured about one hundred men, ten or twelve officers, and one battle flag, the regimental color of the Twenty-first North Carolina, besides killing and wounding a large number of the enemy."[228]

Periodic skirmishes took place throughout the day as the Confederate column began passing through the crossroads of Holt's Corner. However, the hard-riding Union cavalry brigade of Brig. Gen. Charles Smith attacked Anderson's corps at Holt's Corner about five miles from Rice's Station, forcing it to halt, deploy, and deliver concentrated volleys to fend off the enemy horsemen. Anderson then resumed his march, advancing slightly more than a mile past the Hillsman farm, across Little Sailor's Creek, and on to Marshall's Crossroads.

Lee and Longstreet reached Rice's Station on the South Side Railroad at midday and waited. As Longstreet continued his march toward Rice's Station and Anderson stopped to take on Smith's cavalry, a precipitous gap opened between the two commands. Seizing the opportunity, more Union cavalry commanded by George Custer dashed through the gap to block Anderson's advance beyond Marshall's Crossroads. In short order, three divisions of Sheridan's cavalry, eight thousand troopers, were squarely across Anderson's path, outnumbering his two divisions under Pickett and Bushrod Johnson that totaled about six thousand men.

As Ewell came up to Holt's Corner, he noticed that Anderson's progress had slowed to a crawl and heard the sound of rifle fire to his rear. He understood that Gordon was being harassed by Humphreys's II Corps and sent the army's main wagon train up the Jamestown Road toward Lockett's farm in a long movement around the Union encroachments. Sailor's Creek, a tributary of the Appomattox River, flowed northward from the confluence of two smaller streams, Big Sailor's Creek and Little Sailor's Creek. Where these streams came together, the wagons might cross Sailor's Creek and turn back toward Rice's Station. Although he did not receive orders to do so, Gordon followed the wagons as he had been doing throughout the day.

Inadvertently, the Army of Northern Virginia became divided into three distinct segments. None of these were in position to support the others. Ewell and Anderson began to realize that their commands were in imminent danger.

Humphreys remained hot on Gordon's heels and continued his pursuit, veering up the Jamestown Road. "On and on, hour after hour, from hilltop to hilltop, the lines were alternately forming, fighting, and retreating, making one almost continuous shifting battle," remembered Gordon. "The roads and fields and woods swarmed with eager pursuers."[229] Close behind, Wright's VI Corps followed Ewell toward the Hillsman farm.

Sheridan later recorded that the day's work eventually included several hundred wagons destroyed along the road to Rice's Station and sixteen artillery pieces captured. He also asserted that it was pressure from Col. Peter Stagg's brigade of Michigan cavalry and accompanying artillery that compelled Gordon to detour from the Rice's Station road at Holt's Corner.

Sheridan saw a decisive battle looming as the afternoon shadows lengthened. "The complete isolation of Ewell [and Anderson] from Longstreet in his front and Gordon in his rear led to the battle of Sailor's Creek, one of the severest conflicts of the war," he recalled, "for the enemy fought with desperation to escape capture, and we, bent on his destruction, were no less eager and determined."[230]

Although it was already late in the afternoon, there was still time for this momentous Thursday to become one of the blackest days in the history of the Confederacy. The Battle of Sailor's Creek (referred to as "Sayler's" in some texts) is actually a collective term for three separate engagements that had catastrophic results for the Army of Northern Virginia.

As the blocking Union cavalry at Marshall's Crossroads confronted Anderson, Ewell crossed to the west side of Little Sailor's Creek and deployed 5,200 troops, the divisions of Maj. Gen. Custis Lee and Maj. Gen. Joseph Kershaw on the flanks with a contingent of sailors and marines turned soldiers under Cdre. John Randolph Tucker in the center, along a ridgeline southwest of Anderson's corps. Custis Lee's command was a hodgepodge of garrison troops, clerks, and heavy artillerymen whose guns had been abandoned in Richmond.

Ewell detailed a small contingent of Mississippi infantrymen to delay the vanguard of the VI Corps. Facing northeast, the rest of his soldiers hastily threw up earthworks and watched the Federal tide sweep northward from Pride's Church toward the heroic Mississippians.

Sheridan watched as his cavalry kept Ewell busy along the ridge while the VI Corps infantry arrived in force. One of the general's staff officers saw Stagg's cavalry brigade go into action. "Stagg's men moved out gallantly for a mounted charge," remembered Lt. Col. Frederic C. Newhall, "and, as seen from the knoll where General Sheridan was, there never was a prettier panorama of war in miniature than when this brave brigade trotted across the valley and began to go up the slope on which the enemy's infantry was now entrenched. A heavy fire met them, but they pressed on boldly, as if they had an army at their back, and the piff! paff! Of their carbines echoed the sputtering fire from the enemy's hillside."[231]

As the battle around the Hillsman farm took shape, the family of the owner, Confederate Capt. James M. Hillsman of Lee's sharpshooters, sought shelter. The captain, however, had been captured at Spotsylvania Court House in May 1864, and was sitting in a northern prison.

To Ewell's dismay, he could also see five batteries of Union artillery, twenty guns under the command of VI Corps artillery chief Maj. Andrew Cowan, unlimbering astride the Rice's Station Road near the Hillsman house. Soon shot and shell began falling on the Confederate positions. For a moment, the projectiles flew harmlessly overhead and exploded well beyond the entrenchments. However, when the Union gunners found the range, the Rebels clawed into the ground and endured the bombardment. Ewell had not artillery on hand to reply, and for nearly half an hour the Federal guns blasted the ridge from a distance of only eight hundred yards.

Two Union divisions, about seven thousand soldiers commanded by Brig. Gen. Frank Wheaton and Brig. Gen. Truman Seymour, deployed left to right on the east side of Little Sailor's Creek near the Hillsman house and began their advance down into the shallow valley before them. Swollen by the recent rains, the creek was difficult to ford. Some men waded through waist-high water. Others stepped into mud so thick that they needed help from comrades to extricate themselves. They clambered up the other side of the creek bank and saw Ewell's thin line.

The Union soldiers were ordered not to fire until they were within two hundred yards of the Confederate positions, and many of them were convinced that the enemy in front of them could not withstand the pending onslaught. With that, some men of Brig. Gen. Oliver Edwards's brigade of Wheaton's division began to wave white handkerchiefs at the Rebels, asking them to lay down their arms to avoid unnecessary loss of life. During the march, the center of the Union line moved across open ground, driving back the Rebel skirmishers, while the flanks were delayed in thick underbrush.

The response to the surrender invitation was swift, and the center of the Union advance, including the 2nd Rhode Island and 49th Pennsylvania regiments, absorbed the brunt of two volleys fired from the top of the ridge. Among the Confederates delivering the devastating fire were former heavy artillerymen under the command of Maj. Robert Stiles. He remembered that the front rank of blue-clad riflemen simply folded to the ground.

Colonel Elisha Hunt Rhodes of the 2nd Rhode Island received orders from General Edwards to advance. His diary entry for the day after the battle reads, "As I rode back to the regiment Captain Charles W. Gleason stepped up and said: 'Colonel, are we to fight again?' I answered: 'Yes,' 'Well,' said he, 'This will be the last battle if we win, and then you and I can go home. God bless you colonel.' I replied: 'God bless you, captain. I hope to meet you after the battle.' Poor Gleason, he was shot through the head a few minutes after and killed. He was a gallant fellow, and I thought the world of him."[232]

The 2nd Rhode Island began taking fire as soon as it was exposed, and the men struggled across Little Sailor's Creek. "The Rebels opened upon us soon as we reached the river, but we jumped in with the water up to our waists and soon reached the opposite side," Colonel Rhodes recorded in his diary. "Here we formed and advanced up a slight hill towards a piece of wood, the

Rebels retreating from our front. When within about fifty yards of the woods a Rebel officer stepped out and shouted: 'Rise up, fire!' A long line of Rebels fired right into our faces and then charged through our line and then getting between us and the river."[233]

The center of the Union line staggered and then reeled backward. Georgians of Stiles's command and the 18th Georgia Brigade, under Maj. William S. Basinger, leaped from their earthworks and grappled hand to hand with the Federal soldiers that did not immediately retire. Bayonets flashed and fists flew as the Rebels tumbled down the hill and toward the creek bank in pursuit of the enemy. Cowan's artillery barked, spewing canister at the charging Confederates and finally forcing them back to the ridge.

As Wheaton's advanced regiments wavered, Seymour's division, covering a somewhat greater distance, crossed the creek and formed in line of battle. The two divisions then advanced together as the men of the 37th Massachusetts of Edwards's brigade worked their Spencer repeating rifles and put up a sheet of smoke, flame, and lead. Major Stiles rallied his former artillerymen and became the sixth soldier to hoist his battalion colors.

Stiles's immediate superior, Col. Stapleton Crutchfield, rode away to find Custis Lee and receive new orders. He was killed by a single bullet through the head. Only twenty-nine years old, Crutchfield had lost a leg while serving as Stonewall Jackson's artillery commander at the Battle of Chancellorsville in May 1863. At first, it appeared that the war was over for him. However, during the darkest days of the Confederacy he was one of many disabled soldiers who answered a second call to duty.

The firepower of the two advancing Federal divisions began to have a telling effect on Ewell's men, some of whom had never previously been in action. The length of the Federal line overlapped both of Ewell's flanks, and the commander realized that the outcome of the desperate struggle was inevitable. The Confederates were soon pressed on three sides, and their tenuous flanks folded.

One Rebel officer recalled, "The battle degenerated into a butchery . . . of brutal personal conflicts. I saw . . . men kill each other with bayonets and the butts of muskets, and even bite each others throats and ears and noses, rolling on the ground like wild beasts."[234]

During the vicious struggle, Colonel Edwards witnessed the extraordinary exploits of Pvt. Samuel Eddy of the 37th Massachusetts. According to Edwards, a Confederate colonel in the act of surrendering changed his mind and attacked adjutant John Bradley, the Union officer to whom he was giving up moments before. Bradley was shot twice, first through the shoulder, and then in the thigh as the two men struggled on the ground.

Edwards wrote, "Samuel E. Eddy, private Co. D shot the rebel Colonel as he was about to shoot Bradley through the head with his pistol. A rebel who saw the man who killed his Colonel—put his bayonet through private Eddy's body, the bayonet passing through the lung and coming out near his spine. Eddy dropped his gun, and tore the bayonet out from his body, then in a hand to hand struggle with his foe temporarily disabled him and crawled to his gun, and with it killed his antagonist."[235]

William Shaw, another member of the 37th Massachusetts, saw Eddy sitting on the ground after the fighting ended. Shaw remembered, "I says to him, 'Are you wounded?' He said, 'They have run a bayonet through me.' I looked and saw where it entered his body and came out on his back. He said it did not hurt so very much when it went through, but the man twisted it when withdrawing it but the man never bayoneted another soldier, for Mr. Eddy was so indignant that he shot him then and there."[236]

Eddy was carried to a field hospital at the Hillsman farm and then transferred to another facility at Burkeville. Several days later, he was taken by rail to the Depot Field Hospital at City Point. He recovered and was mustered out of the army on June 9, 1865. Thirty-two years later, on September 10, 1897, he received the Medal of Honor for his actions at Sailor's Creek. Eddy died in Chesterfield, Massachusetts, at the age of eighty-six on March 7, 1909.

The sheer number of Union attackers overwhelmed Ewell's Rebels, and they began to hold their rifle butts in the air as a sign of surrender. Approximately 3,400 prisoners were taken, including 6 Confederate generals—Ewell, who surrendered to a sergeant of the 5th Wisconsin Regiment near the home of farmer Swep Marshall, Custis Lee, Joseph Kershaw, Dudley Du Bose, Seth Barton, and James Simms. Strewn across the field were 150 dead Rebels, while 84 Union soldiers were killed and 358 wounded.

The capture of Custis Lee, the eldest son of Robert E. Lee, generated some controversy that has persisted for a century and a half. According to official records, Cpl. Harris S. Hawthorn of the 121st New York Regiment submitted a sworn statement that he took Custis Lee into custody. That statement was submitted with an application for the Medal of Honor, which was subsequently presented to Hawthorn in December 1894. However, Frank E. White, the great-great grandson of Pvt. David D. White of the 37th Massachusetts, asserts that it was actually his ancestor who captured Custis Lee.

Frank White has extensively researched the events surrounding the celebrated capture and written a book supporting his claim. David White did not, by the way, apply for the Medal of Honor. In 1897, supporters of White disputed the awarding of the medal to Hawthorn and applied for White to receive it. They failed in both efforts. Hawthorn has his advocates as well. In the summer of 2011 the US Army agreed to review the circumstances surrounding the capture of Custis Lee, and the outcome is pending.

While Ewell's command fought desperately to no avail, Anderson faced the three cavalry divisions of Custer, Devin, and Crook, operating under the direction of Maj. Gen. Wesley Merritt and blocking the road to Rice's Station. Throughout the day, the Union cavalry had harassed Anderson, but each charge had been successfully thrown back. He had advanced about three-quarters of a mile from Holt's Corner to Marshall's Crossroads when he discovered the Union cavalry to his front.

Anderson placed Pickett's division on his left and Johnson's on his right. Facing due south, his men had their backs to Ewell's troops, fighting for their lives against the VI Corps.

As Anderson's artillery began to fire on the massing Union horsemen blocking the road, Sheridan directed Merritt to organize the heaviest cavalry assault of the day. Merritt and his staff officers heard the cannon and rifle fire to northeast and knew that Wright had gone into action against Ewell. Within minutes, Union horsemen were thundering forward.

Crook's column trotted off into heavy woods while Custer's men galloped forward. The two divisions came abreast of one another as Crook burst from the cover of the forest and appeared on Custer's left. Major Henry Tremain watched the awe-inspiring sight as Custer's horsemen gained momentum. "Away now to the charge dashed Custer's troopers," he recalled. "Squadrons of 'red cravats' bore down upon the ensconced foe. But the victory was not thus easy."[237]

Tremain continued:

Waiting until the horsemen were almost near enough to leap over the slight breastworks, the quiet line of dingy grays suddenly sprang into life, planted their rebel flags almost within the reach of the bold troopers, and with their peculiar faint cheer delivered into our ranks a most destructive volley. Saddles were emptied; horses plunged in the struggles of death, and amid din and dust, conflict and confusion, vim and valor, the charge was over. The rebels remained in their old lines, and when the smoke and dust cleared from the field Custer was reforming his lines and preparing to renew the strife.[238]

Devin moved in to reinforce Custer, who renewed his attack on Pickett's Virginia brigades commanded by Brig. Gen. Montgomery Corse, Brig. Gen. Eppa Hunton, and Col. Joseph Mayo. Finally, the Confederates gave way.

Custer with his gay red and white headquarters pennant, and surrounded by a small staff, and orderlies bearing captured rebel colors, was on the right directing the movements of his two brigades under Wells and Pennington. . . . The spring flowers smiling coyishly through the grass were literally trodden under the iron hoof of war. . . . So began the charge. No wonder that when the hostile lines approached, the very sight shook the rebel center. One, two, then three, then little groups of men in gray were seen hurrying back from the light breastwork. This was enough. . . . All was dust and confusion; horses and men fell dead across the rebel works. . . . The rebel line was gone, and squads, companies, and regiments were flying over the hills.[239]

During the brisk charge that broke the Confederate front, Capt. Thomas Custer displayed exceptional courage for the second time in a week. As the Union cavalry surged forward, he spurred his horse through a hail of rifle fire and then up and over the earthworks. In an instant, he was surrounded by Rebel soldiers but fired to both right and left, forcing the enemy soldiers back. When he noticed a rallying point where the Rebel battle flag was waving, he charged ahead.

Colonel Charles E. Capehart, a brigade commander, watched in amazement. He wrote of the younger Custer's exploits in a letter to General George Custer's wife, Libbie.

"I saw your brother capture his second flag," Capehart noted. "It was a charge made by my brigade at Sailor's Creek, Virginia, against General Ewell's corps. Having crossed the line of temporary works in the flank road, we were confronted by a supporting line. It was from the second line that he wrested the colors, single-handed, and only a few paces to my right. As he approached the colors he received a shot in the face which knocked him back on his horse, but in a moment he was upright in his saddle. Reaching out his right arm, he grasped the flag while the color bearer reeled. The bullet from Tom's revolver must have pierced his heart. As he was falling Captain Custer wrenched the standard from his grasp and bore it away in triumph."[240]

Custer bled profusely, but the wound was not life threatening. Thomas rode to his brother and offered the enemy flag with words to the effect that the damned Rebels had shot him but he had his trophy. He reportedly refused to seek medical attention, ignoring General Custer's order. When Thomas turned to rejoin the fight, he was placed under arrest and sent to the rear with an escort. He received a second Medal of Honor for the Sailor's Creek action.

Colonel J. Irvin Gregg's brigade of Pennsylvania cavalry thundered toward the extreme right of the Confederate line, where Brig. Gen. Matthew Ransom's North Carolina brigade waited with fixed bayonets. Bowling into the Rebels, the Pennsylvanians swept around and through Ransom's position, outflanking the line and causing it to crumble. Confederate wagons were looted and burned, and two more Rebel generals, Hunton and Corse, were taken prisoner. The Union cavalry divisions suffered only 30 dead and 142 wounded and missing. Anderson escaped, but 2,600 of his men were killed or captured.

Ewell's and Anderson's commands collapsed within a short time of one another, and some of their fleeing soldiers became intermingled. The Virginia brigade of Brig. Gen. Henry Wise and South Carolinians under Brig. Gen. William Wallace managed to hold back the Union cavalry briefly northwest of Marshall's Crossroads and then slipped away toward Farmville.

As the sun set, Commodore Tucker's sailors and marines, previously marched off into a thickly wooded area and unaware of Ewell's surrender, nearly bagged Union Brig. Gen. J. Warren Kiefer, whose brigade had overrun Ewell's left flank little over an hour earlier. Kiefer was riding alone when several navy men pointed their weapons at him. A Confederate officer pushed the barrel of the nearest rifle aside, and Kiefer turned away, riding to safety at top speed. He returned some time later accompanied by enough force to convince Tucker to surrender.

While Anderson and Ewell were coming to grief, Gordon's troops marched northwest and then turned slightly southwest in the wake of the long wagon train. Three miles from Holt's Corner, Gordon reached high ground at Lockett's farm, above a pair of bridges that span Big Sailor's Creek and Little Sailor's Creek at their confluence forming Sailor's Creek south of the Appomattox River. Known as the Double Bridges, the two spans were narrow, and Gordon saw wagons crowding the crossings in the swampy valley, some with their wheels mired deeply in mud.

Obliged to defend not only himself against Humphreys's approaching II Corps, but also the helpless wagons, Gordon set about forming a battle line around the Lockett farmhouse and across the ridgeline above the bridges on the east side of Sailor's Creek. Hearing the sounds of gunfire, the frightened family of James Lockett descended into the basement of the white frame house, affectionately known to them as Piney Grove, and cowered among piles of potatoes that hid a stash of preserved meat intended as gifts for relatives that might pass through while fighting in the ranks of the Army of Northern Virginia.

As daylight began to fade, the vanguard of the II Corps hove into view. Two divisions under Maj. Gen. Nelson Miles and Brig. Gen. Francis Barlow deployed in line of battle. One Union skirmisher remembered approaching the Lockett home and taking shelter from intermittent Confederate rifle fire.

"I found some protection behind the house," the soldier recounted. "I called Sergeant Percival's attention to what I thought was a better position near the hen coop, fifteen feet distant, but he ordered me to remain where I was. I thought I could get better aim from the other position. I had been hit just before reaching the house and wounded slightly. We had notified the occupants of the house to adjourn to the cellar; bullets came pattering against it."[241]

The storm of battle burst with the two Federal divisions driving Gordon's men from the ridgeline as more bullets slapped the clapboards and chimney of the Lockett house. Firing as they withdrew, Gordon's troops were forced back among the wagons already clogging the Double Bridges. Confusion reigned as Rebel soldiers took cover, teamsters leaped from their wagons or struggled to hold their reins, and horses wild-eyed with terror broke and ran. A few

Confederate cannon opened on the advancing Union troops and slowed their progress until officers urged the men forward with renewed vigor.

"The enemy came upon our rear in great force," recalled one soldier, and another observed that the engagement soon degenerated into an every-man-for-himself affair.[242]

Gordon did well to prevent the complete disintegration of his corps. Those who escaped clambered up the western slope of the small valley and continued on toward Farmville during the night. Still, Gordon's losses were staggering. The Federals claimed 1,700 prisoners along with three hundred wagons, three artillery pieces, and thirteen battle flags captured.

For several hours on April 6, Lee anxiously watched as the stream of soldiers reaching Rice's Station slowed to a trickle. By late afternoon, roughly half his army was yet to arrive. Growing impatient as the sounds of battle drifted to his ears, he turned to retrace his morning route. Ordering Maj. Gen. William Mahone's division to follow, he rode Traveller about two miles to the east and paused on the crown of a small hill about a mile from Sailor's Creek. The chaotic scene that was unfolding before his eyes took the old commander aback. The extent of the rout was apparent. Soldiers without weapons fled while wagons darted helter-skelter, and few officers, if any, seemed to be attempting to restore order.

"My God!" Lee gasped. "Has the army been dissolved?"

Mahone was nearby and heard Lee's lament. He answered, "No, General, here are troops ready to do their duty."

Lee composed himself, gestured toward the oncoming enemy, and said, "Yes, General, there are some true men left. Will you please keep those people back?"[243] Lee ordered Mahone to form a defensive line. He then raised a battle flag aloft, and some of the retreating soldiers stopped in their tracks, rallying to the old, white-haired general.

Even if Lee and Longstreet had been aware of the dire situation sooner, there was little that could be done to salvage it. To keep the road to Farmville open, Longstreet had to hold Rice's Station, and Ord's Army of the James was coming up from Burkeville to the southeast. With VI Corps northeast and II Corps due east, the Army of Northern Virginia was being assailed on three fronts and shunted away from any hope of a rendezvous with Johnston's army in North Carolina.

Lee's army was fighting for survival, and only faint hope remained. There was food at Farmville. It would, however, require another grueling nocturnal march. Gordon's corps absorbed the remnants of Anderson's and Ewell's shattered commands, and Mahone's division was attached as the rear guard. Gordon was ordered to cross the Appomattox River at High Bridge and then march westward to Farmville. If his men could manage to cross the Appomattox and burn the bridges behind them, they could reach the town and possibly rest after finally eating their fill. Longstreet's corps was to move northwest along the road to Farmville from Rice's Station.

April 6, 1865, had been a disaster. Nine generals were captured, and nine thousand soldiers, nearly a quarter of the Army of Northern Virginia, were gone in an afternoon. The general officers included Ewell, Custis Lee, Joseph Kershaw, and Brig. Gens. Eppa Hunton, Dudley Du Bose, Montgomery Corse, Seth Barton, James Simms, and Meriwether Lewis Clark Sr., the son of William Clark of the famed Lewis and Clark expedition of 1804 to 1806.

Well after midnight, John Sergeant Wise at long last located General Lee, north of Rice's Station and east of High Bridge. Fence rails had been pulled down to feed a low-burning campfire, and the young lieutenant strode up to the general while he dictated orders to Col. Charles Marshall, sitting in an ambulance and writing at a lap desk. Marshall, along with Lt. Col. Walter Taylor and Lt. Col. Charles Venable, was one of Lee's closest aides. He was a great-grandnephew of John Marshall, chief justice of the US Supreme Court from 1831 to 1835, and the uncle of Gen. George C. Marshall, President Franklin D. Roosevelt's closest military advisor and army chief of staff during World War II, secretary of state, and architect of the Marshall Plan for the postwar economic recovery of Europe.

Lee rested one arm on a wheel and propped one foot on the end of a log. Wise produced his order signed by President Davis and waited for any information Lee might wish to provide. Years later, Wise recalled Lee's comments that followed. "Then, with a long sigh, he said: 'I hardly think it is necessary to prepare written dispatches in reply. They may be captured. The enemy's cavalry is already flanking us to the south and west. You seem capable of bearing a verbal response. You may say to Mr. Davis that, as he knows, my original purpose was to adhere to the line of the Danville Road. I have been unable to do so and am now endeavoring to hold the Southside Road as I retire in the direction of Lynchburg."[244]

With the impetuosity of youth, Wise asked whether Lee had a specific objective. "'No,' said he slowly and sadly, 'no; I shall have to be governed by each day's developments.' Then, with a touch of resentment, and raising his voice, he added, 'A few more Sailor's Creeks and it will all be over—ended—just as I have expected it would end from the first.'"[245]

The finality of Lee's words stunned Wise. Lee told the young man to get some rest and to find him the following morning in case he changed his mind and decided to send something to Davis in writing. Wise inquired of his father, but Lee did not know whether the old man had escaped from Sailor's Creek. General Wise crossed the High Bridge over the Appomattox River with the rest of Gordon's corps, and the following morning father and son enjoyed a brief reunion in Lee's presence.

Lee wrote a few lines on a scrap of paper, relating to Davis only that he had spoken with the younger Wise, who would deliver a verbal report on the army's situation. With that, the scout was on his way, dodging Union cavalry and infantry once again, and securing a fresh horse from his brother, an Episcopal priest in the town of Halifax Court House. On the evening of April 8, he rode into Danville and delivered his report to President Davis.

After the war, John Sergeant Wise earned a law degree from the University of Virginia and practiced in Richmond. He was elected to Congress in 1883, and later established a law practice in New York City. He fathered nine children and authored four books before his death in 1913 at the age of sixty-six.

Throughout his life, Wise pondered his meeting with Robert E. Lee in the early morning hours of April 7. Wistfully, he wrote more than thirty years later, "As I rode along in search of the ford to which General Lee had directed me, I felt that I was in the midst of the wreck of that immortal army which, until now, I had believed to be invincible."[246]

CHAPTER 10

CROSSING THE RIVER, BURNING THE BRIDGES

In the aftermath of the Battle of Sailor's Creek, dead and wounded men of both sides littered the valley, the banks of the streams, and the neighboring fields, hillocks, and farmyards. Union surgeons occupied the Hillsman house, setting up an operating table in the main hallway. Wounded Union officers were brought inside the house and laid in the various rooms, their blood staining the floors. Wounded soldiers, Union and Confederate, were clustered outside and received medical care as it was available. Shallow graves were dug in the yard, and the dead hastily interred. Three days later, ambulances arrived to carry the injured to a hospital at Burkeville.

The scene was similar at the Lockett farm, where Union soldiers established a field hospital and wounded men were brought inside or laid on the front porch and in the yard. Burial details gathered bodies and interred them across the road. From his headquarters in the field, Phil Sheridan dispatched a staff officer, Col. Redwood Price, to Grant with a report of the events of April 6. Details of the great victory trickled in for several hours, and Sheridan's spirits soared. Just before midnight, he telegraphed Grant. "I sent a dispatch giving the names of the generals captured," recalled

Sheridan. "In the same despatch I wrote: 'If the thing is pressed, I think that Lee will surrender.'"[247]

Grant was cheered by the good news and as was his habit forwarded battlefield updates to President Lincoln at City Point. When Lincoln read Sheridan's assessment of the situation, he dashed off a reply to Grant that noted concisely, "Gen. Sheridan says 'If the thing is pressed I think that Lee will surrender.' Let the thing be pressed. A. LINCOLN."[248]

Before sunrise on April 7, the powerful Federal armies resumed a three-pronged pursuit of the ragged Army of Northern Virginia. Humphreys's II Corps dogged Gordon on his northeastward march to High Bridge, while Maj. Gen. George Crook's cavalry division ranged ahead of Ord's Army of the James rapidly advancing from Rice's Station toward Farmville. Sheridan's other cavalry divisions, under Brig. Gen. George Custer and Brig. Gen. Thomas Devin, were riding westward to Prince Edward Court House, where they could block any move Lee made south toward Danville.

Amid the gloom of a disastrous defeat and the gathering darkness of April 6, General Robert E. Lee rode back to Rice's Station. The trek to Farmville commenced immediately, and the battered Confederate soldiers trudged on through the night and into the late morning of April 7. "About sundown, the enemy at Rice's showed a disposition to advance, and Lee soon gave orders to resume our retreat," recalled I Corps artillery commander E. Porter Alexander. "In the morning we might have gone on toward Danville, but now we turned to the right and took the road to Lynchburg. I remember the night as one peculiarly uncomfortable. The road was crowded with disorganized men and deep in mud."[249]

The quick reaction of James Longstreet early on April 6 saved Gordon's route of retreat across High Bridge during the night. At the head of the Army of Northern Virginia, Longstreet arrived at Rice's Station late that morning and was greeted with the alarming news that a large body of Union infantry and cavalry had passed through the small town a short time earlier. As far as Longstreet could determine, a force moving at the rapid pace described could only be attempting to do one thing—destroy High Bridge and the adjacent wagon bridge across the Appomattox River to prevent the Confederates from using them during their withdrawal.

Both bridges were three miles north of Rice's Station where the South Side railroad line crossed the river and ran westward to Lynchburg. While the wagon bridge was functional but unimpressive, the High Bridge railroad trestle was something of a marvel. Constructed in 1853 to span the half-mile floodplain of the Appomattox, High Bridge was 2,400 feet long, and the track rested on twenty-one brick piers that soared to a height of 125 feet.

As General Ord and the Army of the James reached Burkeville, it became apparent that High Bridge might serve as an avenue of escape for the Rebels. He detailed two infantry regiments, the 54th Pennsylvania and the 123rd Ohio, and three companies of the 4th Massachusetts Cavalry, about eighty troopers, to burn the bridges. Col. Francis Washburn led this force of about nine hundred men quickly out of Burkeville, hoping to clear Farmville before Longstreet got there.

The Federal raiding party was a mile from its objective when Longstreet learned of its passage. He ordered Brig. Gen. Thomas Rosser and Brig. Gen. Thomas Munford to take more than a division of cavalry toward High Bridge and hunt down the enemy. Meanwhile, Ord learned that more than 1,500 Rebel horsemen were in pursuit of his raiders and sent his adjutant, Brig. Gen. Theodore Read, riding hell-for-leather with a warning for Washburn.

Read caught up with Washburn, and the two made the fateful decision to continue the mission as their men drove off a few militia guarding the bridges. Within minutes of their meeting, the Confederate cavalry appeared, cutting off the Union soldiers' escape route. The Federal infantry was a half mile from the scene of the opening action, lodged atop a hill near Chatham, the home of the James Watson family. Some of the Confederate cavalrymen were ordered to dismount, and one of Munford's brigades moved into position for a frontal assault on the Union infantry while Rosser sent two mounted brigades through thick woods to hit their right flank.

Washburn was not sure how large the enemy force confronting him actually was but nevertheless ordered his Massachusetts cavalrymen to charge in what became a show of tragic bravado. Major Edward T. Bouvé of the 4th Massachusetts remembered the bravery of Washburn's band of cavalrymen. "The little battalion swept down the slope . . . pressing close behind their knightly leader and their blue standard. They crashed through three lines of their advancing enemies, tearing their formation asunder as the tornado cuts its way through the forest. But now order and coherence were lost, and the troopers mingled with the Confederates in a bitter hand-to-hand struggle."[250]

Initially, Munford's dismounted troopers were thrown back, but Rosser's mounted men charged into the fray. Sabers rose and fell, men were unhorsed, and savage hand-to-hand fighting ensued. The highest ranking officers on the field were said to have engaged in direct combat with one another.

Washburn and twenty-five-year-old Confederate Brig. Gen. James Dearing, commanding the Laurel Brigade of Rosser's division, slashed at one another with their sabers. Then a Confederate trooper shot Washburn in the mouth. He fell to the ground and was struck a death blow with another saber. Dearing recognized Read and killed him with a shot from his revolver. Then Dearing was shot through both lungs and fell mortally wounded.

Within minutes, all eleven officers of the 4th Massachusetts were out of action. Three had their horses shot from under them, and eight were dead or wounded. Washburn's battered body was found on the field the following day as the Army of the James resumed its advance.

While their accompanying cavalry was decimated, the Union infantry regiments maintained their position on the nearby hill. Munford and Rosser hit them hard. Rosser's 6th Virginia Cavalry Regiment and 35th Virginia Cavalry Battalion, under Brig. Gen. John McCausland, charged the hill on its front and flank. The Federals broke, retiring toward High Bridge, and as the Rebel horsemen closed the gap they surrendered.

The Confederates captured eight hundred prisoners, six battle flags, an ambulance, and strangely enough, a full brass band. As he was being led away, a Union colonel was defiant. He shouted, "Never mind boys! Old Grant is after you! You will all be in our predicament in forty-eight hours!" The colonel's prediction was eerily accurate.[251]

For the time being, High Bridge remained in Rebel hands, but the price was high. Colonel Reuben Boston of the 6th Virginia was killed in the attack on the hill, while Maj. James Thompson of the Stuart Horse Artillery and Maj. John Locher Knott of the 12th Virginia Cavalry were among nearly one hundred Confederate dead.

Barely able to speak and gasping for breath, General Dearing was taken to Chatham and laid in a bed. He was later moved to the Ladies Aid Hospital in Lynchburg and lingered in great pain until

April 23, the last Confederate general to die of wounds received in action during the Civil War.

The defeats at Five Forks and Sailor's Creek and mounting fatigue were taking their toll on Lee, who believed that provisioning at Farmville and reuniting the two columns of the Army of Northern Virginia on the north side of the Appomattox River with the bridges destroyed behind them would buy a brief respite from the relentless Federal pursuit. Once the soldiers had rested and eaten, Lee intended to continue west toward Lynchburg. Eventually, he might still turn the army south to meet Johnston.

During the night, Gordon's troops tramped across High Bridge and the wagon bridge below. At times the crossing became disorderly as a shot rang out or a phantom Federal formation was spotted, alarming men and horses. One incident resulted in such a rush to cross that a soldier lost his footing and fell from the tall span. It was still dark when the last of Gordon's troops crossed the Appomattox and headed southwest toward Farmville. Men of Mahone's rear guard remained to burn the bridges.

Due to an unexplained delay, both High Bridge and the wagon bridge were intact when the leading elements of Humphreys's II Corps came boiling over the horizon from the east at about 7:00 a.m. on April 7. Quickly, the handful of Rebels set both spans alight and took to the north bank of the Appomattox, some of them stopping to pepper the first Union troops to reach the other bank with rifle fire.

The fires were growing livelier by the minute, and one Union soldier watched the drama unfold. "Our pioneers tried to reach the burning end of the railroad bridge, but were driven back by the enemy skirmishers, whose purpose it was to get the flames so well under way that we could not stop them," he said. "The fire had about wrapped up three spans and was at work on a fourth. The superstructure of the bridge was of wood which was tarred, and it was a truss ten or twelve feet high, the top was floored with boards and covered with tin."[252]

The heroic effort finally got the fire under control, but High Bridge had sustained serious damage. The soldier continued, "The men tore up the tin, cut through the floor, and then cut off the timbers one by one. . . . Others brought water from several half hogsheads which had been placed at intervals on the bridge. . . . It seemed as if the flames would catch on the fifth span when the fourth span fell, leaving the fifth untouched by the flames."[253]

Union engineers went to work on the damaged High Bridge, sawing, hammering, and laying planks. Shortly after 9:00 a.m., Union troops were crossing the river at a brisk pace. At the wagon bridge, soldiers drew water from the rain-swollen river to douse the flames, using their canteens, buckets, dippers, boxes, hats, and canvas tents to carry it. The wagon bridge was saved with slight damage.

Alexander was with Lee and Longstreet as the first Confederate soldiers reached the objective of their long march. Four boxcars packed with rations were waiting. "About sunrise we got to Farmville and crossed the river to the north side of the Appomattox," recalled Alexander, "and here we received a small supply of rations."[254]

The ragged ranks of Gordon's vanguard trudged in from the northeast and joined Longstreet's soldiers at the open boxcar doors. They began receiving rations, lighting campfires, and cooking. Around 11:00 a.m., while many of the men were still waiting for food, the sound of gunfire erupted along a ridgeline east of Farmville. Crook's cavalry was riding toward the town, and both Lee and Longstreet knew that the heavy infantry columns of General Ord's Army of the James were not far behind.

The boxcar doors slammed shut, and the train was sent west along the South Side Railroad. Opposing cavalry clashed briefly in the town, and Confederate soldiers stuffed food into their mouths, their shirts, and their pockets as they scrambled across the two bridges over the Appomattox River. The Rebels took positions on the high ground of the north bank and faced the emerging threat.

Both Longstreet and Alexander questioned Lee's decision to move the entire Army of Northern Virginia to the north side of the Appomattox River. While remaining to the south might bring on a fight, the route west was shorter. Moving north of the river would require a longer march to reach Lynchburg and abandon the most direct westward route to the enemy. In the meantime, Lee's army would be marching away from the railroad and its source of supply. There would be no opportunity to turn south again until the Confederates reached the headwaters of the river near Appomattox Court House.

Alexander wrote years later, "Indeed, no man who looked at our situation on a map, or who understood the geography of the country, could fail to see that General Grant had us completely in

In this photograph by Timothy O'Sullivan, the impressive High Bridge belonging to the South Side Railroad stretches across the Appomattox River near Farmville, Virginia. The failure of Confederate troops to destroy the High Bridge allowed Union troops to cross the Appomattox in pursuit of the Army of Northern Virginia without the appreciable delay for which Gen. Robert E. Lee had hoped. *Library of Congress*

a trap. . . . We were now in a sort of jug shaped peninsula between the James River and the Appomattox and there was but one outlet, the neck of the jug at Appomattox Court House, and to that Grant had the shortest road!"[255]

Nevertheless, Lee was already agitated by the failure of Mahone's men to thoroughly destroy the High Bridge and the wagon bridge to impede Humphreys's II Corps. He ordered Alexander to burn the two bridges across the Appomattox at Farmville and brushed aside the artillery officer's concerns, offering only, "Well, there is time enough to think about that." Longstreet advised that burning the Farmville bridges would do little to impede the Federal advance. He remarked later, "I reminded him [Lee] that there were fords over which his [the enemy's] cavalry could cross, and that they knew of or would surely find them."[256]

While the Army of the James advanced toward Farmville, Humphreys divided his II Corps after its crossing of the Appomattox River. The divisions of Miles and de Trobriand moved in a northwesterly direction from High Bridge in an attempt to cut Lee off, while the division of Brig. Gen. Francis Barlow pursued the Confederate rear guard in a direct line along the railroad.

Late in the gray morning, Barlow's division brushed with Gordon's wagon train as it departed Farmville. In the skirmish that followed, the Union troops destroyed a number of wagons but sustained more than 130 killed, wounded, and captured.

Among the casualties was Brig. Gen. Thomas A. Smyth, an Irish immigrant whose journey to America was similar to those of so many others who crossed the Atlantic during the mid-nineteenth century. Smyth heard gunfire to his front and rode forward to investigate. To protect the wagons, Confederate infantry and artillery had opened on the Union advance, and sharpshooters searched the horizon for enemy officers on horseback.

Major David Maull, the division surgeon, recalled the general's habit of leading from the front and the sporadic rifle fire that met Smyth as he surveyed the area. "He was mounted, with his staff about him: it was now about 11 o'clock in the morning, with a cold, disagreeable rain falling. There was an irregular fire of musketry going on. Suddenly he was seen to fall on the right side of his horse; his staff quickly dismounted and caught him."[257]

A bullet from a Confederate sharpshooter's rifle struck the general, resulting in a horrific wound. "A small conical ball had entered the left side of the face, about an inch from the mouth, cutting away a tooth," Maull continued. "The ball continued its course to the neck, fracturing a cervical vertebra, and driving a fragment of the bone upon the spinal cord. Entire paralysis resulted."[258]

Maull watched as General Smyth was carried by a "relay of sorrowing men" to a nearby farmhouse where the II Corps hospital had been established. On the morning of April 8, he was being transferred twelve miles to Burkeville Station when he began to fail noticeably. It was decided to move him into the home of the Burke family, two miles from the original destination. He died at 4:00 a.m. on April 9, just hours before hostilities ended.

A native of Ballyhooley, County Cork, Ireland, General Smyth immigrated to the United States in 1854 and worked in his uncle's carriage making business in Philadelphia. With an inclination toward the military, he served with a mercenary unit in Nicaragua in the mid-1850s. When the Civil War broke out, Smyth enlisted in the 24th Pennsylvania and then transferred to the 1st Delaware in October 1861. He participated in the Peninsula Campaign and the battles of Antietam and Fredericksburg, rising to the rank of colonel.

During the Battle of Gettysburg, Smyth's brigade fought at the stone wall on Cemetery Ridge during the repulse of Pickett's Charge. He was wounded in the nose and head by shell fragments, and when another officer mentioned the resulting disfigurement, he responded that he would gladly give his nose for the sake of his country.

After leading the legendary Irish Brigade during the Battle of the Wilderness, Smyth returned to the II Corps and his former brigade. He was called upon to serve as temporary division commander several times during General Gibbons's extended illness.

He was promoted to brigadier general in October 1864, and at the age of thirty-three was the last Union general to die as the result of hostile fire during the Civil War.

Lee's route of retreat toward Appomattox Station initially proceeded north and then west along the Richmond-Lynchburg Stage Road, passing the rural Cumberland Presbyterian Church about three and one-half miles from Farmville. He desperately hoped to reach Appomattox Station ahead of the Federals, distribute rations, and then turn south once again on a route to Danville through Campbell Court House and Pittsylvania County.

Well aware that Humphreys's II Corps was on the move from High Bridge, Lee ordered Mahone to entrench along a ridgeline east of the church to protect the Confederate withdrawal. Longstreet's corps and Fitzhugh Lee's cavalry took positions to the west to protect the wagons during their slow trek to the northwest and secure Mahone's right flank.

Miles and de Trobriand marched their divisions about five miles from High Bridge and came upon Mahone's entrenchments at midafternoon, while some Rebel soldiers were still digging. Around 1:00 p.m., the Union advance encountered Rebel skirmishers and a strong defensive position comprised of several thousand veteran infantrymen of the Army of Northern Virginia and the sixteen guns of Col. William T. Poague's artillery battalion, which, at the direction of Lee, Alexander had ordered to unlimber in support of Mahone.

General de Trobriand remembered, "General Humphreys, with my division and that of Miles, continued energetically to pursue the greater part of the Confederates by the road to Appomattox Court House. We came up with them five or six miles further on, in a strong position, where they had already covered themselves with intrenchments and awaited our approach. I had the left and Miles the right. The skirmishers deployed in advance met everywhere a stubborn resistance, and, from the extent and solidity of the enemy's line, it became apparent that we had before us all that remained of Lee's army."[259]

For nearly three hours, Union commanders positioned their troops for an assault against the Confederate positions around Cumberland Church. Humphreys did not realize that other Union forces were still south of the Appomattox River and unable to rapidly cross at Farmville and requested that Meade send reinforcements. He also sent word to Barlow to come up from the south if possible.

As the afternoon wore on, Humphreys heard distant rifle fire and believed that reinforcements were indeed on the way.

General Nelson Miles's division opened the Federal attack around 4:00 p.m. against Mahone's front and soon threatened the open Confederate left flank. In a letter written from Washington, DC, in 1890, in response to an inquiry from Longstreet, Mahone described his efforts to repulse the Union thrust:

> Genl. Miles came up and made a direct but feeble attack on my front which was easily repulsed. Subsequently he seeing that Poague was unsupported by Infantry made a skirmish line attack in force upon his guns and for the moment took them— but in the nick of time I caught up a body of North Carolina troops—Genl. Gaines' Division I believe, which had come up from Farmville and flung them in upon the enemy and recovered Poague's guns—all of them. Meanwhile Genl. Longstreet came up and took position on our right. Later in the day Genl. Miles took my left, unprotected, with a large brigade of Federals. I saw the movement and sent to Genl. Longstreet for two brigades. Unfortunately only one reached me in time. The Federal brigade had gotten fully around my left flank and came pouring into the rear of my line, when the brigade from Genl. Longstreet cut them off and quite annihilated it, in its attempts to get back.[260]

De Trobriand watched the repeated assaults at Cumberland Church and concluded that the entrenched Rebels could not be dislodged without substantial reinforcements, which were not forthcoming. "The day was passing away," he recalled. "In the impossibility of turning either flank of the position, a charge was ordered of three regiments of the First Division. It was repulsed with loss. We had to do with too strong a force."[261]

Rather than reinforcements coming up, the rifle fire that Miles heard, prompting him to attack Mahone, was actually a skirmish between elements of Crook's cavalry and Fitzhugh Lee's horsemen protecting the rear of Longstreet's wagon train. Just as Longstreet had predicted, Crook found a ford across the Appomattox River. As they splashed across, the Union cavalrymen spotted the wagons and attacked.

In the engagement that followed, the Confederates turned the tables on their pursuers. Robert E. Lee watched with approval as

Fitzhugh Lee met the Union cavalry head-on while Rosser's horsemen struck the exposed enemy flank. Within minutes, the attackers were routed and streamed back toward the ford they had discovered. The old general's spirits were lifted, and he remarked to his son Rooney, "Keep your command together and in good spirits, general. Don't let them think of surrender. I will get you out of this."[262]

During the fighting that swirled around Cumberland Church and the Appomattox River on April 7, Union casualties totaled nearly 700, while Confederate losses amounted to about 250. Brig. Gen. J. Irvin Gregg, one of Crook's aggressive cavalry commanders, was among the Union troops taken prisoner, scooped up by Fitzhugh Lee's cavalry during the abortive strike at Longstreet's wagon train. Mahone's stand at Cumberland Church and the dazzling Confederate cavalry action have been collectively described as the last victory of the Army of Northern Virginia.

Darkness ended the fighting near Farmville, and Lee's army proceeded on its third night march in three days and its fourth since the evacuation of Richmond and Petersburg. Rations had been sent from Lynchburg and were now waiting at Appomattox Station, twenty-six miles to the west. While Gordon and Fitzhugh Lee's cavalry moved south and then swung north and west on the Richmond-Lynchburg Stage Road, Longstreet's corps marched north and then turned west on a plank road that ran parallel to Gordon's route. Mahone maintained his position at Cumberland Church until 11:00 p.m. and then marched his command down a "terrible muddy road."[263]

During his brief stay in Farmville, Lee set up his headquarters at the Prince Edward Hotel. A little before noon on April 7, Grant arrived in the town and occupied the same location where his adversary had been just a few hours earlier. Information on the day's skirmishes began trickling in to Grant. Ord's Army of the James came up and bivouacked for the night. Sheridan's two cavalry divisions and Griffin's V Corps had arrived from the south. As night fell, Wright's VI Corps followed orders to cross a pontoon bridge to the north side of the Appomattox.

The morale of the Union troops was high, and the VI Corps crossing soon developed into a torchlight review with Grant watching from the hotel porch. "Notwithstanding their long march that day, the men sprang to their feet with a spirit that made everyone marvel at their pluck, and came swinging through the main street of the village with a step that seemed as elastic as on the first day of their toilsome tramp," wrote Horace Porter. "It was now dark, but they spied the general-in-chief watching them with evident pride from the piazza of the hotel as they marched past."[264]

The spontaneous parade gathered momentum, and more than thirty years after the event, Porter's memory of it was vivid. "Then was witnessed one of the most inspiring scenes of the campaign," he continued. "Bonfires were lighted on the sides of the street; the men seized straw and pine-knots, and improvised torches; cheers arose from their throats, already hoarse with shouts of victory; bands played, banners waved, and muskets were swung in the air."[265]

Sheridan advised Grant that seven trains of Rebel rations were at Appomattox Station and that he intended to undertake another forced march to cut the Confederates off and destroy their supplies. Early in the evening, generals Ord and Gibbon paid Grant a visit at the Prince Edward Hotel. Gibbon remembered that Grant was pensive and as their conference ended the commander-in-chief observed, "I have a great mind to summon Lee to surrender."[266]

Grant had also met a local doctor named Smith, who presented himself as a relative of General Ewell, captured at Five Forks. Smith informed Grant that he had spoken with Ewell, who believed that the cause was lost and that "for every man that was killed after this in the war somebody is responsible, and it would be but very little better than murder."[267]

Sheridan's news seemed to indicate like nothing previously that the end was indeed in sight, and Grant reasoned, "This fact, together with the incident related the night before by Dr. Smith, gave me the idea of opening correspondence with General Lee on the subject of the surrender of his army. I therefore wrote to him on this day, as follows:

HEADQUARTERS ARMIES OF THE U.S.,
5 P.M., April 7, 1865

General R.E. Lee,
Commanding C.S.A.

The results of the last week must convince you of the hopelessness of further resistance on the part of the Army of Northern
Virginia in this struggle. I feel that it is so, and regard it as my

duty to shift from myself the responsibility of any further effusion of blood, by asking of you the surrender of that portion of the Confederate States army known as the Army of Northern Virginia.

U.S. Grant,
Lieut.-General.[268]

Adjutant General Seth Williams was summoned and given instructions to ride to Humphreys's II Corps front, believed to be the closest to Lee's rear guard, and deliver the message through the picket lines.

At City Point, President Lincoln received numerous telegrams reporting the progress of the Union armies, one of which came from Humphreys and detailed the tally at Sailor's Creek, and forwarded them to Secretary of War Stanton. He notified General Weitzel in Richmond to inform Confederate emissaries Campbell and Myers that he would allow the Virginia legislature to meet for the purpose of repealing the state's ordinance of secession and possibly compelling Robert E. Lee and all Virginians in the Confederate armies to lay down their arms.

Lincoln informed Grant of this political decision, added that he did not believe anything would come of it, and then quipped to Assistant Secretary of War Charles A. Dana that Sheridan seemed to be removing Virginia soldiers from the war more rapidly than any legislature could act. The president reviewed troops, shook hundreds of hands, and returned to City Point that evening to meet with two Congressmen, his friend Elihu Washburne of Illinois and James G. Blaine of Maine.

Meanwhile, Jefferson Davis remained largely uninformed. A surreal routine dragged on in Danville in spite of the presence of the highest ranking government officials and the town's newly elevated status as the Confederate capital. Wild rumors cropped up, sometimes sparking a fleeting hope that the Army of Northern Virginia might yet emerge victorious.

Departing Richmond on horseback, Secretary of War Breckinridge had traveled toward Danville with Ewell's wagon train. An experienced general in his own right, Breckinridge directed the protection of the wagons against harassing Union cavalry. He met General Lee at Farmville, and the two discussed the tactical situation. Then Breckinridge rode on, finding a telegraph station on the

Richmond & Danville Railroad the following morning and finally sending a reliable report to Davis.

Breckinridge wrote that the Federals were still pursuing the Army of Northern Virginia, that a serious defeat had occurred at Sailor's Creek, and the Union II Corps had crossed the Appomattox River at High Bridge. He noted that Lee "will still try to move around toward North Carolina," but added, "The straggling has been great, and the situation is not favorable."[269]

At dusk, Lee found a small cottage behind Mahone's surprisingly sturdy line, where he might rest for a few hours. Unknown to the old general, a group of his senior commanders had already met to candidly discuss the rapidly deteriorating situation. General Gordon was not among those who initially gathered, but he was soon apprised of the matters discussed.

Gordon recalled the limited options available to the remnants of the Army of Northern Virginia:

> 1. To disband and allow the troops to get away as best they could, and reform at some designated point. This was abandoned because a dispersion over the country would be a dreadful infliction upon our impoverished people, and because it was more improbable that all the men would reach the rallying-point.
>
> 2. To abandon all trains, and concentrate the entire Confederate army in a compact body, and cut through Grant's lines. This proposition was in turn, discarded, because without ammunition trains we could not hope to continue the struggle many days.
>
> 3. To surrender at once.
> It was decided that this last course would be the wisest, and these devoted officers felt that they should do all in their power to relieve General Lee by giving him their moral support in taking the step.[270]

The generals realized the seriousness of their overture, which was against protocol, and that even the suggestion of surrender might be punishable by death. The burden of approaching Lee with the controversial proposal fell to Brig. Gen. William N. Pendleton, the army's chief of artillery. Gordon advised Pendleton that Longstreet should be informed before any discussion was had with General Lee.

After the war, conflicting reports of the ensuing drama emerged. Longstreet recalled speaking with Pendleton on the morning of April 8 and reminding him of the severe penalties to which officers were liable if they suggested surrender. He railed, "If General Lee doesn't know when to surrender until I tell him, he will never know!"[271]

Pendleton asserted that Longstreet eventually came around and wished to be counted among the petitioners. However, Longstreet firmly denied that assertion. Alexander wrote that Longstreet said "his duty was to help hold up Lee's hands, not to beat them down; that his Corps could still whip twice its number and as long as that was the case he would never be the one to suggest surrender."[272]

Pendleton did present the stance of the officers to Lee and later told Gordon that the old general responded, "Oh no. I trust that it has not come to that. We have too many bold men to think of laying down our arms."[273]

The discussion ended abruptly as Pendleton assured Lee that every officer involved in the petition was prepared to do his duty to the fullest.

Grant described the accommodations at the Prince Edward Hotel as a building "almost destitute of furniture . . . which had probably been used as a Confederate hospital."[274] Suffering from a horrific headache, he walked outside on the morning of April 8 and was greeted by a strange sight.

"I found a Confederate colonel there," Grant recalled, "who reported to me and said that he was the proprietor of that house, and that he was a colonel of a regiment that had been raised in that neighborhood. He said that when he came along past home, he found that he was the only man of the regiment remaining with Lee's army, so he just dropped out, and now wanted to surrender himself. I told him to stay there and he would not be molested."[275]

The Army of Northern Virginia was indeed crumbling. A single prisoner of war—tired, defeated, and already back home—would have made little difference as the end drew closer with each passing hour.

PART VI

TO APPOMATTOX COURT HOUSE

CHAPTER 11

A THOUSAND DEATHS

Seth Williams rode through dangerous country in the darkness. His orderly rode beside him, and as they approached Mahone's picket line the orderly was shot dead before the two could identify themselves as coming under a flag of truce. When his purpose was understood, Williams delivered Grant's surrender overture and one other item. Mahone wrote to Longstreet in 1890:

Capt. Patterson the Provost Marshal of my Division was sent over to receive the flag and he brought from Genl. Miles two things—one a letter from Genl. Grant to Genl. Lee—which turned out to be Grant's first letter to Lee, suggesting that the time had come when the latter should end the unhappy struggle by the surrender of his army, and the other was my wife's miniature with Genl. Miles' compliments. After handing over the letter Capt. Patterson said with the compliments of Genl. Miles I have something else for you.

I replied, hold Captain; I have a presentiment and I can tell you what it is You have for me—It is my wife's daguerreotype. And straightaway he pulled the miniature out of his coat pocket and I said, then Genl. Miles' command got my waggon [*sic*]: it is not burned; this miniature was in my trunk, in the top of which I had stowed away two hundred and sixty-five thousand brand new issued Confederate notes—money. I returned my card of thanks to Genl. Miles for the courtesy.[276]

While Mahone marveled at the recovery of his wife's photograph, Lee and Longstreet received Grant's message at about 9:30 p.m. Lee read silently and then passed the note to Lt. Col. Charles Venable, one of his staff officers. Venable advised that he would not reply to such a communication. Lee responded, "Ah, but it must be answered."[277]

Without another word, Lee passed the message to Longstreet, who later remarked, "After reading it, I gave it back, saying, 'Not yet.'"[278]

Then, Lee wrote in response:

7th Apl '65

Genl

I have rec'd your note of this date. Though not entertaining the opinion you express of the hopelessness of further resistance on the part of the Army of N. Va. —I reciprocate your desire to avoid useless effusion of blood, & therefore before considering your proposition, ask the terms you will offer on condition of its surrender.

Very respy your obt. Servt
R.E. Lee
Genl[279]

Williams waited at the picket line, and when Lee's reply was handed to him, he chose to take a safer but more circuitous route via High Bridge back to Grant at Farmville. His head pounding, Grant was sleeping fitfully when Williams arrived at the Prince Edward Hotel in the predawn hours of April 8. He rose from his bed and came downstairs. He read intently, determining that the response was "not satisfactory" but nevertheless deserving of another letter.

Grant replied:

April 8, 1865

GENERAL R.E. Lee,
Commanding C.S.A.
Your note of last evening in reply to mine of same date, asking
the condition on which I will accept the surrender of the Army
of Northern Virginia is just received. In reply I would say that,
peace being my great desire, there is but one condition I would
insist upon, namely: that the men and officers surrendered shall
be disqualified for taking up arms again against the Government
of the United States until properly exchanged. I will meet you,
or will designate officers to meet any officers you may name for
the same purpose, at any point agreeable to you, for the purpose
of arranging definitely the terms upon which the surrender of
the Army of Northern Virginia will be received.

U.S. GRANT,
Lieut.-General.[280]

The march toward Appomattox Station was grueling for the bone-
weary soldiers who remained with the Army of Northern Virginia.
Sometime after 11:00 p.m., the movement began, Gordon on the
Richmond-Lynchburg Stage Road and Longstreet marching through
the town of Curdsville. The columns converged a few miles to the west
at New Store, where the roads came together and seriously slowed the
stumbling retreat. Men threw their rifles and knapsacks away. Some
fell prostrate by the roadside unable to go any further and simply
waiting for the inevitable arrival of Federals to take them prisoner. The
only solace was that little enemy action disrupted the movement.

"The enemy left us a quiet day's march on the 8th, nothing disturbing the rear guard," wrote Longstreet. "We passed abandoned wagons
in flames, and limbers and caissons of artillery burning sometimes in
the middle of the road. One of my battery commanders reported his
horses too weak to haul his guns. He was ordered to bury the guns
and cover their burial-places with old leaves and brushwood. Many
weary soldiers were picked up and many came to the column from the
woodlands, some with, many without, arms, —all asking for food."[281]

When the converging columns reached New Store, still twenty
miles from Appomattox Station, Lee ordered Gordon to take the lead
and Longstreet to assume responsibility for the rear guard, screened

by Fitzhugh Lee's cavalry. General Lee also dealt with a command issue that had arisen during the long retreat. Richard Anderson, George Pickett, and Bushrod Johnson were generals whose commands had virtually ceased to exist, their troops killed, wounded, or captured in the continual skirmishing and the calamities at Five Forks and Sailor's Creek. Lee relieved all three generals, allowing them to go home or to any other location they desired. Apparently, Pickett did not immediately receive his orders and remained with the army.

Late in the morning, Fitzhugh Lee sent word to the commanding general that his rear guard was two miles behind Longstreet and that Federal infantry was two miles further back. Ranging Confederate horsemen also reported that Union cavalry had reached Prospect Station, about twenty miles east of Appomattox. Clearly, the stretch run would be close. It appeared that enemy forces might well reach Appomattox by the next morning.

Before sunrise, the Union bivouacs around Farmville were alive with activity. Grant was impressed with the urgency that Sheridan's cavalry displayed and remarked that their pursuit of the Rebels was such a driving force that the men ignored fatigue and hunger. He also noted that the spring in the step of the infantry was representative of a fighting army that sensed the ultimate victory was at hand.

Humphreys's II Corps marched across the Cumberland Church battleground and followed Gordon, while Wright's VI Corps took up the chase behind Longstreet. Ord's Army of the James, Griffin's V Corps from the Army of the Potomac, and the bulk of Sheridan's cavalry remained south of the Appomattox River, following the tracks of the South Side Railroad and availing themselves of the shorter route to Appomattox Station.

The commander of all Union armies in the field crossed the Appomattox with his staff and trailed the two powerful infantry corps. By the afternoon, however, Grant's headache had become so painful that riding a horse for an extended period was more than he could bear. The general and his officers had ridden far ahead of their commissary and baggage trains, sharing food from Meade's hospital mess and taking shelter where they could. A few miles down the Richmond-Lynchburg Stage Road, the large white farmhouse known as Clifton became Grant's refuge.

Built in 1842 by prosperous plantation owner John Sheppard, Clifton was occupied at the time by Sheppard's sister and brother-in-law, Joseph Crute, who used a small adjacent building as an office for the extensive farming operation. Grant found a sofa in the sitting room to the left of the main hall and collapsed on it for a while. He then set about trying to rid himself of the debilitating headache.

"On the 8th I had followed the Army of the Potomac in rear of Lee," he wrote later. "I was suffering very severely with a sick headache, and stopped at a farmhouse on the road some distance in the rear of the main body of the army. I spent the night in bathing my feet in hot water and mustard, and putting mustard plasters on my wrists and the back part of my neck, hoping to be cured by morning."[282]

Grant took off his coat and boots and tried to rest while his staff officers made themselves as comfortable as possible on the floors throughout the structure. Headquarters troops camped on the grounds, lighting fires to ward off the chill of an early spring evening. The II Corps marched through New Store during the day, and the VI Corps camped in the vicinity that night.

One Union infantryman who passed through the area remembered that New Store consisted of a single house and substantial surrounding acreage. Inside the house, a large cache of flour was discovered, and the soldiers helped themselves. A second discovery was at first thought to be an open barrel of molasses. A soldier recalled that the word of "'Molasses, molasses,' ran along the line, and tin cups were quickly loosed from haversacks. As the barrel was reached cups made a hurried dip, but you can imagine the strength of the language used when, instead of Porto Rico, it was found to be tar!"[283]

Sheridan's cavalry was active early on April 8. Crook sent word of the misfortune that had befallen General Gregg on the previous evening, convincing "Little Phil" that the Confederates were headed for Lynchburg via Appomattox Court House and that Lee had temporarily given up on turning southward toward Danville.

"Resolving to throw my cavalry again across his path, and hold him till the infantry could overtake him, I directed everything on Appomattox depot," Sheridan related.[284] He ordered Crook to Prospect Station and directed a reconnaissance along the rail line to Lynchburg. By daybreak, Merritt's cavalry divisions and the cavalry division of the Army of the James, under Brig. Gen. Ranald S. Mackenzie, had converged on Prospect Station and undertaken a rapid ride to the west toward the South Side Railroad depot at Appomattox. The heavy infantry columns of Ord and Griffin followed the horsemen.

As the cavalry pursuit was just getting underway, one of Sheridan's Jessie Scouts, a Sergeant White, rode up to the general with news that four trains had chugged to Appomattox Station from Lynchburg, presumably in response to the ruse that Henry Young's scouts had initiated on April 4 with the intercepted communication from the Confederate commissary general.

"Sergeant White, who had been on the lookout for the trains ever since sending the dispatch, found them several miles west of Appomattox depot, feeling their way along, in ignorance of Lee's exact position," related Sheridan. "As he had the original dispatch with him, and took pains to dwell upon the pitiable condition of Lee's army, he had little difficulty in persuading the men in charge of the trains to bring them east to Appomattox Station."[285]

Around noon, Crook's cavalry reached Pamplin Station in a cloud of dust and captured the provision-laden wagons that Lee had ordered away from Farmville on April 7. George Custer sent two regiments forward at a gallop to break up the South Side Railroad tracks west of Appomattox to prevent the escape of the Lynchburg trains and then seize them at the station.

With the 2nd New York Cavalry leading the way that afternoon, Custer's troopers advanced on the wagon road that paralleled the rail line to Appomattox and swept from the southeast toward their objective. Three of the trains were quickly captured, their engineers surprised by cavalry carbines. The fourth train actually came rolling into the station just as the Federals arrived and reversed toward Lynchburg so rapidly that several couplings broke, stranding some of its cars.

One of the first officers on the scene was Col. Alanson Randol. As he was directing his troopers, a hand came to rest on his shoulder. Randol turned to see Custer, who yelled, "Go in, old fellow! Don't let anything stop you! Now is the chance for your stars! Whoop 'em up! I'll be after you!"[286]

While Custer's men were taking control of the locomotives—those with railroad experience volunteering to run them—artillery shells began crashing down around the Union soldiers. Startled, they turned toward the threat and discovered the reserve artillery of the Army of Northern Virginia, ordered ahead of Lee's retreat to prevent it from impeding the progress of the infantry columns. Brigadier General Reuben Lindsay Walker commanded the Confederates, who were not expecting enemy cavalry. When the alarm was raised,

Walker was sitting on a stump with one of his men giving him a shave. Most of the Rebels were cooking evening rations.

Walker's hodgepodge command consisted of about one hundred artillerymen and a handful of military engineers who were serving as infantry, the three regiments of Brig. Gen. Martin Gary's cavalry brigade, including the 24th Virginia, 7th Georgia, and 7th South Carolina, protecting close to one hundred artillery pieces, a hospital wagon train, and roughly two hundred wagons carrying supplies and baggage.

Caught completely off-guard, Walker rallied his confused forces in a large semicircle and managed to get some of the guns unlimbered to fire on the enemy horsemen visible around the station. True to form, Custer ordered his cavalry to charge only to find that the unfamiliar ground was not favorable for such a movement. Several attempts to overrun the Rebel position were broken up by the difficult terrain and Confederate canister.

Finally, sometime after 8:00 p.m., Custer organized a charge with enough muscle to succeed. A New York cavalryman remembered that his regiment thundered down a narrow dirt lane and into an open field. He related, "A tornado of canister-shot swept over our heads, the next instant we were in the battery."[287]

Fighting raged among the guns, and William Davis, the color bearer of the famed Washington Artillery of New Orleans, was killed as trooper Barney Sheilds of the 2nd West Virginia Cavalry captured the flag. Among the Union dead was Maj. Sesch Howe of the 1st West Virginia Cavalry, the fifth member of his family to die during the Civil War.[288]

As the firing subsided, Custer's men counted twenty-five guns captured and scores of Confederates killed and wounded. Although Union casualties were fewer than fifty, many of them were serious as the horsemen were highly vulnerable to the Rebel canister, which exploded like giant shotgun shells, scattering lead balls indiscriminately and inflicting ghastly wounds on men and horses alike. Those Confederates who were able fled with the remainder of the artillery, either north in the direction of Oakville, or west toward Lynchburg. Custer sent the captured railcars eastward.

On the night of April 8, Lee made camp with Gordon's corps at Rocky Run, north of Appomattox Court House. Artillery Chief Pendleton rode ahead to Appomattox Station and was temporarily caught in Custer's attack. He managed to slip away and intended to request infantry support for Walker; however, as he made his way back to Lee the sound of cannon and rifle fire faded. He correctly deduced that Walker's command had been defeated.

At about 9:00 p.m., Lt. Col. August Root led a contingent of the 15th New York Cavalry into the town of Appomattox Court House. The horses jumped a rail fence and galloped down the Richmond-Lynchburg Stage Road. As they entered the town, the New Yorkers captured a few wagons and ran smack into General Gordon's pickets. One of the horsemen gunned down Jesse Hutchens, a soldier of the 5th Alabama Battalion, in front of the courthouse building.

Root swept past astride his handsome charger, and another soldier of the 5th Alabama took aim, shooting him from the saddle. With a bullet in his neck, Root fell dead in front of Robert Rosser's blacksmith and wheelwright shops about fifteen feet from the courthouse. Gordon's pickets stood firm near the Peers cabin and delivered a volley that compelled the enemy cavalry to withdraw.

Although it was not a battle conducted on a grand scale, the action at Appomattox Station was significant. The Federal cavalry had destroyed the rations Lee was counting on, occupied the high ground west of Appomattox Court House about three miles to the northeast, and cut the Richmond-Lynchburg Stage Road—the way west on which the survival of the Army of Northern Virginia depended. Custer had slammed the door on Robert E. Lee.

Sheridan rode into Appomattox Station as the fighting ended. Anxious for infantry support to arrive, he sent a dispatch to Grant.

Major General George Armstrong Custer posed for this portrait in Matthew Brady's Washington, DC, gallery on January 4, 1865. The flamboyant Custer earned a reputation for bravery and recklessness during the Appomattox Campaign and was instrumental in bringing about the eventual surrender of the Army of Northern Virginia. His daring, however, proved his undoing at the Little Bighorn in 1876. *Library of Congress*

"If General Gibbon and the Fifth Corps can get up to-night, we will perhaps finish the job in the morning. I do not think Lee means to surrender until compelled to do so."[289]

The Army of the James, which included both white and black troops, was actually the closest to Appomattox Court House and had covered thirty miles in the past twenty-four hours. Sheridan sent several couriers in the direction of Ord to hopefully speed him along. "On the night of the 8th, I made my headquarters at a little frame house just south of the station," he recalled. "I did not sleep at all . . . Merritt, Crook, Custer, and Devin were present at frequent intervals during the night, and everybody was overjoyed at the prospect that our weary work was about to end so happily."[290]

When Lee reached Rocky Run, he held in his hand the second message from Grant, written early that morning at Farmville. The day's events were somewhat encouraging. The troops had been largely unmolested during their march, but Lee was not yet aware of the presence of Federal cavalry at Appomattox Station. The battle din of Custer's ultimately successful charge did not reach his ears until about 9:00 p.m., and Pendleton did not confirm the event until nearly 1:00 a.m. Lee did not discuss the content of Grant's note but sat down wearily to compose a reply:

8th Apl '65

Genl

I rec'd at a late hour your note of today. In mine of yesterday I did not intend to propose the surrender of the Army of N. Va. —but to ask the terms of your proposition. To be frank, I do not think the emergency has arisen to call for the surrender of this Army, but as the restoration of peace should be the sole object of all, I desired to know whether your proposals would lead to that and I cannot therefore meet you with a view to surrender the Army of N. Va. —but as far as your proposal may affect the C.S. forces under my command & tend to the restoration of peace, I shall be pleased to meet you at 10 A.M. tomorrow on the old stage road to Richmond between the picket lines of the two armies.

Very respy your Obt Sevt
R. E. Lee
Genl.[291]

At midnight, in the light of a moon that was nearly full, Lee gathered his senior commanders for a council of war, which, as it turned out, would be the last of the Army of Northern Virginia. Distant Federal campfires were visible on three sides. The II and VI corps of the Army of the Potomac were to the east. To the south and west, the fires of the XXIV Corps of the Army of the James, Griffin's V Corps, and Sheridan's cavalry divisions glowed.

Robert E. Lee, Longstreet, Gordon, and Fitzhugh Lee gathered near a fire of fence rails, and the old general asked the others for their thoughts. Those present understood that if only Federal cavalry barred the way at Appomattox Court House, it might be pushed aside. However, if heavy infantry columns had arrived, it meant the end. The army could turn north into oblivion, disperse, or surrender. Only the latter alternative would make any real sense.

A wide-ranging discussion took place, including speculation as to the fate of the Southern people should the Confederate armies and their government cease to function. Fitzhugh Lee and Gordon believed that Federal infantry blocked the way toward Lynchburg. Even so, the quartet agreed that one more battle, an attempt to break through the Federal cordon, would decide the fate of the Army of Northern Virginia.

Lee ordered Gordon and Fitzhugh Lee to attack to the west at dawn, their preparatory movements commencing at 1:00 a.m. Turning south, Gordon was to open a gap for the few remaining wagons to pass through. Then Longstreet would follow and hold the position so that the retreat could continue. Success was a forlorn hope, but honor and duty required the effort.

Fitzhugh Lee asked that his cavalry be allowed to act independently in the event that a surrender was forthcoming or if Union infantry was found to block the way forward. As long as it did not compromise any agreement between Lee and Grant or jeopardize a cease-fire arrangement, he wanted the opportunity to ride toward Lynchburg and then turn south to North Carolina and Johnston's army. His request was granted.

Gordon remembered, "If all that was said and felt at that meeting could be given it would make a volume of measureless pathos. In no hour of the great war did General Lee's masterful characteristics appear to me so conspicuous as they did in that last council. We knew by our own aching hearts that his was breaking.

Yet he commanded himself, and stood calmly facing and discussing the long-dreaded inevitable."[292]

Gordon had ridden some distance when he sent a staff officer back to Lee asking if there were specific instructions as to where his advancing corps should stop for the night after breaking through the Union line. Lee was momentarily taken aback and then facetiously remarked, "Yes; tell General Gordon that I should be glad for him to halt just beyond the Tennessee line."[293]

Gordon immediately understood the implication of Lee's comment. "That line was about two hundred miles away," he acknowledged. "His purpose was to let me infer that there was little hope of our escape and that it did not matter where I camped for the night."[294]

The headquarters baggage had been lost to the enemy cavalry, and General Lee had no tent to pitch that night along the road near Rocky Run. Longstreet remembered, "General Lee made his head-quarters near the rear-guard, and spread his couch about a hundred feet from the saddle and blanket that were my spread for the night. If he had a more comfortable bed than mine I do not know, but I think not."[295]

Abraham Lincoln desperately wanted to be at City Point among the troops when the final surrender of the Army of Northern Virginia was announced. However hopeful the dispatches from the commanding generals were, he decided on April 8 to return to Washington, DC, and await the outcome of Grant's campaign in the capital city.

On his last day at City Point, the president welcomed the Marquis de Chambrun and other dignitaries who had come there with Mrs. Lincoln aboard the *River Queen*, showing them the salon where the discussions with the Confederate emissaries had taken place in January and describing the conference. The group traveled to Petersburg by train and toured the bleak and largely abandoned city. In the afternoon, Lincoln led the party to the sprawling Depot Field Hospital to offer good wishes to the sick and those wounded during the recent fighting.

One of the patients Lincoln met that afternoon was Confederate Col. Henry L. Benbow of the 23rd South Carolina Infantry, wounded and captured at Five Forks. As the president stretched out his hand, the colonel hesitated and inquired, "Mr. President, do you know to whom you offer your hand?" When Lincoln answered that he did not know, Colonel Benbow informed him that he was a Confederate officer who had done his utmost in a cause that Lincoln believed was unjust. The president answered, "I hope a Confederate colonel will not refuse me his hand." Benbow was said to have then extended both of his own hands in a warm greeting.[296]

That evening, a military band came aboard the *River Queen* and performed a concert for the president and his guests. After several tunes were played, Lincoln requested the *Marseillaise* in honor of the Marquis de Chambrun, commenting that the Marquis had traveled a great distance to hear the revolutionary song that was banned by the government of the French Second Empire. Lincoln enjoyed the first rendition of the French anthem so much he asked the band to play it through a second time.

"He then asked me if I had ever heard *Dixie*, the rebel patriotic song to the sound of which all their attacks had been conducted," the Marquis later wrote. "As I answered in the negative, he added, 'That tune is now Federal property; it belongs to us, and, at any rate, it is good to show the rebels that with us they will be free to hear it again.' He then ordered the somewhat surprised musicians to play it for us."[297]

It was nearly 11:00 p.m. when the *River Queen* slipped away from City Point, gaining steam as the bustling depot, temporarily quiet during the night, faded from sight. President Lincoln stood alone on the deck for some time, no doubt contemplating the continuing hazards of war and the anticipated hazards of peace.

Nearly 150 miles southwest of City Point, Jefferson Davis called his cabinet members together at Danville on the evening of April 8. The implications of Breckinridge's report received earlier in the day dominated the dinner conversation. At about 8:00 p.m., John Wise's tired horse clip-clopped across the bridge that spanned the Roanoke River at Danville. It had taken the better part of two days for the young messenger to complete the perilous return trip from Lee's camp near High Bridge.

Stopped by a sentry, Wise explained his mission and was allowed to pass. President Davis's servant greeted him at the front door. In a few moments, he was ushered into the dining room and asked to report to the cabinet members present. Wise admitted:

> I felt rather embarrassed by such a distinguished audience, but Mr. Davis soon put me at ease. They sat around a large

dining-table, and I stood at the end opposite Mr. Davis . . . One question I answered as I felt. "Do you think General Lee will be able to reach a point of safety with his army?"

"I regret to say, no. From what I saw and heard, I am satisfied that General Lee must surrender. It may be that he has done so to-day. In my opinion, Mr. President, it is only a question of a few days at furthest, and, if I may be permitted to add a word, the sooner the better; for, after seeing what I have seen of the two armies, I believe the result is inevitable, and postponing the day means only the useless effusion of noble, gallant blood."

I am sure none of them had heard such a plain statement of this unwelcome truth before. I remember the expression of face—almost a shudder—with which what I said was received. I saw that, however convinced they might be of the truth of it, it was not a popular speech to make.[298]

Wise was given a meal of milk, corn coffee, rolls, butter, and cold turkey. He gulped the milk and coffee and stuffed food into his haversack. He found a stable for his horse and climbed into the loft for a night's sleep. Davis had asked him to make a return trip to General Lee. The next morning the president wrote out credentials so that Wise would not be mistaken as a spy and handed him several dispatches. This mission was one that Wise was not destined to complete.

General Edward O. C. Ord needed no prodding from Sheridan. As his hard marching troops pushed toward Appomattox, Ord exhorted the tired men. "I promise you boys that this is the last day's march you will have to endure. One good steady march, and the campaign is ended."[299]

Sometime during the night, Ord arrived at Sheridan's headquarters and advised that his column was coming up rapidly. Around 4:00 a.m., the first of his foot soldiers tramped into the vicinity of Appomattox Court House. With Ord on the field, Sheridan was no longer the senior commander and could not direct the dispositions of the infantry. However, more confident than ever that the end was near, he was more than willing to offer Ord his opinion.

Grant was still at Clifton trying to shake his awful headache and get some sleep when Col. Charles Whittier of Humphreys's II

Corps staff brought in the relay of Lee's letter written at Rocky Run. An aide cracked the door of Grant's room, and the general said, "Come in; I am awake. I am suffering too much to get any sleep." Porter, meanwhile, lit a candle and stepped in with Lee's communication. Grant read the lines and shook his head in disappointment. "It looks as if Lee still intends to fight," he pronounced. "I will reply in the morning."[300]

It was apparent that Lee had changed his tone. Rather than discussing only the surrender of the Army of Northern Virginia, he seemed to be attempting to stretch the discussion beyond military matters. Grant remembered Lincoln's admonition that his efforts should concentrate on securing the surrender of Lee's army in the field. Porter reflected, "General Grant kept steadily in mind the fact that he was simply a soldier, and could deal only with hostile armies. He could not negotiate a treaty of peace without transcending his authority."[301]

A couple of hours before sunrise, Porter stepped once again into Grant's room at Clifton. It was empty. He found the general pacing in the yard, holding both hands to his head. Several officers came outside and convinced Grant that a cup of coffee might do him some good. They walked over to Meade's camp. The general drank some of the steaming liquid and responded to Lee:

April 9, 1865

General: Your note of yesterday is received. As I have no authority to treat on the subject of peace, the meeting proposed for 10 A.M. to-day could lead to no good. I will state, however, general, that I am equally anxious for peace with yourself, and the whole North entertains the same feeling. The terms upon which peace can be had are well understood. By the South laying down their arms they will hasten that most desirable event, save thousands of human lives, and hundreds of millions of property not yet destroyed. Sincerely hoping that all our difficulties may be settled without the loss of another life, I subscribe myself, etc.,

U.S. GRANT,
Lieutenant-general
GENERAL R.E. Lee.[302]

After composing his note to Lee, Grant decided to ride to Sheridan's front at Appomattox Court House. He was only about three miles away, but a direct route would have taken him through the Confederate lines. The longer route he followed took him out of direct communication with Lee for several hours, and historians have speculated as to why he chose to leave Meade. Some assert that he wanted to be close to Sheridan, who had pursued the Rebels with such panache, others that he wanted to exclude Meade from any surrender discussions. In his memoirs, he said only that he wanted to reach the "head of the column."[303]

Although he still suffered from the headache, Grant declined to ride in an ambulance. Instead, he climbed aboard Cincinnati, his handsome stallion standing seventeen hands tall and his favorite of three horses, including Egypt and Jeff Davis, that he rode during the spring of 1865.

In the predawn hours of April 9, Sheridan ordered the cavalry brigade of Brig. Gen. Charles H. Smith to occupy a low ridge less than a mile west of Appomattox Court House. The Maine, New York, and Ohio cavalrymen dug shallow breastworks that commanded the Richmond-Lynchburg Stage Road and the Bent Creek Road, leading north. Smith instructed Lt. James Lord to place a pair of guns on the heights, and soon these cannon were lobbing shells at the Confederate positions visible through deep fog. Confident that the day was to be theirs, Sheridan and Merritt brought the rest of their cavalry up with the divisions of Devin on the right, Crook in the center, Mackenzie on the left, and Custer in reserve.

Gordon formed a battle line with the remnants of three divisions, Brig. Gen. Clement Evans on the left, Brig. Gen. James Walker in the center, and Maj. Gen. Bryan Grimes on the right. To the rear, the small division of Brig. Gen. William H. Wallace remained as a ready reserve. Fitzhugh Lee's cavalry, under Rooney Lee, Thomas Munford, and Thomas Rosser, took up positions on the right, and artillery under Col. Thomas Carter unlimbered in support.

As the sun rose, the Union defensive positions were clearly visible, but it was difficult to determine whether the blue-clad soldiers who occasionally showed themselves were infantry or dismounted cavalrymen. Infantry meant that Gordon would spearhead the attack. Cavalry gave Fitzhugh Lee the responsibility for going in first. As the two generals engaged in a heated exchange over who would lead the attack, Grimes rode up and interjected that someone had to do the job.

"I will undertake it," Grimes told the other two. "Well, replied Gordon, "Drive them off!" When Grimes added that his single division would not be enough to dislodge the Federals, Gordon shouted, "You can take the other two divisions of the corps!"[304]

Gordon's depleted corps began forming at 5:00 a.m. A mere shadow of its former grandeur and combat prowess, the soldiers nevertheless stepped smartly into line. Observers reminisced momentarily as the sight conjured memories of earlier days when Stonewall Jackson inspired the corps to great deeds on the battlefield. Just before 8:00 a.m., the "Yip! Yip!" of the Rebel yell raised shrilly from soldiers' throats.

Brigadier General William Roberts's North Carolina cavalry brigade rolled forward and captured Lord's two guns that had harassed the Confederate encampment during the previous hours. The ragged Rebel infantry pushed ahead while the horsemen attacked the Union left flank and the Rebel cannon boomed. Gordon, too, recalled that the scene was reminiscent of the days of old. "I take especial pride," he said, "in recording the fact that this last charge of the war was made by the footsore and starving men of my command with a spirit worthy of the best days of Lee's army."[305]

The Confederate infantry pivoted to the left like a door on hinges, and Smith's advanced position was outflanked and overrun. Clearing the Richmond-Lynchburg Stage Road, these troops moved south and west, running into a stronger second line of defense under Maj. Gen. George Crook, where the fighting became hand-to-hand. Rooney Lee's cavalry engaged in charge and countercharge with Mackenzie's cavalry and the Pennsylvania cavalry of Col. Samuel B. Young, leading the brigade in the absence of the recently captured General Gregg. Munford and Rosser headed west to further clear the escape route.

Sheridan rode to the sound of the guns and realized that a continuing stand by his cavalry would result in unnecessary casualties. The XXIV Corps of the Army of the James was nearby, and he ordered his horsemen to provide space for the infantrymen. "Riding to a slight elevation where a good view of the Confederates could be had, I there came to the conclusion that it would be unwise to offer more resistance than that necessary to give Ord time to form, so I directed Merritt to fall back, and in retiring to shift Devin and Custer to the right so as to make room for Ord now in the woods to my rear."[306]

Although accounts differ somewhat—the Confederates attributing their progress to fighting spirit while Sheridan seems to conclude that his cavalry gave ground while fighting a delaying action—it was, in the end, the presence of Ord's Army of the James and Griffin's V Corps of the Army of the Potomac to Ord's right that stymied Gordon's advance. As the Union cavalry executed a fighting withdrawal to more defensible positions, Gordon's foot soldiers and Fitzhugh Lee's cavalry rushed ahead and did, in fact, find the open road to Lynchburg. Their exultation was short-lived. As they reached the crest of a low ridge, thousands of Federal infantrymen were shifting into line of battle.

Gordon soon received reports of Federal infantry approaching on his right and moving toward his vulnerable rear. The XXIV Corps divisions of Brig. Gen. Robert Foster and Brig. Gen. John Turner moved forward toward the Richmond-Lynchburg Stage Road and the Confederate artillery positions. Two brigades of United States Colored Troops from XXV Corps moved up along with Griffin's V Corps, slanting northward in the vicinity of the courthouse building itself.

Concerned about Gordon's progress after three hours of fighting, General Lee sent Colonel Venable to find out what was happening. Gordon grasped the hard fact that his situation was rapidly deteriorating—the Federals were not in retreat, heavy infantry was to his front and flank, and Custer and Devin were moving their cavalry toward the gap between his own lines and those of Longstreet, which were fighting nearly back to back.

When Venable rode up, Gordon responded to his inquiry with disheartening news. "Tell General Lee that my command has been fought to a frazzle, and unless Longstreet can unite in the movement, or prevent these forces from coming upon my rear, I cannot long go forward."[307]

Fitzhugh Lee's cavalry could offer only token resistance against massed infantry, and soon his horsemen were disengaging across the field and, according to his prearrangement with generals Lee and Gordon, turning west toward Lynchburg at a gallop. Longstreet was in no position to assist Gordon. Two Federal corps that had dogged the retreat for the last week, Humphreys's II and

Wright's VI, were preparing for an assault against his positions northeast of Gordon near New Hope Church.

Just after Fitzhugh Lee ordered his men to head west, he turned to the staff officers gathered nearby and whisked them in the same direction. The firing remained brisk, and one of the Confederate officers fell to the ground seriously wounded. The young man writhed in pain and begged for someone to shoot him to end his misery.

Fitzhugh Lee was dismayed to discover that the wounded soldier was his favorite aide, Lt. Charles Minnigerode, who had joined the army three years earlier at the age of sixteen and without the permission of his father, Reverend Charles Minnigerode of Saint Paul's Episcopal Church in Richmond. Lee believed the wound was fatal and asked someone to pin a note to the young man's coat to identify his body. Bleeding profusely, the lieutenant managed to write a short note to his mother in Richmond. "I am dying—but I have fallen where I expected to fall. Our cause is defeated but I do not live to see the end of it."[308]

When the fighting was over, a Union soldier found Minnigerode lying on the field. Barely alive, the wounded officer begged the man to shoot him. "No I won't Johnny Reb, you might get well," came the reply. Carried to a field hospital in Farmville, Minnigerode wrote to his father on April 13, saying, "I suffer intensely, but my hopes of recovery are good."[309] Minnigerode indeed survived, married, and fathered seven children. He committed suicide in 1888 at the age of forty-two.

Venable rode rapidly back to General Lee and delivered the report from Gordon that caused the old general to momentarily forget that staff officers were close at hand. He murmured, "Then, there is nothing left me to do but to go and see General Grant, and I would rather die a thousand deaths."[310]

One last time, Lee sought the counsel of his lieutenants and staff officers. He called for Longstreet, who arrived to find a cluster around the dying embers of the roadside fire. Mahone was close to General Lee, shivering, but he assured those present that it was not due to fear, only the chill of the morning. After his customary courteous greeting, Lee described the dire straits of the Army of Northern Virginia.

Lee asked Longstreet for his thoughts, and the Old War Horse inquired as to whether the sacrifice of the army would benefit the Confederacy on some other field or in the political arena. When Lee responded that he did not think so, Longstreet said, "Then your situation speaks for itself."[311]

Mahone advised Lee to surrender.

Only E. Porter Alexander dissented. "If we surrender this army," he reasoned, "all will go like a row of bricks."[312] He asserted that the army could disband and individual soldiers make their way to the governments of their respective states. The suggestion raised the prospect of a prolonged guerrilla war.

Lee would have none of it. He replied,

> General, you and I as Christian men have no right to consider only how this would affect us. We must consider its effect on the country as a whole. Already it is demoralized by the four years of war. If I took your advice, the men would be without rations and under no control of officers. They would be compelled to rob and steal in order to live. They would become mere bands of marauders, and the enemy's cavalry would pursue them and overrun many sections they may never have occasion to visit. We would bring on a state of affairs it would take the country years to recover from. And, as for myself, you young fellows might go to bushwhacking, but the only dignified course for me would be to go to General Grant and surrender myself and take the consequences of my acts.[313]

Alexander was speechless. Writing decades later, he reflected, "I had not a single word to say in reply. He had answered my suggestion from a plane so far above it, that I was ashamed of having made it."[314]

Prepared to meet General Grant between the lines on Longstreet's front, Lee mounted Traveller and trotted off toward the expected rendezvous.

CHAPTER 12

FURL THE FLAGS

In full dress uniform, Robert E. Lee presented a striking figure, the personification of military bearing, dignity, and honor.

That is how Longstreet found him in the early morning of Palm Sunday, April 9, 1865. "He was dressed in a suit of new uniform," Lee's Old War Horse remembered, "sword and sash, a handsomely embroidered belt, boots, and a pair of gold spurs. At first approach his compact figure appeared as a man in the flush vigor of forty summers, but as I drew near, the handsome apparel and brave bearing failed to conceal his profound depression."[315]

When General Pendleton inquired as to why he was so formally attired, Lee answered, "I have probably to be General Grant's prisoner and thought I must make my best appearance."[316]

Around 8:30, Lee started toward his anticipated meeting with Grant between the lines of Longstreet's corps and Humphreys's II Corps on the Richmond-Lynchburg Stage Road. Colonels Marshall and Taylor and Sergeant Tucker, the courier who had been with A. P. Hill when the latter was killed on April 2, accompanied Lee. The party had ridden only a half mile when a Federal skirmish line came into view. Tucker rode ahead with a flag of truce as Taylor and Marshall rode beside Lee expecting to find Grant.

Tucker halted. Marshall dismounted, took off his sword, and waved a handkerchief as he walked toward the opposing skirmish line. Instead of Grant, Marshall met Lt. Col. Charles A. Whittier of Humphreys's staff with Grant's letter written about four hours earlier at Clifton. Whittier offered to wait in the event that Lee wished to reply, and Marshall walked about a hundred yards back to Lee and read Grant's letter aloud.

It was apparent that Grant intended only to deal with the surrender of the Army of Northern Virginia and no issues concerning a larger peace would be entertained. Marshall stood silently while Lee pondered the inevitable. "After a few moments' reflection," the colonel later wrote, "he said, 'Well, write a letter to General Grant and ask him to meet me to deal with the question of the surrender of my army, in reply to the letter he wrote me at Farmville.'"[317]

Marshall sat down and wrote the following reply to Grant:

> HEADQUARTERS ARMY OF NORTHERN VIRGINIA
> April 9th, 1865
>
> Lieut.-Gen. U.S. Grant, Commanding United States Armies,
> General, –
>
> I received your note this morning in the picket line, whither I had come to meet you and ascertain definitely what terms were embraced in your proposition of yesterday with reference to the surrender of this army.
> I now request an interview in accordance with the offer contained in your letter of yesterday for that purpose.
> Very respectfully, your obedient servant
>
> R.E. LEE, General[318]

After Lee reviewed and signed the letter, Marshall returned to Whittier, handed over the reply, and asked for a suspension of hostilities. When Whittier responded that he did not believe his commanding officer had the authority to order a truce, Marshall asked Whittier to request that the commanding officer read the content of Lee's letter, which would justify such an action. Although Grant and Lee were corresponding, both Meade and Humphreys had been instructed to proceed with their attacks.

Lee lingered, waiting for confirmation of a truce. None seemed to be forthcoming, and a Federal horseman rode out to warn the Confederates that a skirmish line was approaching and they were in imminent danger. Reluctantly, Lee turned back and rode through Longstreet's positions still hoping for acknowledgment of the requested cease-fire. After some delay, Meade, who was still quite ill, assented to a one-hour truce and suggested that Lee send another communication to Grant through Sheridan's lines close to Appomattox Court House.

As word of the cease-fire spread through both armies, sporadic firing continued, and the tragedy of the resulting casualties, so close to the end of hostilities, was heightened. Private John L. Smith of the 118th Pennsylvania recalled after the war, "It seems to me everyone was more scared than ever, from the fact that we knew the war was nearly over, and we did not want to be killed at the end of the war."[319]

Late in the morning, the 185th New York of Joshua Chamberlain's brigade advanced from a ridgeline through the yard of the house belonging to Mariah Wright, a widow whose husband Pryor had built the structure in 1823. The cannon of the Richmond Howitzers, an artillery unit that had been with the Confederate armies in the field since the first major battle of the war at Bull Run in 1861, were unlimbered around the frame house belonging to George Peers on a hill overlooking the town.

The Richmond Howitzers fired some of the last shots of the war, and Lt. Hiram Clark was one of the unfortunate victims, killed by a shell during the last minutes of the fighting at Appomattox. A soldier observed the poignant scene that followed and remarked, "A group of sad-eyed officers gathered around the body, and it seemed, under the circumstances, a particularly hard fate."[320]

The 185th New York Regiment was raised in the central part of the state in the vicinity of Syracuse and Onondaga and Cortland counties. Several soldiers maintained a regular correspondence with the newspapers back home, and on April 11 one of them wrote to the *Onondaga Standard*, "But fate had destined that the 185th should lose another of its officers before the end. Lieut. Hiram Clark, of Co. G. was struck by a shell from a gun of the enemy's and killed instantly, the shell passing through his body and afterwards taking off a foot of a member of the 198th Pennsylvania Vols. Lieut. C. was an excellent officer, a perfect gentleman, highly respected by all who knew him. . . . It was one of the last shells fired by the enemy that caused his untimely end. The shell, which did not explode, has been found and is now in Capt. Barber's possession, who intends to retain it."[321]

The 185th New York had participated in the siege of Petersburg and several skirmishes along the road to Appomattox. Another account of Clark's death reveals the random, haphazard nature of war. "Members of the 185th saw the 'white flag come out and was [sic] glad to see it.' First Lieutenant Hiram Clark of Marathon gathered his men and sang 'Hail Columbia.' As the men settled against a rail fence, a shell came over and killed Clark."[322]

Among other Union casualties on the last day of fighting was nineteen-year-old Pvt. William Montgomery of the 155th Pennsylvania, mortally wounded by an artillery round. In the Confederate cemetery at Appomattox the remains of eighteen Confederate soldiers, several from Virginia, Louisiana, Alabama, and Georgia and ten of them unknown, are buried along with one unknown Union soldier. These men died on April 8 or 9, some of the last soldiers to lose their lives on the battlefields of Virginia.

Grant and his staff were riding toward Sheridan about nine miles east of Appomattox Court House when Lt. Charles E. Pease of Meade's staff delivered Lee's latest request for a meeting. Pease also brought a note from Meade saying that he had authorized a cease-fire after reading Lee's message to Grant at Marshall's request. Grant read the brief note and then handed it to his chief of staff, Brig. Gen. John Rawlins, asking the officer to read it aloud. The moment was stunning, but a call for three cheers received only a weak answer.

"When the officer reached me I was still suffering with the sick headache; but the instant I saw the contents of the note I was cured," Grant recalled. "I wrote the following note in reply and hastened on:

April 9, 1865.

GENERAL R.E. LEE,
Commanding C.S. Armies.
Your note of this date is but this moment (11:50 A.M.) received, in consequence of my having passed from the Richmond and Lynchburg road to the Farmville and Lynchburg road. I am at this writing about four miles west of Walker's Church and will push forward to the front for the purpose of meeting you. Notice

sent to me on this road where you wish the interview to take place will meet me.

U.S. Grant,

Lieutenant-General.[323]

Aware that Gordon was still fighting to his front, Lee met Longstreet and requested that an officer ride to Gordon with a message that he should also request a cease-fire. Captain Robert M. Sims tied a fringed white dishtowel to his sword, rode to Gordon, and then proceeded toward the Union lines. Lee confided in Longstreet that he was concerned about harsher surrender terms than Grant had offered previously at Farmville. The Union commander's last letter had said nothing of terms.

Longstreet tried to assure Lee that he had known Grant before the war and that his old friend would offer terms as magnanimous as Lee would offer if the roles were reversed. Still, Lee felt compelled to dash off another note to Grant:

9th April 1865

General,

I ask a suspension of hostilities pending the adjustment of the terms of the surrender of this army, in the interview requested in my former communication today.

Very respectfully,
Your obt. servt.,

Lt. Gen. U.S. Grant

R.E. Lee

Comdg. U.S. Army. Genl.[324]

Lee and his small entourage rested near the Appomattox River within sight of the town of Appomattox Court House. The old general had been in the saddle for several hours, and he was exhausted. Fence rails were thrown on the ground beneath an apple tree, and blankets were spread across them. Lee lay down and went to sleep.

When Captain Sims reached the Union lines, he asked to be conducted to General Ord. Instead, he was guided to Custer's command. Some accounts state that Custer sent two staff officers back with Sims to demand Gordon's surrender; however, Gordon made no mention of a preliminary surrender demand in his memoirs. He did, however, vividly remember his ensuing encounter with Custer himself. Gordon wrote:

> [Sims] returned to me accompanied by an officer of striking picturesque appearance. This Union officer was slender and graceful, and a superb rider. He wore his hair very long, falling almost to his shoulders . . . he galloped to where I was sitting on my horse and, with faultless grace and courtesy, saluted me with his sabre and said:
>
> "I am General Custer and bear a message to you from General Sheridan. The general desires me to present to you his compliments, and to demand the immediate and unconditional surrender of all troops under your command." I replied: "You will please, general, return my compliments to General Sheridan, and say to him that I shall not surrender my command."
>
> "He directs me to say to you, general, if there is any hesitation about your surrender, that he has you surrounded and can annihilate your command in an hour."[325]

Gordon reminded Custer that Lee and Grant were communicating with one another and that if Sheridan chose to continue fighting in the presence of a flag of truce, the responsibility for further bloodshed rested with the Union forces. To help spread the word of the tenuous truce, Gordon sent three more white flags into the Federal lines. He also recalled that Sheridan came riding forward and only Gordon's personal intervention prevented Sheridan from being shot from his horse by a "weak-minded but strong-hearted" Confederate private.

In a second heated exchange Gordon produced the letter he had received from Lee and convinced Sheridan to agree to a cessation of hostilities. "Our respective staff officers were despatched to inaugurate this temporary armistice, and Sheridan and I dismounted and sat together on the ground," said Gordon.

One of Gordon's brigades far to the left had not been notified, and firing was heard in the distance. Gordon wrote later that he had no staff officer at hand to deliver another cease-fire message. Sheridan offered to lend Lt. Vanderbilt Allen of his own staff for the purpose. Gordon wrote no more on the topic, but Sheridan recalled that a general named Geary confronted Allen, ignored his message, and took Allen prisoner.

The officer was actually Brig. Gen. Martin Gary, who had instructed the young Capt. Clement Sulivane to blow Mayo's Bridge in Richmond to hell and fought Custer's cavalry at Appomattox Station a day earlier. Sheridan concluded that Gary blustered to Allen, "'I do not care for white flags: South Carolinians never surrender.' By this time Merritt's patience being exhausted, he ordered an attack, and this in short order put an end to General Geary's [sic] 'last ditch' absurdity, and extricated Allen from his predicament."[326]

Gordon was frank in his appraisal of Sheridan's demeanor, writing, "Truth demands that I say of General Sheridan that his style of conversation and general bearing, while never discourteous, were far less agreeable and pleasing than those of any other officer of the Union army whom it was my fortune to meet."[327]

Meanwhile, Custer was not satisfied and apparently before Sheridan arrived he requested to be taken to Longstreet, who was waiting for Lee to return from his ride toward Humphreys's lines. The weary senior Confederate corps commander was in no mood to receive the brazen Custer in a breach of military protocol. Longstreet remembered:

> Down they came in a fast gallop, General Custer's flaxen locks flowing over his shoulders, and in brusk, excited manner, he said, "In the name of General Sheridan I demand the unconditional surrender of this army."
>
> He was reminded that I was not the commander of the army, that he was within the lines of the enemy and without authority, addressing a superior officer, and in disrespect to General Grant as well as myself; that if I was the commander of the army I would not receive the message of General Sheridan. He then became more moderate, saying it would be a pity to have more blood upon that field. Then I suggested that the truce be respected, and said, "As you are now more reasonable, I will say that General Lee has gone to meet General Grant, and it is for him to determine the future of the armies."[328]

Lieutenant General James Longstreet commanded I Corps, Army of Northern Virginia for much of the Civil War. He was Robert E. Lee's senior corps commander, and Lee's affection for Longstreet was readily apparent, referring to the corps commander as his "Old War Horse." Due to Longstreet's association with the Republican Party and acceptance of government appointments after the war, he became the target of Lost Cause advocates who blamed him for the defeat at Gettysburg and ultimately for the downfall of the Confederacy. *Library of Congress*

Longstreet may have mellowed in his later years or believed that he should downplay the incident. Others recall that Longstreet erupted in response to Custer's demands. When Custer admonished that Longstreet would be responsible for any ensuing bloodshed, Longstreet dismissed the cavalryman with a wave of his hand and thundered, "Go ahead and have all the bloodshed you want."[329]

His staff officers hovering around him, Lee had slept under the apple tree for about an hour when a rider approached. Lieutenant Colonel Orville E. Babcock and his orderly, Capt. William M. Dunn, brought Grant's assent to meet at a place of Lee's choosing. "General Lee got up and talked with Babcock for a little while," recalled Marshall, "and at last he called me and told me to get ready to go with him."[330]

Lee asked Colonel Walter Taylor, another of his close subordinates, to accompany him to Appomattox Court House to assist with arrangements for the meeting with Grant. Taylor could not come to terms with the task that lay ahead and declined. Years later, the sting of disappointment, not only in the surrender of the Army of Northern Virginia but also in his own conduct, distressed Taylor, who wrote in his 1877 memoirs, "I shrank from this interview, and while I could not then, and cannot now, justify my conduct, I availed myself of the excuse of having taken the two rides through the extent of our lines and to those of the enemy . . . and did not accompany my chief in this trying ordeal."[331]

Somewhat disheveled, Marshall borrowed a sword, gauntlets, and clean shirt collar from his friend, Col. Henry Young, the army's judge advocate general, and refreshed himself. Then, the party of five, General Lee resplendent with his deep crimson sash visible from a distance, Marshall and his aide Pvt. Joshua O. Johns, Babcock, and Dunn, set out for the town.

Lee ordered Marshall to ride ahead and find a place that was suitable for the meeting with Grant. The first person Marshall encountered was Wilmer McLean, a merchant and trader who speculated in sugar and supplied the scarce commodity to the Confederate military. The fifty-one-year-old McLean was a veteran of the Virginia militia and a native of Alexandria, Virginia. He married in 1853 and settled in the town of Manassas, a few miles outside Washington, DC.

The opening battle of the Civil War, known as Bull Run or Manassas, occurred on July 21, 1861, and McLean's home was commandeered as General Beauregard's headquarters. A witness to the fighting, McLean was shaken by the experience. In the spring of 1863, about the time that his wife, Virginia, gave birth to their second daughter (the first was six years old), McLean sold his Manassas home and moved his family 120 miles south, to a two-story brick home on the Richmond-Lynchburg Stage Road near the small town of Appomattox Court House.

Marshall hailed McLean and asked for help locating an appropriate place where Lee and Grant might confer. "He took me into a house that was all dilapidated and that had no furniture in it," Marshall wrote. "I told him it wouldn't do. Then he said, 'Maybe my house will do!' He lived in a very comfortable house, and I told him I thought that would suit."[332]

Marshall sent Johns to bring Lee and the others to the house. Babcock dispatched Captain Dunn to direct Grant to the proper place. Soon, Lee and Babcock joined Marshall in the parlor and engaged in pleasant conversation as they waited for Grant.

"General Grant arrived about 1 o'clock in the afternoon," said Sheridan. "Ord and I, dismounted, meeting him at the edge of the town, or crossroads, for it was little more. He remaining mounted, spoke first to me, saying simply, 'How are you, Sheridan?' I assured him with thanks that I was 'first-rate,' when, pointing toward the village, he asked, 'Is General Lee up there?' and I replied, 'There is his army down in that valley, and he himself is over at that house . . . waiting to surrender to you.' The General then said, 'Come, let us go over,' this last remark being addressed to both Ord and me."[333]

After waiting a half hour, Marshall heard horses outside the McLean House. In a moment, Grant entered the front door. Sheridan, Ord, and several staff officers remained outside. Lee came to his feet, and the two commanders shook hands. Grant hardly cut the figure of the conqueror.

"When I left the camp that morning I had not expected so soon the result that was then taking place, and consequently was in rough garb," Grant remembered. "I was without a sword, as I usually was when on horseback on the field, and wore a soldier's blouse for a coat, with the shoulder straps of my rank to indicate to the army who I was."[334]

In his memoirs, Grant noted with a tinge of pride that he had known Lee in the "old army" and had "served with him in the Mexican War." However, Grant "did not suppose, owing to the difference in our age and rank, that he would remember me; while I would more naturally remember him distinctly, because he was the chief of staff of General Scott in the Mexican War."[335] On the date of their historic meeting, Lee was fifty-eight years old. Grant was nearing his forty-third birthday.

Grant took a seat near the center of the room in an old armchair that looked more like it belonged in an office than a parlor, and Lee faced Grant, sitting near the front window in an armchair with a cane back and seat, next to a small marble-topped table. Colonel Marshall stood at Lee's left, his arm resting on the fireplace mantel. In a moment, Grant motioned to Babcock to bring the other Union officers inside.

"Colonel Babcock came to the front door, and, making a motion with his hat toward the sitting-room, said: 'The general says come in,'" remembered Horace Porter. "It was then about half-past one on Sunday, the 9th of April. . . . We walked in softly, and ranged ourselves quietly about the sides of the room, very much as people enter a sick-chamber when they expect to find the patient dangerously ill. Some found seats on the sofa standing against the wall between the two doors and on the few plain chairs which constituted the furniture, but most of the party stood."[336]

The meeting lasted ninety minutes, and during that time it is likely that a number of Union officers, including Capt. Robert Todd Lincoln, entered and exited the parlor, gathering on the colonnaded porch or in the yard. General Custer was present but did not enter the room.

Grant admitted that he was a bundle of conflicting emotions. "What General Lee's feelings were I do not know," he mused. "As he was a man of much dignity, with an impassible face, it was impossible to say whether he felt inwardly glad that the end had finally come, or felt sad over the result, and was too manly to show it. Whatever his feelings, they were entirely concealed from my observation; but my own feelings, which had been quite jubilant on the receipt of his letter, were sad and depressed. I felt like anything rather than rejoicing at the downfall of a foe who had fought so long and valiantly, and had suffered so much for a cause, though that cause was, I believe, one of the worst for which a people ever fought, and one for which there was the least excuse."[337]

Grant was somewhat uneasy and began the conversation with remarks about their chance meeting in Mexico. Lee was polite, and Porter heard him comment that he knew the two had met but that Lee could not remember what Grant looked like saying, "I could never recall a single feature."[338] Marshall later wrote that Lee recognized Grant immediately when the two met face to face.

The discussion was cordial and even began to drift a bit. After nearly half an hour, it was left to Lee to return to the topic at hand. He remarked, "I suppose, General Grant, that the object of our present meeting is fully understood,"[339] and then said, "I have come to meet with you in accordance with my letter to you this morning, to treat about the surrender of my army, and I think the best way would be for you to put your terms in writing."[340]

Grant replied, "Yes. I believe it will."[341]

Lieutenant Colonel Ely S. Parker, an attorney and Native American of the Seneca tribe, born Hasanoanda, who joined Grant as his adjutant during the Chattanooga campaign in the autumn of 1863, brought forward a small oval table. Grant set his order book on it and wrote the terms in pencil. He reviewed the draft with Parker, crossing out the word "their," which had been repeated.

Grant then turned with the order book in his right hand and stretched to offer the book to Lee. Porter was standing between the generals and took the book from his commander, passing it to the Confederate general. Lee moved a few books and a pair of brass candlesticks out of the way, wiped his glasses, placed the order book on the marble table, and began to read. The word "exchanged" had been omitted in the draft, and Lee asked permission to insert it in the appropriate place. He searched his coat for a pencil, borrowed one from Porter, and began to twirl it between his fingers and tap it on the marble tabletop. Lee returned the pencil at the end of the meeting, and Porter treasured the memento for the rest of his life.[342]

As he reviewed the terms, Lee came across the section that stated only public property was to be surrendered. Officers were allowed to retain their side arms and any personal baggage. He remarked, "That will have a very happy effect."[343]

Lee then asked for one concession, saying, "General, our cavalry-men furnish their own horses; they are not Government horses, some of them may be, but of course you will find them out any property that is public property, you will ascertain that, but it is nearly all private property, and these men will want to plough ground and plant corn."[344]

Grant replied that as the terms were written such an allow-ance was not possible. Then, the victor's compassion for the defeated prompted a generous allowance. He remembered, "I then said to him that I thought this would be about the last battle of the war—I sincerely hoped so; and I said further I took it that most of the men in the ranks were small farmers. The whole country had been so raided by the two armies that it was doubtful whether they would be able to put in a crop to carry themselves and their families through the next winter without the aid of the horses

Colonel Horace Porter served as an aide and personal secretary to Gen. Ulysses S. Grant both during and after the Civil War. He also served on the staff of Gen. William T. Sherman during Sherman's tenure as Commanding General of the United States Army. After the war, Porter became a railroad executive and US ambassador to France. His memoir of the Civil War, *Campaigning with Grant*, provides a detailed description of the surrender discussion in the parlor of the McLean House at Appomattox. *Library of Congress*

they were then riding. The United States did not want them and I would, therefore, instruct the officers I left behind to receive the paroles of his troops to let every man of the Confederate army who claimed to own a horse or mule take the animal to his home. Lee remarked again that this would have a happy effect."[345]

Grant then summoned Col. Theodore S. Bowers, his secretary and a former newspaper editor from Illinois, to copy the final terms in ink. Bowers was too nervous to comply. "He turned the matter over to Colonel Parker, whose handwriting presented a better appearance than that of any one else on the staff," said Porter.[346]

Parker carried the book and the oval table to the back of the room. He dipped his pen in Wilmer McLean's stoneware inkstand and found the ink dried and unusable. Marshall came forward and offered his own. "I had a screw boxwood inkstand that I always carried with me in a little satchel that I had at my side," Marshall recalled, "and I gave that to Colonel Parker, and he copied General Grant's letter with the aid of my inkstand and my pen."[347]

Sheridan and Brig. Gen. Rufus Ingalls, the supply chief whose bustling center at City Point had delivered the overwhelming industrial capacity of the Union to the battlefield, were seated on the small sofa against the wall. Marshall walked over and sat on the sofa's arm. Sheridan commented, "This is very pretty country," and Marshall replied, "General, I haven't seen it by daylight. All my observations have been made by night and I haven't seen the country at all myself."[348]

Sheridan laughed, and while their conversation continued Lee informed Grant that the Confederates held a thousand or more Union soldiers prisoner and that there was nothing to eat, either for the prisoners or for the starving men of the Army of Northern Virginia. Grant asked Sheridan about the availability of rations from his command and assured Lee that twenty-five thousand would be ordered up.

Parker finished his copy of the surrender terms, and the two pages read:

APPOMATTOX COURT-HOUSE, VA., APRIL 9, 1865.

GENERAL R.E. LEE, Commanding C.S.A.
GENERAL: In accordance with the substance of my letter to you of the 8th inst., I propose to receive the surrender of the Army of Northern Virginia on the following terms, to wit: Rolls of all the officers and men to be made in duplicate, one copy

to be given to an officer to be designated by me, the other to be retained by such officer or officers as you may designate. The officers to give their individual paroles not to take up arms against the Government of the United States until properly [exchanged], and each company or regimental commander to sign a like parole for the men of their commands. The arms, artillery, and public property to be parked and stacked and turned over to the officers appointed by me to receive them. This will not embrace the side-arms of the officers, nor their private horses or baggage. This done, each officer and man will be allowed to return to his home, not to be disturbed by the United States authorities so long as they observe their paroles and the laws in force where they may reside.

Very respectfully,
U.S. GRANT,
Lieutenant-general.[349]

Marshall drafted a letter of acceptance. "I began it in the usual way," the colonel remembered, "'I have the honor to acknowledge the receipt of your letter of such a date,' and then went on to say the terms were satisfactory. I took the letter over to General Lee, and he read it and said: 'Don't say, "I have the honor to acknowledge the receipt of your letter of such a date"; he is here; just say, "I accept these terms." I then wrote: –

HEADQUARTERS OF THE ARMY OF NORTHERN VIRGINIA

April 9, 1865
I received your letter of this date containing the terms of the surrender of the Army of Northern Virginia proposed by you. As they are substantially the same as those expressed in your letter of the 8th instant, they are accepted. I will proceed to designate the proper officers to carry the stipulations into effect.

"Then General Grant signed his letter, and I turned over my letter to General Lee and he signed it. Parker handed me General Grant's letter, and I handed him General Lee's reply, and the surrender was accomplished. There was no theatrical display about it. It was in itself perhaps the greatest tragedy that ever occurred in the history of the world, but it was the simplest, plainest, and most thoroughly devoid of any attempt at effect, that you can imagine."[350]

When the formalities were concluded, the commanding generals again shook hands. Grant introduced Lee to the Union officers present. He shook hands with those who were close and bowed slightly to those distant around the parlor. Among the Union officers was Brig. Gen. Seth Williams, the erstwhile courier, who had also served as Lee's adjutant at West Point when he was the superintendent there in the early 1850s.

"After that," said Marshall, "a general conversation took place of a most agreeable character. I cannot describe it. I cannot give you any idea of the kindness, and generosity, and magnanimity of those men. When I think of it, it brings tears to my eyes."[351]

In his book *An Aide-de-Camp of Lee*, Marshall footnoted an intriguing observation as the meeting concluded. Grant was, no doubt, self conscious about his appearance. He asked Lee to excuse the fact that he was without his sword and not in his best uniform. Marshall wrote, "This little conversation is of peculiar interest because Lee first met Grant when he was a captain [*sic*] on General Scott's staff in the Mexican War, and Grant was a lieutenant of infantry. General Scott had issued an order that officers coming to headquarters were to do so in full dress. Grant had been making a reconnaissance and came to headquarters to report the result in his field dress, plentifully covered with the dust of Mexico, evidently thinking in 1847, as he did in 1865, that time was of more importance than appearance. Lee had to tell Grant to go back to his tent and return in full dress. One wonders whether, when apologizing to Lee for his informal costume, Grant remembered what had happened eighteen years before."[352]

At about 3:00 p.m., Lee left the room, walked across the porch, and stood on the lowest step while Traveller was bridled. Perhaps without much thought, he pounded his right fist into his left hand three times and looked down the valley toward his army. By the time Lee mounted his horse, Grant had made his way to the porch. He raised his hat in salute, and Lee returned the same gesture. The officers present followed Grant's lead, and Lee acknowledged their salutes as well.

As so often occurs in the wake of momentous events, myths and misconceptions emanated from the surrender meeting at the McLean House. One of these involved Lee supposedly relinquishing his handsome sword, with its scabbard of gold and leather, which had been

The fine brick home of merchant Wilmer McLean was the setting for the meeting between Gens. Ulysses S. Grant and Robert E. Lee on Palm Sunday, April 9, 1865, as the Confederate Army of Northern Virginia surrendered to the overwhelming strength and resources of three Union armies arrayed against it. Grant's terms were generous. At the conclusion of the proceedings, Union officers paid McLean for many of the items in the parlor where the meeting had taken place, including candlesticks, an inkwell, and the tables and chairs used by the commanders. *Library of Congress*

presented to him by an admiring group of English ladies. The story goes that Lee handed his sword to Grant, who then handed it back.

Marshall called the story "absurd," and Grant wrote in his memoirs, "The much talked of surrendering of Lee's sword and my handing it back, this and much more that has been said about it is the purest romance. The word sword or side arms was not mentioned by either of us until I wrote it in the terms."[353]

A second and probably more enduring myth since the scene was immortalized in a popular postwar Kurz and Allison print is that Lee met Grant under an apple tree and the surrender took place there. This notion probably arose from Lee having spent part of the morning resting under the apple tree where Colonel Babcock found him. Grant alluded to Babcock's encounter with Lee and made short shrift of the tale, writing, "Wars produce many stories of fiction, some of which are told until they are believed to be true. . . . The story had no other foundation than that. Like many other stories, it would be very good if it was only true."[354]

In their zeal following the surrender at the McLean House, souvenir hunters hacked the apple tree where Lee rested to pieces, along with several others.

News of the surrender spread rapidly, and Union artillery began firing in celebration. Grant was annoyed and sent an order for the guns to cease. He said, "The war is over; the rebels are our countrymen again; and the best sign of rejoicing after the victory will be to abstain from all demonstrations in the field."[355]

Shortly after Lee's departure, Grant dashed off the news of his victory in a message to Stanton. It was a masterpiece of brevity and understatement.

HEADQUARTERS APPOMATTOX C.H., VA.,
April 9th,
1865, 4:30 p.m.

HON. E.M. STANTON, Secretary of War, Washington.
General Lee surrendered the Army of Northern Virginia this afternoon on terms proposed by myself. The accompanying additional correspondence will show the conditions fully.

U.S. GRANT,
Lieut.—General.[356]

Grant was concerned about the continuing procurement of supplies for the Union armies in Virginia and decided to travel to Washington to put a stop to the "useless outlay of money."[357] He spent the night at Appomattox and then traveled with a few members of his staff to Burkesville Station. Railroad track had just been laid from Burkesville Station to City Point, and on the soft ground the train slipped from the track several times, resulting in an uncomfortable journey of nearly two days. From City Point, Grant took a dispatch boat to Washington. He noted that by April 14, he had substantially completed a significant load of administrative duties.

Before he left Appomattox, Grant sought a final meeting with Lee on the morning of April 10. Grant rode toward Lee's camp with a bugler and a staff officer carrying a white flag. "Lee soon mounted his horse, seeing who it was, and met me," Grant reflected. "We had there between the lines, sitting on horseback, a very pleasant conversation of over half an hour."[358]

During the conversation, Lee expressed concerns that the Confederacy encompassed a large area of land and that Union armies might be required to continue their military operations for some time before the war finally ended. Grant proposed that Lee exert his influence with the Confederate military and the people of the South to convince the Rebel armies to capitulate. Lee replied that he could not take such a step without consulting President Davis, and Grant did not pursue the topic further. Meanwhile, officers of both sides asked permission to cross into the other's lines to seek out old army friends.

"They went over," Grant said, "had a very pleasant time with their old friends, and brought some of them back with them when they returned . . . the officers of both armies came in great numbers, and seemed to enjoy the meeting as much as though they were friends separated for a long time while fighting battles under the same flag."[359]

For Abraham Lincoln, the long day's journey aboard the *River Queen* was monotonous, and the president occupied his time reading aloud from Shakespeare, avoiding political discussions with Senator Sumner, whose Radical Republican agenda was well known. Of particular interest was Lincoln's selection of a passage from *Macbeth*, the story of the general tormented by guilt after murdering King Duncan and usurping the throne of Scotland.

The Marquis de Chambrun remembered that the haunting lines caused Lincoln to pause. The president began to "explain to us how true a description of the murderer that one was," said the Marquis.

"When, the dark deed achieved, its tortured perpetrator came to envy the sleep of his victim; and he read over again the same scene."[360]

The *River Queen* arrived in Washington, DC, at sundown. The streets were filled with people. Bonfires glowed throughout the city. Lincoln learned of the surrender of the Army of Northern Virginia and visited injured Secretary of State Seward, stretching out on the secretary's bed to briefly converse about the future and the defeat of the remaining Confederate armies. As Seward fell asleep, Lincoln departed.

Crowds gathered around the White House and clamored for the president to make an appearance. A wild cheer went up as Tad came to a second-story window and brandished a Confederate flag. Lincoln finally appeared and, expecting a more formal celebration to follow the next day, briefly offered, "I shall have nothing to say if you dribble it all out of me before." He turned to the bandleader and asked for a rendition of *Dixie*, saying that it was "one of the best tunes I ever heard . . . a lawful prize . . . we fairly captured it."[361]

For Robert E. Lee, the hours following the meeting with Grant were quite different. As he rode back to his camp, the general was initially greeted with cheers. However, in a few moments these drifted away on the afternoon breeze. The soldiers broke ranks and surged toward him, some shouting that they loved him and would follow him anywhere he wished the army to go. Others asked the hardest question. Had the army really surrendered? They pressed toward their beloved commander, their eyes brimming with tears.

For just a moment, the old general came to a halt, and he said, "Men, we have fought the war together, and I have done the best I could for you. You will all be paroled and go to your homes until exchanged."[362] As he told the soldiers of their fate, Lee remained unsure of his own.

Longstreet remembered Lee's striking image. "Those that could find voice said good-by, those who could not speak, and were near, pressed their hands gently over the sides of Traveller," he wrote. "He rode with his hat off, and had sufficient control to fix his eyes on a line between the ears of Traveller and look neither to right nor left until he reached a large white-oak tree, where he dismounted to make his last headquarters."[363]

That night, Lee and several of his officers sat together near his tent, a bright fire burning. During the discussion, Lee asked Colonel Marshall to prepare a farewell order to the troops. Marshall approached the task with hesitation. In the early morning rain of April 10, he struggled to write, but the comings and goings of men and constant interruptions kept him from concentrating. When Lee discovered at 10:00 a.m. that the order had not been written, he sequestered Marshall in an ambulance with a guard posted.

Shortly, Marshall produced a draft. Lee read, deleting a paragraph that he believed might contribute to continuing ill will between North and South and making a couple of minor changes, and handed the draft back to Marshall. It was rewritten, handed to the adjutant general's office to be copied in ink, and then signed by Lee for distribution. It read:

Hd. Qrs. Army of N. Va.
April 10, 1865

General Orders
No. 9

After four years of arduous service marked by unsurpassed courage and fortitude, the Army of Northern Virginia has been compelled to yield to overwhelming numbers and resources.

I need not tell the brave survivors of so many hard fought battles, who have remained steadfast to the last, that I have consented to this result from no distrust of them; but feeling that valor and devotion could accomplish nothing that could compensate for the loss that must have attended the continuance of the contest, I determined to avoid the useless sacrifice of those whose past services have endeared them to their countrymen.

By the terms of the agreement, officers and men can return to their homes and remain until exchanged. You will take with you the satisfaction that proceeds from the consciousness of duty faithfully performed; and I earnestly pray that a Merciful God will extend to you His blessing and protection.

With an unceasing admiration of your constancy and devotion to your country, and a grateful remembrance of your kind and generous consideration for myself, I bid you all an affectionate farewell.

R.E. Lee
Genl.[364]

Responsibility for feeding, disarming, and paroling the surrendered soldiers was assigned to Union generals Gibbon, Griffin, and Merritt, and Confederate generals Longstreet, Gordon, and Pendleton. Through the day on April 10 and 11, a field printing press belonging to the Army of the Potomac turned out parole forms. More than twenty-eight thousand officers and men would receive them.

Then, they would make their way home. Some walked several hundred miles, uncertain what they would find when they got there. Lee returned to Richmond and the house at 707 East Franklin Street, arriving on April 15. Along the way, he stopped to visit his brother, Charles Carter Lee, who lived along the route at a farm named Windsor. The general did not wish to inconvenience his brother and pitched his tent for the last time along the roadside.

Colonel Taylor concluded, "Thus terminated the career of the Army of Northern Virginia—an army that was never vanquished; but that, in obedience to the orders of its trusted commander, who was himself yielding obedience to the dictates of a pure and lofty sense of duty to his men and those dependent on them, laid down its arms, and furled the standards never lowered in defeat."[365]

On April 26, 1865, Gen. Joseph Johnston surrendered to Gen. William T. Sherman at Bennett Place, near Durham, North Carolina. In May, Confederate commands in Mississippi, Alabama, Florida, Georgia, and in the Trans-Mississippi region surrendered. On June 23, Cherokee soldiers under their general, Stand Watie, capitulated in Oklahoma.

Finally, in November the Confederate naval raider CSS *Shenandoah*, after circumnavigating the globe and wreaking havoc among the Union merchant and whaling fleets, sailed into the harbor of Liverpool, England, the crew surrendering to British authorities.

With the end of the Civil War, a nation once torn in two set off on the long road to Reconstruction and reconciliation. There were indeed other surrenders that brought the day of peace; however, the end of the Army of Northern Virginia, accomplished at Appomattox, extinguished the heart and laid to rest the soul of the Southern Confederacy.

EPILOGUE

The Army of Northern Virginia executed its last march on the cold, overcast morning of April 12, 1865. Before his departure for Washington, Grant directed that a surrender ceremony should be arranged. It was not to be an elaborate affair; however, he believed that one should take place rather than allowing the paroled Confederate soldiers to stack arms and furl their colors in their camps and walk away.

Brigadier General Joshua Lawrence Chamberlain and troops of the V Corps were given the honor of receiving the surrender. Chamberlain assembled the soldiers along the Richmond-Lynchburg Stage Road as it passed through the town of Appomattox Court House. The men were in place by 9:00 a.m. There were no martial music, celebratory discharges of weapons, or shouts of joy. The victors awaited the vanquished in the quiet of the morning. Chamberlain looked down the road toward the Confederate camp, both reticent and somewhat anxious.

"And now they move," he wrote later. "The dusky swarms forge forward into gray columns of march. On they come with the old swing route step and swaying battle flags. . . . Before us in proud humiliation stood the embodiment of manhood . . . with eyes looking level into ours, waking memories that bound us together as no other bond;—was not such manhood to be welcomed back into a Union so tested and assured?"[366]

Gordon rode at the front of the Army of Northern Virginia, his head bowed. Then, on Chamberlain's order, a bugle sounded and the Federal soldiers lining the road snapped from order arms to carry. Rifles went to shoulders, and Gordon recognized the unmistakable clack-clack of the salute.

Chamberlain remembered that Gordon wheeled superbly "making with himself and his horse one uplifted figure, with profound salutation as he drops the point of his sword to the boot toe; then facing to his own command, gives word for his successive brigades to pass us with the same position of the manual; —honor answering honor. On our part not a sound of trumpet more, nor roll of drum; not a cheer, nor word nor whisper of vainglorying, nor motion of man standing again at the order, but an awed stillness rather, and breath-holding, as if it were the passing of the dead!"[367]

For Gordon, the day had begun with profound depression, but he recalled nearly forty years later that Chamberlain was "one of the knightliest soldiers of the Federal army," whose moving gesture contributed mightily to the work of reconciliation. He added, "As my men marched in front of them, the veterans in blue gave a soldierly salute to those vanquished heroes—a token of respect from Americans to Americans, a final and fitting tribute from Northern to Southern chivalry."[368]

The ceremony continued for hours, until the last Confederate rifle and battle flag had been laid down sometime after 4:00 p.m. When it was over, Chamberlain's men counted hundreds of rifles and at least a hundred battle flags. Both sides had lost heavily in the war, and among those who surrendered with the remnants of the Army of Northern Virginia were approximately 50 men of the original 1,196 of the 12th Alabama Infantry. The venerable Stonewall Brigade numbered fewer than two hundred soldiers.

"After being convinced that General Lee had really surrendered, I said to the boys who were with me, 'Well, it's all over now,' and could not refrain from crying like a child," wrote 1st Lt. Nathan Bachman of the 63rd Tennessee Infantry. "It would be hard for me to write anything that would adequately describe my feelings, for up to the very moment that this news came my faith in General Lee's being able to defeat Grant with all odds against him was firm and unshaken. Within an hour or less time, perhaps, the bluecoats were mixing among us, dividing rations with our starving boys and jollying us for being so hard to 'hem in.' As soon as parole papers could be prepared we began our homeward journey."[369]

As the Southern soldiers headed to homes both close to the surrender scene and hundreds of miles away, Meade took field command of the Army of the Potomac and the Army of the James and, on Grant's instructions, retired temporarily to Burkesville Station before heading to the nation's capital. After Johnston's surrender in North Carolina, Sherman's triumphant troops moved north as well. On May 23 and 24, 1865, a grand review of the victorious armies took place in Washington, DC. The soldiers marched down Pennsylvania Avenue, their ranks stretching from the Capitol to the White House.

After the war, Joshua Lawrence Chamberlain returned to Maine and won election to four one-year terms as governor of the state. He resumed his academic career and served as president of Bowdoin College for twelve years. In 1893, he received the Medal of Honor for his heroism at Little Round Top during the Battle of Gettysburg, thirty years after the action took place. With the outbreak of the Spanish-American War in 1898, he volunteered for service at the age of seventy and was rejected.

Chamberlain suffered from his war wounds for the rest of his life, enduring periodic infections and high fevers. Nevertheless, he was a prolific writer and speaker. He attended reunions of his old comrades and often returned to Gettysburg, the last time in the spring of 1913 during planning for the fiftieth anniversary of the battle. He died on February 24, 1914, at the age of eighty-five, one of the most celebrated heroes of the Civil War.

Ulysses S. Grant and his wife, Julia, reunited in Washington, DC, and the two wanted to travel to Burlington, New Jersey, to visit their children who were attending school there. President and Mrs. Lincoln extended an invitation to the Grants to join them at Ford's Theater on the night of April 14, to enjoy the production of *Our American Cousin* starring British actress Laura Keane. Grant recalled that he hoped to finish his work in Washington that day and wrote sadly, "I did get through and started by the evening train on the 14th, sending Mr. Lincoln word, of course, that I would not be at the theatre."[370]

That night, the sixteenth President of the United States, perhaps the most beloved in American history, was fatally shot by assassin John Wilkes Booth. Lincoln lingered until 7:22 the following morning. While Grant was traveling through Philadelphia en route to New Jersey, he received the news of the president's death.

For a short time after the Civil War, Grant served controversially as secretary of war in the administration of President Andrew Johnson. In 1868, he was elected to the first of two terms as President of the United States. Although Grant was not implicated in any wrongdoing, his administration was wracked with corruption and plagued by scandal.

At the conclusion of his second term as president, Grant embarked on a two-year world tour. He was hailed as a hero and dined with heads of state, but misfortune followed. In 1884, due to dealings with an unscrupulous investment banker, he lost more than one hundred thousand dollars. He borrowed from tycoon William Henry Vanderbilt and lost more money. To repay Vanderbilt, he sold many of his personal mementos from the Civil War.

Grant struggled financially, and in the spring of 1885 Congress reinstated the military pension that he had given up when elected president. To supplement his income he wrote articles on the war for the *Century Magazine,* earning five hundred dollars apiece for them.

Grant, meanwhile, learned that he was suffering from throat cancer and became determined to write his two-volume autobiography, *Personal Memoirs of U.S. Grant,* and to complete the project to ensure his family's financial future. He worked steadily, both at home in New York City and on the porch of a cabin at Mount McGregor, near Saratoga, New York, finishing a few days before he died on July 23, 1885, at the age of sixty-three.

A quarter of a million people paid their respects to Grant during the two days preceding his funeral, and thousands of veterans attended the services. Among the pallbearers were Union generals William T. Sherman and Phil Sheridan, Admiral David Dixon Porter, and Confederate generals Simon Bolivar Buckner and Joseph E. Johnston. He and his wife, who died in 1902, are entombed at the General Grant National Memorial in Upper Manhattan. The busts of five generals—William T. Sherman, Phil Sheridan, E. O. C. Ord, James McPherson, and George Thomas—keep vigil within the tomb.

The legacy of Gen. William T. Sherman is that of a brutal proponent of total war. He did understand that victory would only be achieved when the South's capacity to wage war was crippled sufficiently. Sherman was sharply criticized for the generous surrender terms he offered to Johnston in North Carolina and devoted much of his energy to defending his perspective on the political and military situation at the time the terms were offered.

Sherman served as commanding general of the United States Army from 1869 to 1883, fought Indians, refused to run for president, wrote his memoirs, remained in contact with veterans' organizations, and was known for his financial assistance to old soldiers who had served under him. He retired from the army in 1884 and died in New York City at the age of seventy-one on February 14, 1891. His old adversary Joseph Johnston attended the funeral, served as an honorary pallbearer, and refused to place his hat on his head as a bitterly cold wind swirled outside the church.

"If I were in [Sherman's] place and he were standing here in mine, he would not put on his hat," the eighty-two-year-old Johnston told a worried friend.[371] Johnston died of pneumonia a month later.

Major General George Meade held various commands including the Military Division of the Atlantic and governor of the Third Military District, encompassing Georgia, Alabama, and Florida, during Reconstruction. He remained on active duty until his death in Philadelphia at the age of fifty-six on November 6, 1872, from pneumonia and complications of old wounds suffered during the Seven Days Battles. The people of Philadelphia gave his widow, Margaretta, a house at 1836 Delancy Place. She died in 1886. They are buried side by side in the city's Laurel Hill Cemetery.

Two months after completing his two-volume memoirs, General Phil Sheridan suffered several serious heart attacks. He died in Massachusetts on August 5, 1888, at the age of fifty-seven. During Reconstruction, the general was appointed military governor of Texas and Louisiana; however, President Andrew Johnson considered his administration too severe and removed him from the post.

In August 1867, General Grant appointed Sheridan to command the Department of the Missouri with responsibility for forcing the Plains Indians onto reservations. Sheridan relentlessly pursued the Cheyenne, Comanche, Kiowa, Sioux, and other tribes and promoted the slaughter of the bison, the primary source of food for the Native Americans, to starve his adversaries.

After the devastating Chicago Fire of 1871, Sheridan supervised the military relief effort. He was also a proponent of the establishment of Yellowstone National Park and was the ninth president of the National Rifle Association.

In 1883, Sheridan followed Sherman as commanding general of the US Army. He rose to the rank of General of the Army of the

United States, equal to that of Sherman and Grant. He is buried in Arlington National Cemetery.

Sheridan's protégé, George Armstrong Custer, reverted to his permanent rank of captain after the war. By the mid-1870s, he had risen to lieutenant colonel of the 7th Cavalry Regiment. On June 25, 1876, Custer, along with his brothers, Capt. Thomas Custer and twenty-seven-year-old Boston Custer, was killed in the battle popularly known as Custer's Last Stand against the Lakota Sioux and Cheyenne in the valley of the Little Bighorn River in Montana. Also killed was Custer's eighteen-year-old nephew, Henry Armstrong Reed. George Custer was thirty-six.

Major General Andrew A. Humphreys, commander of the II Corps, Army of the Potomac, returned to the army's engineers after the war. In 1866, he became chief of engineers. Humphreys was a philosopher and scientist and a founder of the National Academy of Sciences. He died at the age of seventy-three on December 27, 1883, and is buried in the Congressional Cemetery in Washington, DC.

Major General Horatio Wright, commander of the VI Corps, Army of the Potomac, succeeded Humphreys as chief of engineers in 1879, and was known chiefly for contributions to the construction of the Brooklyn Bridge and the Washington Monument. Wright died on July 2, 1899, at the age of seventy-nine. He is buried in Arlington National Cemetery beneath an obelisk facing the Washington Monument placed by veterans of the VI Corps.

Major General Edward O. C. Ord, commander of the Army of the James, held several posts during the Reconstruction period, including command of the Army of Occupation in Richmond. He later accepted a position with the Mexican and Southern Railroad, owned by General Grant and railroad magnate Jay Gould. Ord contracted yellow fever while working in Mexico and died in Havana, Cuba, at the age of sixty-four on July 22, 1883. He is buried in Arlington National Cemetery a few yards from the door to the former home of Robert E. Lee.

Horace Porter continued to serve Grant after the war as an aide and personal secretary. He also served as aide-de-camp to Sherman. He resigned from the army in 1873 and became vice president of the Pullman Palace Car Company and later president of the West Shore Railroad. He served as US ambassador to France from 1897 to 1905 and paid for the repatriation of the body of Revolutionary War naval hero John Paul Jones to the United States. He received the Medal of Honor in 1902 for heroism during the Battle of Chickamauga and was prominent in the construction of the General Grant National Memorial. His book *Campaigning with Grant* is considered a classic of the Civil War. Porter died in New York City on May 29, 1921, at the age of eighty-four.

Colonel Ely S. Parker achieved the rank of brevet brigadier general. He served as President Grant's commissioner of Indian Affairs from 1869 to 1871 and was influential in the implementation of the president's policies toward Native Americans. Parker lost heavily in the collapse of the stock market during the Panic of 1873. He worked with the police department in New York City but lived his last years virtually destitute. He died in Fairfield, Connecticut, on August 31, 1895, aged about sixty-seven.

Seth Williams was appointed assistant adjutant general of the Military District of the Atlantic in 1866 and promoted to brevet major general of volunteers. Soon after his appointment, Williams became seriously ill. He died in Boston on March 23 at the age of forty-four. The cause was listed as brain inflammation.

In the autumn of 1867, Wilmer McLean and his family returned to the Manassas area of Northern Virginia, later moving to Alexandria. He commissioned a print and tried to sell the artwork to earn a living, worked for the Internal Revenue Service from 1873 to 1876, and died on June 5, 1882, at the age of sixty-eight. He is buried in Saint Paul's Episcopal Cemetery in Alexandria.

Financially ruined by the war, McLean could rightly claim that the conflict had indeed begun in his front yard and ended in his parlor. In another startling coincidence, McLean actually knew Brig. Gen. E. Porter Alexander, artillery chief of the I Corps, Army of Northern Virginia. Alexander wrote for the *Century Magazine*:

> When I first joined the Army of Northern Virginia in 1861, I found a connection of my family, Wilmer McLean, living on a fine farm through which ran Bull Run, with a nice farmhouse about opposite the center of our line of battle along the stream . . . The first hostile shot which I ever saw fired was aimed at this house, and about the third or fourth went through its kitchen, where our servants were cooking dinner for the headquarters staff.
>
> . . . I had not seen or heard of McLean for years, when, the day after the surrender I met him at Appomattox Court House, and asked with some surprise what he was doing there. He replied with much indignation: "What are you doing here? These

armies tore my place on Bull Run all to pieces, and kept running over it backward and forward till no man could live there, so I just sold out and came here . . . hoping I should never see a soldier again. And now, just look around you! Not a fence rail is left on the place, the last guns trampled down all my crops, and Lee surrendered to Grant in my house." McLean was so indignant that I felt bound to apologize for coming back, and to throw all the blame for it upon the gentlemen on the other side.[372]

McLean defaulted on his bank loans, and the house at Appomattox was sold at auction in November 1869. Purchased by John L. Pascoe, it appears that the house was rented to the family of Nathaniel Ragland, who bought the property for $1,250 on January 1, 1891. After Ragland's death, his widow sold the house to Capt. Myron Dunlap of New York for $10,000.

Dunlap and a group of investors intended to profit from the history of the McLean House and devised at least two plans to do so. These involved dismantling the structure and reassembling it at the 1893 World's Columbian Exposition in Chicago or in Washington, DC, and charging admission. The house was dismantled completely, but financial problems ended the speculative venture. The structure remained in pieces, neglected for half a century.

Immediately after the surrender, soldiers seeking souvenirs of the momentous occasion ravaged the house. Wilmer McLean could not stop the frenzy as General Ord insisted on paying forty dollars for the table Lee used and General Sheridan offered twenty dollars in gold for Grant's table. When McLean refused Sheridan's money, he apparently took the table anyway and threw the gold coin to the floor. Sheridan gave the table to George Custer as a gift to his wife. Another officer claimed the pair of brass candlesticks for ten dollars, while Sheridan's brother procured the stone inkstand.

The chairs the generals occupied were passed through a succession of owners and eventually were given to the Smithsonian Institution along with Grant's table. Lee's table remained in Ord's family until the general's death. It was sold to Chicago businessman C. F. Gunther and then donated to the Chicago Historical Society, now the Chicago History Museum.

A little girl's doll was found in the McLean parlor, and several junior officers tossed the toy around while referring to it as the "silent witness." Captain Moore of Sheridan's staff took the doll home to New York, and it remained in his family for years before finally being returned to Appomattox.

On April 10, 1940, Congress authorized the preservation of 970 acres at Appomattox Court House to create a national monument. Excavations uncovered the original foundation of the McLean House, but World War II interrupted the restoration of the town and reconstruction of the house in late 1941.

Work resumed in November 1947, and on April 9, 1949, the eighty-fourth anniversary of the surrender, the house was opened to the public. Major General Ulysses S. Grant III and Robert E. Lee IV, grandson and great grandson of the principal actors in the surrender drama, were present during dedication ceremonies attended by twenty thousand people on April 16, 1950.

Born in Ahrensburg, Westphalia, Germany, Reverend Charles Minnigerode became pastor of Saint Paul's Episcopal Church in Richmond, sometimes referred to as the "Cathedral of the Confederacy," in 1856. He served in that capacity for the next thirty-three years. In addition to Jefferson Davis, his congregation included numerous high-ranking Confederate soldiers and politicians. He presided over the funeral of Maj. Gen. Jeb Stuart in 1864, visited Davis in prison at Fortress Monroe, and addressed the mourners at the Confederate president's funeral.

Minnigerode is perhaps less known for his role in bringing a German custom to America. While staying at the Williamsburg, Virginia, home of St. George Tucker, an attorney and law professor at the College of William & Mary, he introduced the tradition of the Christmas tree, which was subsequently popularized throughout Tidewater Virginia and beyond. Minnigerode died in 1894 and was buried in Richmond's Hollywood Cemetery.

When courier John Sergeant Wise set out with President Davis's dispatches to find General Lee on the morning of April 9, he headed to Halifax Court House, where his brother Richard informed him that he had cut off from Lee's army since the Battle of Sailor's Creek. The following afternoon, the two learned of Lee's surrender from several soldiers paroled at Appomattox and heading south toward their homes. The brothers turned back toward Danville and found that Davis had evacuated again. They rode on to North Carolina and ended the war with Johnston's army.

Wise practiced law in Richmond after the war and was elected to Congress in 1883. He lost a bid for the governorship of Virginia to Fitzhugh Lee in 1885, and later moved to New York City, where he continued in the legal profession. He died near Princess Anne, Maryland, on May 12, 1913, at the age of sixty-six.

On the day he left Appomattox Court House, General Lee completed a written report to President Davis explaining the circumstances that brought about the surrender of the Army of Northern Virginia. He concluded, "We had no subsistence for man or horse, and it could not be gathered in the country. The supplies ordered . . . from Lynchburg could not reach us, and the men, deprived of food and sleep for many days, were worn out and exhausted."[373]

Eight days later, Lee followed up with a letter from Richmond, urging Davis to seek peace.

> From what I have seen and learned, I believe an army cannot be organized or supported in Virginia, and as far as I know the condition of affairs, the country east of the Mississippi is morally and physically unable to maintain the contest unaided with any hope of ultimate success. A partisan war may be continued, and hostilities protracted, causing individual suffering and the devastation of the country, but I see no prospect by that means of achieving a separate independence. It is for Your Excellency to decide, should you agree with me in opinion, what is proper to be done. To save useless effusion of blood, I would recommend measures be taken for suspension of hostilities and the restoration of peace.[374]

By the time both of Lee's communications were written, Davis had departed Danville for North Carolina. He arrived in Charlotte on April 26, the day that Johnston surrendered to Sherman, and was eventually reunited with his family. He fled into Georgia and was captured near Irwinville on May 10, by detachments of the 4th Michigan and 1st Wisconsin Cavalry Regiments. The apocryphal story that he was captured wearing women's clothing has persisted. Davis was imprisoned for two years at Fortress Monroe in Virginia, where his wife, Varina, and daughter Winnie were later permitted to join him in the officers' quarters.

Davis was indicted for treason but never tried. He was released on a bond of one hundred thousand dollars, living for a while in Tennessee and spending his remaining years near Biloxi,

Mississippi, at an estate named Beauvoir. In 1868, he received a presidential amnesty, and in 1881 his two-volume work titled *The Rise and Fall of the Confederate Government* was published. He maintained his belief in the right of the Confederate states to secede but told a gathering in 1888 that the best course of action was to "lay aside all rancor, all bitter sectional feeling, and to make your places in the ranks of those who will bring about a consummation devoutly to be wished—a reunited country."[375]

Davis worked in the insurance business and was elected to the US Senate from Mississippi but was not seated due to the provisions of section three of the XIV Amendment to the US Constitution. Davis died in New Orleans on December 6, 1889, at the age of eighty-one. He was buried first in New Orleans and then reinterred in Hollywood Cemetery in Richmond. A life-size statue of Davis marks the grave.

Varina Davis moved north after her husband's death. She became friends with Julia Dent Grant and wrote extensively. Her book *Jefferson Davis, A Memoir* was published in 1890. Varina Davis died in New York City at the age of eighty on October 16, 1906. She is buried in Hollywood Cemetery near her husband and daughter.

As Sheridan noted in his memoirs, Gen. Martin Gary was an unrepentant secessionist. He refused to surrender at Appomattox and rode away from the battlefield on the morning of April 9 with about two hundred cavalrymen. During the Confederate president's flight from the Federals, Gary's troopers joined him at Greensboro, North Carolina, and escorted the presidential party as far as Cokesbury, South Carolina, where Gary's mother lived.

After the war, Gary resumed his law practice in Edgefield, South Carolina, and became an outspoken member of the Democratic Party, vehemently opposing cooperation with Republicans or measures favorable to blacks. He was involved in a backroom deal that helped Rutherford B. Hayes to claim the presidency of the United States during the disputed election of 1876 and served as a South Carolina state senator. Governor Wade Hampton opposed Gary's political views and later blocked his appointment to the US Senate. Gary died at the age of fifty, ironically on April 9, 1881, the sixteenth anniversary of the surrender of the Army of Northern Virginia.

General Lee's three trusted aides, Colonels Marshall, Taylor, and Venable, each lived into his seventies. After the war, Venable returned to academia and served as a mathematics professor and chairman of the faculty at the University of Virginia. He wrote math texts and was instrumental in raising state appropriations to expand the university's science department. He died in 1900 at the age of seventy-three and is buried in University Cemetery in Charlottesville.

Taylor returned to banking and law and was elected to the Virginia Assembly. He wrote extensively on the Army of Northern Virginia, attempting to mediate disputes and correct factual discrepancies relating to the army's history. Taylor wrote two significant books on his association with General Lee and the army, titled *Four Years with General Lee* and *Robert E. Lee, His Campaign in Virginia, 1861–1865*. Taylor died of cancer at seventy-seven on March 1, 1916. He is buried in Elmwood Cemetery in Norfolk, Virginia.

Marshall returned to his law practice in Baltimore and wrote *An Aide-de-Camp of Lee*, a fine memoir of the Civil War, which was published in 1927, twenty-five years after his death at age seventy-one. He is buried in Green Mount Cemetery in Baltimore. Marshall spoke during the dedication ceremonies of monuments to Lee in Richmond and Grant in New York City.

General John B. Gordon of Georgia rose to command the II Corps, Army of Northern Virginia during the arduous retreat from Petersburg to Appomattox Court House. Gordon was revered for his bravery and was seriously wounded on several occasions—five times in a single day during the Battle of Antietam. He survived the war, embarked on a political career, and penned a classic memoir titled *Reminiscences of the Civil War*. *Library of Congress*

Lieutenant General James Longstreet, Lee's senior corps commander and beloved Old War Horse, died at the age of eighty-two in Gainesville, Georgia, on January 2, 1904. Longstreet's postwar career is somewhat tragic due to his affiliation with the Republican Party, his acceptance of government appointments during the Grant and Hayes administrations, and his criticism of the generalship of Robert E. Lee. Like other former, high-ranking Confederates, Longstreet received an official pardon from Congress in 1868. He worked in a cotton brokerage and the insurance business. He supported Grant for president in 1868 and was appointed surveyor of customs in New Orleans.

In 1880, Hayes appointed Longstreet ambassador to the Ottoman Empire, and during the McKinley and Theodore Roosevelt administrations he succeeded Wade Hampton as US commissioner of railroads. Longstreet endured vicious attacks from former Confederate leaders, including generals Jubal Early, William Pendleton, and Daniel Harvey Hill. He devoted much energy to preserving his reputation and wrote his memoirs, *From Manassas to Appomattox*, in 1895.

Despite the postwar attacks, Longstreet probably remembered that his former commander-in-chief always held him in high esteem. On January 19, 1866, Lee wrote to him, "I had, while in Richmond, a great many inquiries after you, and learned that you intended commencing business in New Orleans. If you become as good a merchant as you were a soldier, I shall be content. No one will then excel you, and no one can wish you more success and more happiness than I. My interest and affection for you will never cease, and my prayers are always offered for your prosperity."[376] Longstreet is buried in Alta Vista Cemetery in Gainesville, Georgia.

Lieutenant General John B. Gordon was a vigorous opponent of Reconstruction and was defeated in a run for governor of Georgia in 1868. He was believed by some to be associated with the Ku Klux Klan, but such was never proven conclusively. Gordon was elected to the US Senate from Georgia in 1873 and in 1879 became the first former Confederate to preside over the Senate. He was elected governor of Georgia in 1886 and returned to the Senate for another six years in 1891.

Gordon was a champion of an economically vital New South and served as the first commander of the United Confederate Veterans. He developed cordial relations with numerous Union veterans and regularly engaged in public speaking. His relationship with Union General Francis Barlow, particularly the fantastic story of their meeting years after the Battle of Gettysburg, is woven into the fabric of Civil War folklore. Gordon's book *Reminiscences of the Civil War* is considered an outstanding memoir of the conflict. He died at seventy-one on January 9, 1904, while visiting his son in Miami, Florida, and is buried in Oakland Cemetery in Atlanta.

Fearing prosecution for treason, George Pickett fled to Canada for a year after Appomattox. He returned in 1866 and sold insurance, receiving a Congressional pardon in 1874. Pickett never forgave Robert E. Lee for the decimation of his division at Gettysburg. He died at the age of fifty, probably of liver disease, on July 30, 1875, and is buried in Hollywood Cemetery in Richmond.

The fiery young general who volunteered to lead the final assault of the Army of Northern Virginia at Appomattox Court House, Bryan Grimes, returned to his native North Carolina after the war. He was a farmer and trustee of the University of North Carolina. In 1880, he was murdered at the age of fifty-one by a hired assassin to prevent his testifying in an upcoming criminal trial.

General William Mahone resumed his career as a renowned railroad construction engineer and was elected to the US Senate. In late 1865, he was named president of the South Side Railroad, whose High Bridge over the Appomattox River his men had tried to burn earlier in the year. Mahone died in Washington, DC, at the age of sixty-eight on October 8, 1895. He is interred in the family mausoleum in Blandford Cemetery in Petersburg, Virginia.

Cavalry general Thomas Rosser, a close friend of George Custer, avoided the surrender at Appomattox but was taken prisoner on May 4, 1865, near Staunton, Virginia. During the war, Rosser and Custer taunted one another with letters following their cavalry engagements. Rosser became a railroad executive after the war and purchased a large estate near Charlottesville in 1886. With the outbreak of the Spanish-American War in 1898, he was appointed brigadier general of volunteers in the US Army. Rosser died in Charlottesville at seventy-three on March 29, 1910.

Edward Porter Alexander taught mathematics at the University of South Carolina and became a railroad executive after the war. A close friend of President Grover Cleveland, he led a commission to Central America to determine the territorial boundary between Costa Rica and Nicaragua to facilitate the construction of a canal in the region that would join the Atlantic and Pacific oceans.

Alexander was frank in his assessment of the Confederacy's defeat and refused to embrace the postwar sentiment of the Lost Cause. His book *Military Memoirs of a Confederate: A Critical Narrative*, was published in 1907, while *Fighting for the Confederacy: The Personal Recollections of General Edward Porter Alexander* was published for the first time in 1989 and edited by eminent historian Dr. Gary W. Gallagher of the University of Virginia. Both works serve as balanced assessments of the war.

Alexander died in Savannah, Georgia, on April 28, 1910, at the age of seventy-four. He is buried in Magnolia Cemetery in Augusta, Georgia.

Robert E. Lee's nephew Gen. Fitzhugh Lee worked for reconciliation after the war and lived in Stafford County, Virginia. He served as a member of the board of visitors at West Point and was elected governor of Virginia in 1886. He was appointed consul-general in Havana, Cuba, in 1896 and served as a major general of volunteers commanding the VII US Army Corps during the Spanish-American War. He retired from the US Army as a brigadier general and died during a business trip to Washington, DC, at the age of sixty-nine on April 28, 1905. He is buried in Richmond's Hollywood Cemetery.

All three of Robert E. Lee's sons survived the Civil War. George Washington Custis Lee, the oldest, died at eighty on February 18, 1913, in Alexandria, Virginia. He spent his postwar years as a professor at the Virginia Military Institute and succeeded his father as president of Washington and Lee University. In 1877, he filed suit against the US government to regain title to the family estate at Arlington. The case reached the US Supreme Court, and Lee prevailed in a five to four decision. In 1883, he sold Arlington to the US government for $150,000.

William Henry Fitzhugh "Rooney" Lee inherited Ravensworth, the Fitzhugh family estate, in 1873 and farmed the land. He was elected to the Virginia State Senate in 1875 and to the US House of Representatives in 1887. He died at the age of fifty-four in Alexandria.

Robert E. Lee Jr. served as an officer in the Rockbridge Artillery and then as an aide to President Davis during the Civil War. He farmed at Romancoke Plantation in King William County, Virginia, after the war. His memoir of family life titled *Recollections and Letters of General Robert E. Lee* was published in 1904. He died on October 19, 1914, two weeks before his seventy-first birthday.

A few days after his return to Richmond, Robert E. Lee posed for photographer Matthew Brady. The resulting frames are among the iconic images of the Civil War. In defeat, Lee's quiet dignity is evident. The general lived in Richmond only until June, as a steady stream of visitors meant little time for rest.

On May 29, 1865, President Johnson issued a general amnesty for most former Confederates. Lee was among those prominent members of the former rebellious government and military who was excluded. He wrote letters to both Grant and to Johnson, making a direct application for amnesty to the latter in the midst of rumors that he would be indicted for treason along with other prominent ex-Confederates by a grand jury in Norfolk. Lee was indicted but never tried, and the possibility of such an action ended with the second amnesty proclamation of December 1868.

In October 1865, Lee accepted the presidency of tiny Washington College in Lexington, Virginia, with a compensation package that included an annual salary of $1,500, a house and garden, and one-fifth of the tuition collected, which was then $75 per student. He was initially reluctant to accept the position believing that his Confederate military service "might draw upon the College a feeling of hostility." However, he also noted, "I think it the duty of every citizen in the present condition of the country, to do all in his power to aid in the restoration of peace and harmony."[377]

During his tenure, Lee asserted, "We have but one rule here, and it is that every student be a gentleman."[378] He oversaw the construction of a new chapel and home for the presidents of the college. He was largely quiet concerning the politics of the day and held his office until his death at the age of sixty-three on October 12, 1870, two weeks after suffering a stroke.

Within days of Lee's death, the college's board of trustees voted to change its name to Washington and Lee University. The chapel is now known as the Lee Chapel, and the general and members of his immediate family are interred there. The faithful Traveller is buried nearby. Lee's full citizenship was restored posthumously in 1975.

In its October 13, 1870, edition, the *New York Times* published a lengthy obituary. It detailed General Lee's noble lineage and the loyalty to Virginia that prompted him to lead the Army of Northern Virginia during the war. In conclusion, it stated that as president of Washington College he had "devoted himself to the interests of that institution, keeping so far as possible aloof from public notice, and by his unobtrusive modesty and purity of life, has won the respect even of those who most bitterly deplore and reprobate his course in the rebellion."[379]

Lee's coffin was carried to the college chapel the following day, and a long vigil ensued. Cadet William Nalle of the neighboring Virginia Military Institute wrote to his mother on October 16, "Myself and four other cadets . . . sat up all night with the corpse on Friday night, perfect silence was kept the whole night, no one speaking except in a low whisper . . . the day following the funeral procession after marching all around town and through the Institute grounds, formed around the college chapel and he was buried in the chapel under the floor of the basement. The procession was a very large one."[380]

Although Robert E. Lee was larger than life even while he was among the living, he became in death a symbol of honor, nobility, and duty. He embodied the highest qualities of the army that he led, an army that covered itself in glory, legend, and lore on the battlefield in defense of home, hearth, a people, and its perspective on government—sadly tinged with the horrific legacy of the institution of slavery that it also defended.

The last days of the Army of Northern Virginia tell a story of heroism, suffering, and sacrifice, a chronicle of the terrible price of war. The result of those hard days for both North and South was the promise of the future for a revived and reunited nation.

ENDNOTES

[1] Lincoln to Ulysses S. Grant, July 13, 1863, in *Collected Works of Abraham Lincoln*, ed. Roy P. Basler, Marion Dolores Pratt, and Lloyd A. Dunlap, asst. eds., the Abraham Lincoln Association (New Brunswick, NJ: Rutgers University Press, 1953), 4:326.

[2] Geoffrey C. Ward, *The Civil War: An Illustrated History* (New York: Alfred A. Knopf, 1990), 278.

[3] Ulysses S. Grant, *Personal Memoirs of U. S. Grant* (New York: J. J. Little, 1885), 1:38–42.

[4] Ibid., 210.

[5] Ibid., 311.

[6] James Lee McDonough, *Shiloh—in Hell before Night* (Knoxville: University of Tennessee Press, 1977), 183.

[7] Alexander K. McClure, *Abraham Lincoln and Men of War-Times: Some Personal Recollections of War and Politics during the Lincoln Administration* (Philadelphia: Times Publishing Company, 1892), 193–194.

[8] Bruce Catton, *Grant Takes Command* (Boston: Little, Brown, 1968), 124.

[9] Ibid., 126.

[10] Grant, *Personal Memoirs*, 2:115–116.

[11] Jean Edward Smith, *Grant* (New York: Simon and Schuster, 2001), 301.

[12] Douglas Southall Freeman, *Lee: An Abridgment in One Volume* by Richard Harwell of the four-volume *R. E. Lee* (New York: Charles Scribner's Sons, 1961), 16–19.

[13] Time-Life Books, *Lee Takes Command: From Seven Days to Second Bull Run*, The Civil War (Alexandria, VA: Time-Life Books, 1984), 10–16.

[14] Freeman, *Lee*, 105.

[15] Ibid., 106–107.

[16] Ibid., 110.

[17] George Gordon Meade, *The Life and Letters of George Gordon Meade, Major-General United States Army* (New York: Charles Scribner's Sons, 1913), 2:181.

[18] Ward, *The Civil War*, 288.

[19] Gregory Jaynes and Time-Life Books, *The Killing Ground: Wilderness to Cold Harbor*, The Civil War (Alexandria, VA: Time-Life Books, 1986), 88.

[20] Ward, *The Civil War*, 291.

[21] Horace Porter, *Campaigning with Grant* (New York: Century Company, 1897), 174–175.

[22] Jaynes and Time-Life Books, *The Killing Ground*, 158–161.

[23] Grant, *Personal Memoirs*, 2:276.

[24] Grant to Lincoln, March 20, 1865, Robert Todd Lincoln Collection of Abraham Lincoln Papers, *Library of Congress*.

[25] "Grant's Headquarters: Lincoln Waits for War's End," National Park Service, last modified October 25, 2014, www.nps.gov/history/logcabin/html/cp5.html.

[26] Dispatch from Sylvanus Cadwallader, City Point, June 11, 1864, *New York Herald*, June 25, 1864.

[27] Bruce Catton, *A Stillness at Appomattox* (New York: Doubleday, 1957), 321.

[28] "Abraham Lincoln Visits the Wounded at City Point, VA," last modified January 9, 2010, www.waymarking.com/waymarks/WM81H7.

[29] David Herbert Donald, *Lincoln* (New York: Simon and Schuster, 1995), 571–572.

[30] Porter, *Campaigning with Grant*, 406–407.

[31] Ibid., 410.

[32] Ibid., 414.

[33] Donald, *Lincoln*, 572–573.

[34] Ward Hill Lamon, *Recollections of Abraham Lincoln, 1847–1865*, ed. Dorothy Lamon Teillard (published by the editor, Washington, DC, 1911), 114–115.

[35] Ibid., 115.

[36] Ibid.

[37] Ibid., 116–117.

[38] William Tecumseh Sherman quotation, BrainyQuote.com, Xplore Inc, 2014, accessed August 3, 2014, www.brainyquote.com/quotes/quotes/w/williamtec205676.html.

[39] Porter, *Campaigning with Grant*, 417–418.

[40] William T. Sherman, *Memoirs of General William T. Sherman*, 2nd ed., rev. and corrected (New York: D. Appleton, 1889), vol. 2.

[41] Porter, *Campaigning with Grant*, 422–423.

[42] Ibid., 423–424.

[43] Sherman, *Memoirs*, vol. 2.

[44] Ibid.

[45] Ibid.

[46] Donald, *Lincoln*, 574.

[47] John B. Gordon, *Reminiscences of the Civil War* (New York: Charles Scribner's Sons, 1903), 292–293.

[48] Ibid., 294.

[49] Meade, *Life and Letters*, 2:201–202.

[50] William C. Davis and Time-Life Books, *Death in the Trenches: Grant at Petersburg*, The Civil War (Alexandria, VA: Time-Life Books, 1986), 22–25.

[51] "June 4–11: Grant Plans a New Campaign," National Park Service, last modified October 23, 2014, www.nps.gov/history/history/online_books/civil_war_series/11/sec14.htm.

[52] Douglas Southall Freeman, ed., *Lee's Dispatches: Unpublished Letters of General Robert E. Lee, C.S.A., to Jefferson Davis and the War Department of the Confederate States of America, 1862–1865* (New York: G. P. Putnam's Sons, Knickerbocker Press, 1915), 238.

[53] "June 4–11: Grant Plans a New Campaign," National Park Service, last modified October 23, 2014, www.nps.gov/history/history/online_books/civil_war_series/11/sec14.htm.

[54] Grant, *Personal Memoirs*, 2:293–294.

[55] Freeman, *R. E. Lee*, 414.

[56] D. P. Conyngham, *The Irish Brigade and Its Campaigns* (New York: William McSorley, 1867), 558.

[57] Robert Keating, *Carnival of Blood: The Civil War Ordeal of the Seventh New York Heavy Artillery* (Baltimore, MD: Butternut and Blue, 1998).

[58] Freeman, *R. E. Lee*, 416.

[59] P. G. T. Beauregard, *Four Days of Battle at Petersburg*, ed. Robert Underwood Johnson and Clarence Clough Buel, of the Editorial Staff of *The Century Magazine*, based upon "The Century War Series," vol. 4 *Battles and Leaders of the Civil War: Being for the Most Part Contributions by Union and Confederate Officers* (New York: Century Company, 1887–1888), 4:543.

[60] Ibid.

[61] Davis, *The Civil War*, 48.

[62] Captain Augustus C. Brown, *The Diary of a Line Officer* (New York, 1906), 59.

[63] Grant, *Personal Memoirs*, 2:298–299.

[64] Ibid., 297–298.

[65] Alice Rains Trulock, *In the Hands of Providence: Joshua L. Chamberlain and the American Civil War* (Chapel Hill: The University of North Carolina Press, 1992), 215.

[66] J. Gary Laine and Morris M. Penny, *Law's Alabama Brigade in the War between the Union and the Confederacy* (Shippensburg, PA: White Mane, 1996), 284.

[67] Noah Andre Trudeau, *The Last Citadel: Petersburg, Virginia, June 1864–April 1865* (Boston: Little, Brown, 1991), 291–292.

[68] Freeman, *Lee*, 430.

[69] "Petersburg," New York State Military Museum and Veterans Research Center, NYS Division of Military and Naval Affairs, last modified March 14, 2006, www.dmna.ny.gov/historic/reghist/civil/battles/petersburg.htm.

[70] "1865," rootsweb.ancestry.com/~ms19inf/1865.htm.

[71] "The Siege of Petersburg," National Park Service, last modified October, 23, 2014, www.nps.gov/history/history/online_books/civil_war_series/20/sec5.htm.

[72] *The War of the Rebellion: A Compilation of the Official Records of the Union and Confederate Armies*, Series 1, Vol. 46, Part 1 (*Appomattox Campaign*), 381–382.

[73] Beauregard, *Battles and Leaders of the Civil War*, 4:551.

[74] Grant, *Personal Memoirs*, 2:315.

[75] Meade, *Life and Letters*, 2:217–218.

[76] *Official Records*, Series 1, Vol. 40, Part 2, 583.

[77] Davis and Time-Life Books, *Death in the Trenches*, 110.

[78] "Wade Hampton and the Great Beefsteak Raid," Sons of Confederate Veterans, Wadehamptoncamp.org/hist-bs.html.

[79] Trudeau, *The Last Citadel*, 195–201.

[80] Grant, *Personal Memoirs*, 2:424–425.

[81] Henry Kyd Douglas, *I Rode with Stonewall* (Chapel Hill: The University Press of North Carolina, 1940), 327.

[82] Freeman, *R. E. Lee*, 448.

[83] Gordon, *Reminiscences*, 394.

[84] Ibid., 398.

[85] Ibid., 403.

[86] William H. Hodgkins, *The Battle of Fort Stedman* (Boston: privately printed, 1889), 27–28.

[87] Gordon, *Reminiscences*, 411.

[88] Philip H. Sheridan, *Personal Memoirs of P. H. Sheridan, General United States Army* (New York: Charles L. Webster, 1888), 2:119.

[89] Porter, *Campaigning with Grant*, 426.

[90] Ibid.

[91] Ibid.

[92] Jerry Korn and Time-Life Books, *Pursuit to Appomattox: The Last Battles* The Civil War (Alexandria, VA: Time-Life Books, 1987), 81.

[93] Sheridan, *Personal Memoirs*, 140.

[94] Korn and Time-Life Books, *Pursuit to Appomattox*, 81.

[95] Sheridan, *Personal Memoirs*, 142.

[96] Porter, *Campaigning with Grant*, 428.

[97] Ibid., 429.

[98] Douglas Southall Freeman, *Lee's Lieutenants: A Study in Command*, vol 3, *Gettysburg to Appomattox* (New York: Charles Scribner's Sons, 1944), 661.

[99] Porter, *Campaigning with Grant*, 432.

[100] Sheridan, *Personal Memoirs*, 160–161.

[101] Freeman, *Lee's Lieutenants*, 667.

[102] Ibid., 671.

[103] Porter, *Campaigning with Grant*, 437.

[104] Ibid.

[105] Korn and Time-Life Books, *Pursuit to Appomattox*, 90.

[106] Freeman, *Lee's Lieutenants*, 673.

[107] "Confederate War Diary by Captain H. A. Chambers," www.nccivilwar.lostsoulsgenealogy.com/ownwords/diarycapthachambers.htm.

[108] Porter, *Campaigning with Grant*, 442.

[109] Ibid., 443.

[110] A. A. Hoehling and Mary Hoehling, *The Day Richmond Died* (New York: Madison Books, 1981), 111–112.

[111] nps.gov/history/history/online books/hh/33/hh33s.htm

[112] Hoehling and Hoehling, *The Day Richmond Died*, 112.

[113] Jay Winik, *April 1865: The Month That Saved America* (New York: HarperCollins, 2001), 105.

[114] "Varina Davis: First Lady of the Confederate States of America," Civil War Women, last modified June 26, 2010, www.civilwarwomenblog.com/varina-davis.

[115] James I. Robertson Jr., *General A. P. Hill: The Story of a Confederate Warrior* (New York: Vintage Books, 1987), 315.

[116] Ibid., 317.

[117] Ibid., 317–318.

[118] Interview with Cpl. John W. Mauk, *Baltimore American*, May 29, 1892.

[119] Freeman, *R. E. Lee*, 463–464.

[120] Korn and Time-Life Books, *Pursuit to Appomattox*, 93.

[121] Noah Andre Trudeau, *Out of the Storm: The End of the Civil War, April–June 1865* (Boston: Little, Brown, 1994), 53.

[122] Ibid., 54.

[123] Grant, *Personal Memoirs*, 448–449.

[124] Korn and Time-Life Books, *Pursuit to Appomattox*, 99.

[125] John C. Gorman, *Lee's Last Campaign* (Raleigh, NC: William B. Smith, 1866), 6.

[126] Ibid., 7.

[127] William Palmer Hopkins, *The Seventh Regiment Rhode Island Volunteers in the Civil War, 1862–1865* (Providence, RI: Providence Press, 1903), 259.

[128] Grant, *Personal Memoirs*, 2:453.

[129] Hoehling and Hoehling, *The Day Richmond Died*, 31.

[130] "Slavery and Freedom Tour," Richmond Civil War Walking Tours, last modified November 5, 2012, civilwartraveler.com/RichmondTours/SlaveryFreedom.html.

[131] "The Fall of Richmond," Civil War Trust, www.civilwar.org/education/history/warfare-and-logistics/warfare/richmond.html.

[132] G. Powell Hill, "Lieutenant-General A.P. Hill," *Southern Historical Society Papers* 19 (1891): 184–185.

[133] Ibid.

[134] Freeman, *R. E. Lee*, 466.

[135] Hoehling and Hoehling, *The Day Richmond Died*, 133–134.

[136] *Richmond Whig*, April 4, 1865.

[137] Trudeau, *Out of the Storm*, 77–78.

[138] Ibid., 74–77.

[139] Ibid., 78.

[140] William B Arnold, *The Fourth Massachusetts Cavalry in the Closing Scenes of the War for the Maintenance of the Union*, Internet Archive, 27–28, www.archive.org/stream/fourthmassachuse-00arno/fourthmassachuse00arno_djvu.txt.

[141] Phoebe Yates Pember, *A Southern Woman's Story* (New York: G. W. Carleton, 1879), 171–172.

[142] "The Fall of Richmond," Civil War Trust, www.civilwar.org/education/history/warfare-and-logistics/warfare/richmond.html

[143] *Richmond Whig*, April 4, 1865.

[144] Ibid.

[145] *Official Records*, Series 1, Vol. 46, Part 3, 271.

[146] Lincoln, *Collected Works of Abraham Lincoln*, 8:376–377.

[147] Ibid., 8:377–378.

[148] *Official Records*, Series 1, Vol. 46, Part 3, 332.

[149] Ibid., 379.

[150] Lincoln, *Collected Works of Abraham Lincoln*, 8:380.

[151] Ibid., 8:381.

[152] Ibid., 8:385.

[153] Ibid.

[154] Korn and Time-Life Books, *Pursuit to Appomattox*, 108.

[155] Grant, *Personal Memoirs*, 2:459.

[156] "Lincoln in Petersburg: Last Meeting," The Historical Marker Database, last modified October 17, 2011, www.hmdb.org.

[157] Walk in Lincoln's Final Footsteps, www.walkinlincolnsfinalfootsteps.com.

[158] "Lincoln in Petersburg: Last Meeting," The Historical Marker Database, last modified October 17, 2011, www.hmdb.org.

[159] Grant, *Personal Memoirs*, 2:458–459.

[160] Ibid., 460.

[161] Ibid.

[162] Lincoln, *Collected Works of Abraham Lincoln*, 8:385.

[163] Donald, *Lincoln*, 576.

[164] David Dixon Porter, *Incidents and Anecdotes of the Civil War* (New York: D. Appleton, 1885), 295.

[165] Ibid.

[166] Ibid., 297.

[167] "President Lincoln Enters Richmond, 1865," Eyewitness to History, last modified 2000, www. http://eyewitnesstohistory.com/richmond.htm.

[168] William C. Harris, *Lincoln's Last Months* (Cambridge, MA: Harvard University Press, 2004), 205.

[169] *New York Herald*, April 9, 1865.

[170] Donald, *Lincoln*, 577.

[171] Weitzel, Godfrey, *Entry of the United States Forces into Richmond, Virginia, April 3, 1865, Calling Together the Virginia Legislature and Revocation of the Same*, www.mdgorman.com/images/occupied.pdf, 58.

[172] Donald, *Lincoln*, 579.

[173] LaSalle Corbett Pickett, *Pickett and His Men* (Philadelphia: J. B. Lippincott, 1913), 37–40.

[174] Grant, *Personal Memoirs*, 2:454–455.

[175] Freeman, *R. E. Lee*, 467.

[176] "The Campaign to Appomattox," National Park Service, last modified October 25, 2014, www.nps.gov/history/history/online_books/civil_war_series/6/sec2.htm.

[177] Freeman, *Lee's Lieutenants*, 3:689.

[178] *Chesterfield Observer*, April 9, 2008.

[179] "Namozine Church," Civil War Traveler, last modified March 25, 2014, www.civilwartraveler.com/EAST/VA/va-southside/LR-RadioScripts.html#4.

[180] Ibid.

[181] Henry Edwin Tremain, *Last Hours of Sheridan's Cavalry: A Reprint of War Memoranda* (New York: Bonnell, Silver and Bowers, 1904), 101.

[182] Sheridan, *Personal Memoirs*, 2:174.

[183] Freeman, *R. E. Lee*, 469.

[184] Burke Davis, *To Appomattox: Nine April Days, 1865* (New York: Rinehart, 1959), 190.

[185] "The Campaign to Appomattox," National Park Service, last modified October 25, 2014, www.nps.gov/history/history/online_books/civil_war_series/6/sec2.htm.

[186] Davis, *To Appomattox*, 190–191.

[187] Korn and Time-Life Books, *Pursuit to Appomattox*, 112.

[188] Jefferson Davis, *The Rise and Fall of the Confederate Government* (New York: D. Appleton, 1881), 2:671.

[189] Freeman, *Lee's Lieutenants*, 3:690.

[190] Carlton McCarthy, *Detailed Minutae of Soldier Life in the Army of Northern Virginia, 1861–1865* (Cambridge, MA: Riverside Press, 1882), 116–158.

[191] Freeman, *Lee's Lieutenants*, 3:692–693.

[192] Trudeau, *Out of the Storm*, 98.

[193] Korn and Time-Life Books, *Pursuit to Appomattox*, 116.

[194] William M. Owen, *In Camp and Battle with the Washington Artillery of New Orleans* (Boston: Ticknor, 1885), 694.

[195] Trudeau, *Out of the Storm*, 94.

[196] Sheridan, *Personal Memoirs*, 2:175.

[197] "The Campaign to Appomattox," National Park Service, last modified October 25, 2014, www.nps.gov/history/history/online_books/civil_war_series/6/sec2.htm.

[198] Sheridan, *Personal Memoirs*, 2:175.

[199] Grant, *Personal Memoirs*, 2:463–464.

[200] Meade, *Life and Letters*, 2:269–270.

[201] Sheridan, *Personal Memoirs*, 2:177.

[202] Korn and Time-Life Books, *Pursuit to Appomattox*, 114.

[203] Sheridan, *Personal Memoirs*, 2:178.

[204] "Nottoway Court House," Civil War Traveler, last modified March 25, 2014, www.civilwartraveler.com/EAST/VA/va-southside/LR-RadioScripts.html#25.

[205] "Crewe," Civil War Traveler, last modified March 25, 2014, www.civilwartraveler.com/EAST/VA/va-southside/LR-RadioScripts.html#24.

[206] Grant, *Personal Memoirs*, 2:469.

[207] Sheridan, *Personal Memoirs*, 2:179.

[208] Septima M. Collis, *A Woman's War Record, 1861–1865* (New York: G. P. Putnam's Sons, Knickerbocker Press, 1889), 62.

[209] Ibid., 63.

[210] Ibid., 64.

[211] Ibid., 65–66.

[212] Ibid., 67–68.

[213] Ibid., 70.

[214] Trudeau, *Out of the Storm*, 189.

[215] John Sergeant Wise, *The End of an Era* (Cambridge, MA: Houghton Mifflin, Riverside Press, 1901), 415.

[216] Davis, *The Rise and Fall*, 2:677–678.

[217] Wise, *End of an Era*, 416.

[218] Trudeau, *Out of the Storm*, 193.

[219] Wise, *End of an Era*, 419.

[220] Ibid., 420.

[221] Ibid., 421.

[222] Ibid., 421–422.

[223] Ibid., 423–426.

[224] Shelby Foote, *The Civil War: A Narrative; Red River to Appomattox* (New York: Random House, 1974), 915.

225 Sheridan, *Personal Memoirs*, 179.

226 Régis De Trobriand, *Four Years with the Army of the Potomac* (Boston: Ticknor, 1889), 734–735.

227 Ibid., 736–737.

228 "Deatonville," Civil War Traveler, last modified March 25, 2014, www.civilwartraveler.com/EAST/VA/va-southside/LR-RadioScripts.html#8.

229 Gordon, *Reminiscences*, 423, 430.

230 Sheridan, *Personal Memoirs*, 180.

231 Korn and Time-Life Books, *Pursuit to Appomattox*, 122.

232 Robert Hunt Rhodes, ed., *All for the Union: The Civil War Diary and Letters of Elisha Hunt Rhodes* (New York: Orion Books, 1985), 227–228.

233 Ibid., 228–229.

234 "Hillsman House," Civil War Traveler, last modified March 25, 2014, www.civilwartraveler.com/EAST/VA/va-southside/LR-RadioScripts.html#10.

235 "The Campaign to Appomattox," National Park Service, last modified October 25, 2014, www.nps.gov/history/history/online_books/civil_war_series/6/sec3.htm.

236 Ibid.

237 Tremain, *Last Hours of Sheridan's Cavalry*, 146.

238 Ibid., 146–147.

239 Ibid., 151–152.

240 "The Forgotten Custer: Thomas Ward Custer," National Medal of Honor Museum of Military History, www.mohm.org/recipient_pages/moh_recipient_tom_custer.html.

241 "Lockett's House," Civil War Traveler, last modified March 25, 2014, www.civilwartraveler.com/EAST/VA/va-southside/LR-RadioScripts.html#12.

242 Trudeau, *Out of the Storm*, 110.

243 Freeman, *R. E. Lee*, 471.

244 Wise, *End of an Era*, 429.

245 Ibid.

246 Ibid., 436.

247 Sheridan, *Personal Memoirs*, 2:187.

248 Lincoln, *Collected Works of Abraham Lincoln*, 8:392.

249 E. Porter Alexander, *Military Memoirs of a Confederate* (New York: Charles Scribner's Sons, 1907), 597.

250 Arnold A. Rand, *The Fourth Massachusetts Cavalry in the Closing Scenes of the War for the Maintenance of the Union, from Richmond to Appomattox, the Battle at High Bridge*, by Major Edward T. Bouvé, Hollinger, Mill Run, 12.

251 "Cavalry Battle at High Bridge," Civil War Traveler, last modified March 25, 2014, www.civilwartraveler.com/EAST/VA/va-southside/LR-RadioScripts.html#15.

252 "High Bridge," Civil War Traveler, last modified March 25, 2014, www.civilwartraveler.com/EAST/VA/va-southside/LR-RadioScripts.html#18.

253 Ibid.

254 Alexander, *Military Memoirs*, 597.

255 E. Porter Alexander, *Fighting for the Confederacy: The Personal Recollections of General Edward Porter Alexander* (Chapel Hill: University of North Carolina Press, 1989), 527.

256 "The Campaign to Appomattox," National Park Service, last modified October 25, 2014, www.nps.gov/history/history/online_books/civil_war_series/6/sec4.htm.

257 D. W. Maull, M.D., *The Life and Military Services of the Late Brigadier General Thomas A. Smyth* (Wilmington, DE: H. and E. F. James Printers, 1870), 43.

258 Ibid.

259 De Trobriand, *Four Years with the Army*, 744–745.

260 Mahone to James Longstreet, 1890, Auburn University Special Collections and Archives, Transcription of the General William Mahone Letter, RG 242, www.lib.auburn.edu/archive/find-aid/242.htm.

261 De Trobriand, *Four Years with the Army*, 745.

262 Foote, *The Civil War*, 924–925.

263 Mahone to James Longstreet, 1890, Auburn University Special Collections and Archives, Transcription of the General William Mahone Letter, RG 242, www.lib.auburn.edu/archive/find-aid/242.htm.

264 Porter, *Campaigning with Grant*, 458.

265 Ibid.

266 Foote, *The Civil War*, 927.

267 Grant, *Personal Memoirs*, 2:477–478.

268 Ibid., 478–479.

269 Trudeau, *Out of the Storm*, 198.

270 Gordon, *Reminiscences*, 433.

271 Freeman, *Lee's Lieutenants*, 3:720–721.

272 Ibid., 721.

273 Gordon, *Reminiscences*, 433.

274 Grant, *Personal Memoirs*, 2:480.

275 Ibid.

276 Mahone to James Longstreet, 1890, Auburn University Special Collections and Archives, Transcription of the General William Mahone Letter, RG 242, www.lib.auburn.edu/archive/find-aid/242.htm.

277 "The Campaign to Appomattox," National Park Service, last modified October 25, 2014, www.nps.gov/history/history/online_books/civil_war_series/6/sec4.htm.

278 James Longstreet, *From Manassas to Appomattox: Memoirs of the Civil War in America* (Philadelphia: J. B. Lippincott, 1896), 619.

279 Trudeau, *Out of the Storm*, 125.

280 Grant, *Personal Memoirs*, 2:479–480.

281 Longstreet, *From Manassas to Appomattox*, 620.

282 Grant, *Personal Memoirs*, 2:483.

283 "New Store," Civil War Traveler, last modified March 25, 2014, www.civilwartraveler.com/EAST/VA/va-southside/LR-RadioScripts.html#20.

284 Sheridan, *Personal Memoirs*, 2:188.

285 Ibid., 189.

286 "The Campaign to Appomattox," National Park Service, last modified October 25, 2014, www.nps.gov/history/history/online_books/civil_war_series/6/sec4.htm.

287 Schroeder, Patrick, *The Battles of Appomattox Station and Court House, April 8–9, 1865*, www.civilwar.org/battlefields/appomattox-station-history/the-battles-of-appomattox.html.

288 Ibid.

289 Sheridan, *Personal Memoirs*, 2:199.

290 Ibid., 191.

291 Trudeau, *Out of the Storm*, 130–131.

292 Gordon, *Reminiscences*, 435–436.

293 Ibid., 436.

294 Ibid.

295 Longstreet, *From Manassas to Appomattox*, 623.

296 "Abraham Lincoln Visits the Wounded at City Point, VA," last modified January 9, 2010, www.waymarking.com/waymarks/WM81H7.

297 Rufus Rockwell Wilson, assembled and annotated, *Intimate Memories of Lincoln*, (Elmira, NY: Primavera Press, 1945), 585–586.

298 Wise, *End of an Era*, 443–446.

299 "The Campaign to Appomattox," National Park Service, last modified October 25, 2014, www.nps.gov/history/history/online_books/civil_war_series/6/sec4.htm.

300 Porter, *Campaigning with Grant*, 462–463.

301 Ibid., 465.

302 Ibid., 464.

303 Grant, *Personal Memoirs*, 2:484.

304 Freeman, *Lee's Lieutenants*, 727–728.

305 Gordon, *Reminiscences*, 436–437.

306 Sheridan, *Personal Memoirs*, 2:192.

307 Gordon, *Reminiscences*, 437–438.

308 Trudeau, *Out of the Storm*, 139.

309 Ibid., 141.

310 Freeman, *R. E. Lee*, 483.

311 Freeman, *Lee's Lieutenants*, 730.

312 Korn and Time-Life Books, *Pursuit to Appomattox*, 140.

313 Freeman, *R. E. Lee*, 484.

314 Ibid.

[315] Longstreet, *From Manassas to Appomattox*, 624.

[316] Freeman, *R. E. Lee*, 483.

[317] Charles Marshall, *An Aide-de-Camp of Lee, Being the Papers of Colonel Charles Marshall, Sometime Aide-de-Camp, Military Secretary, And Assistant Adjutant General On The Staff Of Robert E. Lee, 1862–1865* (Boston: Little, Brown, 1927), 262–264.

[318] Ibid., 264.

[319] "Final Combat," The Historical Marker Database, last modified April 25, 2010, www.hmdb.org/marker.asp?MarkerID=5970&Print=1.

[320] Korn and Time-Life Books, *Pursuit to Appomattox*, 141.

[321] "185th Infantry Regiment New York Volunteers Civil War Newspaper Clippings," New York State Military Museum and Veterans Research Center, NYS Division of Military and Naval Affairs, last modified August 14, 2008, www.dmna.ny.gov/historic/reghist/civil/infantry/185thinf/185thinfCWN.htm.

[322] Carol Kammen, "African American Men in White NY Civil War Units," *The New York History Blog*, January 4, 2012, www.newyorkhistoryblog.org/2012/01/04/African-american-men-in-white-ny-civil-war-units.

[323] Grant, *Personal Memoirs*, 2:485–486.

[324] Freeman, *R. E. Lee*, 487.

[325] Gordon, *Reminiscences*, 439.

[326] Sheridan, *Personal Memoirs*, 2:197.

[327] Ibid., 440–442.

[328] Longstreet, *From Manassas to Appomattox*, 627.

[329] Korn and Time-Life Books, *Pursuit to Appomattox*, 144.

[330] Marshall, *Aide-de-Camp of Lee*, 268.

[331] Walter H. Taylor, *Four Years with General Lee: Being a Summary of the More Important Events Touching the Career of General Robert E. Lee, in the War between the States; Together with an Authoritative Statement of the Strength of the Army Which He Commanded in the Field* (New York: D. Appleton, 1878), 152–153.

[332] Marshall, *Aide-de-Camp of Lee*, 269.

[333] Sheridan, *Personal Memoirs*, 2:200.

[334] Grant, *Personal Memoirs*, 2:489.

[335] Ibid., 488–489.

[336] Porter, *Campaigning with Grant*, 472–473.

[337] Grant, *Personal Memoirs*, 2:489.

[338] Porter, *Campaigning with Grant*, 475.

[339] Ibid.

[340] Marshall, *Aide-de-Camp of Lee*, 270.

[341] Ibid.

[342] Porter, *Campaigning with Grant*, 478.

[343] Marshall, *Aide-de-Camp of Lee*, 270.

[344] Ibid., 270–271.

[345] Grant, *Personal Memoirs*, 2:493.

[346] Porter, *Campaigning with Grant*, 480.

[347] Marshall, *Aide-de-Camp of Lee*, 271.

[348] Ibid., 272

[349] Porter, *Campaigning with Grant*, 477.

[350] Marshall, *Aide-de-Camp of Lee*, 272–273.

[351] Ibid., 274.

[352] Ibid.

[353] Grant, *Personal Memoirs*, 2:494.

[354] Ibid., 2:488.

[355] Porter, *Campaigning with Grant*, 486.

[356] Grant, *Personal Memoirs*, 2:495.

[357] Ibid., 496.

[358] Ibid., 497.

[359] Ibid., 498.

[360] Donald, *Lincoln*, 580.

[361] Ibid., 581.

[362] Freeman, *R. E. Lee*, 494.

[363] Longstreet, *From Manassas to Appomattox*, 629.

[364] Freeman, *R. E. Lee*, 497.

[365] Taylor, *Four Years*, 153.

[366] Joshua Lawrence Chamberlain, *The Passing of the Armies: An Account of the Final Campaign of the Army of the Potomac, Based upon Personal Reminiscences of the Fifth Army Corps* (New York: G. P. Putnam's Sons, Knickerbocker Press, 1915), 260.

[367] Ibid., 261.

[368] Gordon, *Reminiscences*, 444.

[369] "1st Lt. Nathan Bachman," Sixty-Third Tennessee Volunteer Infantry, CSA, www.63rdtennessee.org/Veterans/nathan_bachman.htm.

[370] Grant, *Personal Memoirs*, 2:508.

[371] Ward, *The Civil War*, 409.

[372] www.nps.gov/history/history/online_books/civil_war_series/sec6.htm.

[373] www.usa-civil-war.com/Appomattox/appomattox.html.

[374] Lee to Jefferson Davis, April 20, 1865, Civil War Trust, www.civilwar.org/education/history/primarysources/robert-e-lee-to-jefferson.html.

[375] "Jefferson Davis," Civil War Trust, www.civilwar.org/education/history/biographies/jefferson-davis.html.

[376] "From Manassas to Appomattox: James Longstreet," The War Times Journal, www.wtj.com/archives/longstreet/long.

[377] "Robert E. Lee," Washington and Lee University, www.wlu.edu/presidents-office/about-the-presidents-office/history-and-governance/past-presidents/robert-e-lee.

[378] Ibid.

[379] "Obituary: Gen. Robert E. Lee," *New York Times*, October 13, 1870.

[380] Nalle to Mrs. Thomas Botts Nalle, October 16, 1870, Virginia Military Institute, www.vmi.edu/archives.aspx?id=5517.

BIBLIOGRAPHY

Catton, Bruce. *A Stillness at Appomattox*. New York, NY: Doubleday, 1953.

Calkins, Chris M. *The Appomattox Campaign: March 29–April 9, 1865*. Conshohocken, PA: Combined Books, 1997.

Chamberlain, Joshua Lawrence. *The Passing of the Armies: An Account of the Final Campaign of the Army of the Potomac, Based upon Personal Reminiscences of the Fifth Army Corps*. New York: G. P. Putnam's Sons, Knickerbocker Press, 1915.

Collis, Septima M. *A Woman's War Record, 1861–1865*. New York: G. P. Putnam's Sons, Knickerbocker Press, 1889.

Davis, Burke. *To Appomattox: Nine April Days, 1865*. New York: Rinehart, 1959.

Davis, Jefferson. *The Papers of Jefferson Davis: September 1864–May 1865*. Baton Rouge: Louisiana State University Press, 2003.

Davis, Jefferson. *The Rise and Fall of the Confederate Government*, Volume II. New York: D. Appleton, 1881.

Davis, William C., and Time-Life Books. *Death in the Trenches: Grant at Petersburg*. The Civil War. Alexandria, VA: Time-Life Books, 1986.

De Trobriand, Régis. *Four Years with the Army of the Potomac*. Boston: Ticknor, 1889.

Donald, David Herbert. *Lincoln*. New York: Simon and Schuster, 1995.

Foote, Shelby *The Civil War: A Narrative, Red River to Appomattox* New York: Random House, 1974.

Frassanito, William A. *Grant and Lee, the Virginia Campaigns, 1864–1865*. New York: Charles Scribner's Sons, 1983.

Freeman, Douglas Southall, ed. *Lee's Dispatches: Unpublished Letters of General Robert E. Lee, C.S.A., to Jefferson Davis and the War Department of the Confederate States of America, 1862–1865*. New York: G. P. Putnam's Sons, Knickerbocker Press, 1915.

Freeman, Douglas Southall. *Lee's Lieutenants: A Study in Command. Vol. 3, Gettysburg to Appomattox.* New York: Charles Scribner's Sons, 1944.

Freeman, Douglas Southall. an abridgment in one volume by Richard Harwell of the four volume *R. E. Lee.* Birmingham, AL: Oxmoor House, 1982.

Gerrish, Rev. Theodore. *Army Life, a Private's Reminiscences of the Civil War.* Portland, ME: Hoytt, Fogg and Donham, 1882.

Golay, Michael. *A Ruined Land, the End of the Civil War.* New York: John Wiley and Sons, 1999.

Gordon, John B. *Reminiscences of the Civil War.* New York: Charles Scribner's Sons, 1903.

Gorman, John C. *Lee's Last Campaign.* Raleigh, NC: William B. Smith, 1866.

Grant, Ulysses S. *Personal Memoirs of U. S. Grant.* Vol. 2. New York: Charles L. Webster, 1886.

Harris, William C. *Lincoln's Last Months.* Cambridge, MA: Harvard University Press, 2004.

Hoehling, A. A., and Mary Hoehling. *The Day Richmond Died.* Lanham, MD: Madison Books, 1981.

Hopkins, William Palmer. *The Seventh Regiment Rhode Island Volunteers in the Civil War, 1862–1865.* Providence, RI: Providence Press, 1903.

Humphreys, Andrew Atkinson. *The Virginia Campaigns of '64 and '65.* New York: Charles Scribner's Sons, 1883.

Johnson, Robert Underwood, and Clarence Clough Buel of the editorial staff of the *Century Magazine. Battles and Leaders of the Civil War.* Vol. 4. New York: Century Company, 1888.

Korn, Jerry, and Time-Life Books. *Pursuit to Appomattox: The Last Battles.* The Civil War. Alexandria, VA: Time-Life Books, 1987.

Laine, J. Gary, and Morris M. Penny. *Law's Alabama Brigade in the War between the Union and the Confederacy.* Shippensburg, PA: White Mane, 1996.

Lincoln, Abraham. *Collected Works of Abraham Lincoln.* Edited by Roy P. Basler. New Brunswick, NJ: Rutgers University Press, 1953.

Longstreet, James. *From Manassas to Appomattox: Memoirs of the Civil War in America*. Philadelphia: J. B. Lippincott, 1896.

Marshall, Charles. *An Aide-de-Camp of Lee*. Boston: Little, Brown, 1927.

Maull, D.W., M.D. *The Life and Military Services of the Late Brigadier General Thomas A. Smyth*. Wilmington, DE: H. and E. F. James Printers, 1870.

McCarthy, Carlton. *Detailed Minutae of Soldier Life in the Army of Northern Virginia, 1861–1865*. Cambridge, MA: Riverside Press, 1882.

McClure, Alexander K. *Abraham Lincoln and Men of War-Times, Some Personal Recollections of War and Politics during the Lincoln Administration*. Philadelphia: Times Publishing Company, 1892.

McDonough, James Lee. *Shiloh—in Hell before Night*. Knoxville: University of Tennessee Press, 1977.

Meade, George Gordon. *The Life and Letters of George Gordon Meade, Major-General United States Army*. Vol. 2. New York: Charles Scribner's Sons, 1913.

Owen, William M. *In Camp and Battle with the Washington Artillery of New Orleans*. Boston: Ticknor, 1885.

Pickett, LaSalle Corbell. *Pickett and His Men*. Philadelphia: J. B. Lippincott, 1913.

Porter, David Dixon. *Incidents and Anecdotes of the Civil War*. New York: D. Appleton, 1885.

Porter, Horace. *Campaigning with Grant*. New York: Century Company, 1897.

Rand, Arnold A. *The Fourth Massachusetts Cavalry in the Closing Scenes of the War for the Maintenance of the Union, From Richmond to Appomattox, the Battle at High Bridge, by Major Edward T. Bouvé*. Project Gutenberg, 2010.

Rhodes, Robert Hunt, ed. *All for the Union: The Civil War Diary of Elisha Hunt Rhodes*. New York: Orion Books, 1985.

Robertson, James I., Jr. *General A. P. Hill: The Story of a Confederate Warrior*. New York: Vintage Books, 1987.

Sheridan, Philip. *Personal Memoirs of P. H. Sheridan, General United States Army*. Vol. 2. New York: Charles L. Webster, 1888.

Sherman, William T. *Memoirs of General William T. Sherman.* Vol. 2. New York: D. Appleton, 1889.

Smith, Jean Edward. *Grant.* New York: Simon and Schuster, 2001.

Taylor, Walter H. *Four Years with General Lee: Being a Summary of the More Important Events Touching the Career of General Robert E. Lee, in the War between the States; Together with an Authoritative Statement of the Strength of the Army Which He Commanded in the Field.* New York: D. Appleton, 1878.

Tremain, Henry Edwin. *Last Hours of Sheridan's Cavalry: A Reprint of War Memoranda.* New York: Bonnell, Silver and Bowers, 1904.

Trudeau, Noah Andre. *Bloody Roads South: The Wilderness to Cold Harbor, May–June 1864.* Boston: Little, Brown, 1989.

Trudeau, Noah Andre. *Out of the Storm: The End of the Civil War, April–June 1865.* Little, Brown, Boston, 1994.

In the Hands of Providence: Joshua L. Chamberlain and the American Civil War. Chapel Hill: University of North Carolina Press, 1992.

Ward, Geoffrey C. *The Civil War: An Illustrated History.* New York: Alfred A. Knopf, 1990.

Winik, Jay. *April 1865: The Month That Saved America.* New York: HarperCollins, 2001.

Wilson, Rufus Rockwell, assembled and annotated. *Intimate Memories of Lincoln.* Elmira, NY: Primavera Press, 1945.

Wise, John Sergeant. *The End of an Era.* Cambridge, MA: Houghton, Mifflin, Riverside Press, 1901.

INDEX